WORK AND STRUGGLE

"Even a cursory look at work in the 21st century tells us that we live in radical times. *Work and Struggle* is a collection of poignant writings from some of the greatest radical thinkers of the last two centuries—and required reading for anyone interested in how movements might develop in our own radical times."

—Elaine Bernard, Executive Director of the Labor and Worklife Program, Harvard Law School

"Those who want to revive and reinvigorate labor radicalism in the U.S. will find in Paul Le Blanc's *Work and Struggle* an inspiring resource. Radical labor in this collection comes vividly to life, reminding us that the challenge of alternative ways of living has a long, admirable history."

—Bryan D. Palmer, Editor, *Labour/Le Travail*

"This book offers a great remedy for pessimism over labor's current situation. In every age and despite their status as a beleagured minority, radicals have shaped labor movements that changed the world. Paul Le Blanc's magnificent introduction and these compelling voices from the past provide hopeful and richly rewarding reading to anyone concerned about attaining greater justice in today's world."

—Michael Honey, author of *Going Down Jericho Road: The Memphis Strike, Martin Luther King's Last Campaign*

Work and Struggle: Voices from U.S. Labor Radicalism focuses on the history of U.S. labor with an emphasis on radical currents, which have been essential elements in the working-class movement from the mid-nineteenth century to the late twentieth century. Showcasing some of labor's most important leaders, *Work and Struggle* offers students and instructors a variety of voices to learn from—each telling their story in their own words—through writings, memoirs and speeches, transcribed and introduced here by Paul Le Blanc. This collection of revolutionary voices will inspire anyone interested in the history of labor organizing.

Paul Le Blanc is Professor of History at La Roche College in Pittsburgh, PA, where he served as Dean of the School of Arts and Sciences from 2003 to 2009. He has also worked as a unionized healthcare worker, service employee, shipyard worker, and auto worker. He is author of a number of books on labor and social movements, including *Marx, Lenin and the Revolutionary Experience: Studies of Communism and Radicalism in the Age of Globalization* (Routledge), and was most recently an editor of *The International Encyclopedia of Revolution and Protest: 1500 to the Present.*

NEW YORK CITY—GRAND DEMONSTRATION OF WORKINGMEN, SEPTEMBER 5th—THE PROCESSION PASSING THE REVIEWING-STAND AT UNION SQUARE.—From a Sketch by a Staff Artist.—See Page 50.

New York City—Grand Demonstration of Workingmen. September 5th—The Procession Passing the Reviewing-Stand at Union Square.

WORK AND STRUGGLE

VOICES FROM U.S. LABOR RADICALISM

WRITTEN AND EDITED BY
PAUL LE BLANC

Routledge
Taylor & Francis Group
NEW YORK AND LONDON

First published 2011
by Routledge
270 Madison Avenue, New York, NY 10016

Simultaneously published in the UK
by Routledge
2 Park Square, Milton Park, Abingdon, Oxon OX14 4RN

Routledge is an imprint of the Taylor & Francis Group, an informa business

© 2011 Taylor & Francis

The right of Paul Le Blanc to be identified as the author of this work
has been asserted by him in accordance with sections 77 and 78 of the
Copyright, Designs and Patents Act 1988.

Typeset in Minion and Scala Sans by
Florence Production Ltd, Stoodleigh, Devon
Printed and bound in the United States of America on acid-free paper by
Walsworth Publishing Company, Marceline, MO

Library of Congress Cataloging in Publication Data
Le Blanc, Paul, 1947–
    Work and struggle: voices from U.S. labor radicalism/Paul Le Blanc.
        p. cm.
    Includes bibliographical references and index.
    1. Labor movement—United States—History.   I. Title.
    HD8066.L374 2011
    331.880973—dc22

ISBN13: 978-0-415-87746-6 (hbk)
ISBN13: 978-0-415-87824-1 (pbk)
ISBN13: 978-0-203-83492-3 (ebk)

SUSTAINABLE
FORESTRY
INITIATIVE

Certified Chain of Custody
Promoting Sustainable
Forest Management
www.sfiprogram.org

NSF-SFI-COC-C0004285
The SFI label applies to the text stock.

CONTENTS

PREFACE AND ACKNOWLEDGMENTS

My interest in "work and struggle" is by no means simply academic. Some academics may find this book interesting and useful, but it is my hope that others will also find it interesting and useful: especially those who have to make a living by selling their ability to work for a paycheck, and those who struggle for meaning in their lives, for dignity, and for decent living conditions and decent working conditions.

This book is intertwined with lifelong interests and commitments rooted, first of all, in the fact that my parents and many of my favorite relatives were an integral part of the particular working-class traditions (and what I call here the "labor–radical sub-culture") that this book deals with. My father, Gaston ("Gus") Le Blanc, was a union organizer long before I came into this world and right up to the very moment when he took his leave from us.

Among the artifacts that I got from my father was a left-wing history of U.S. labor, published in 1937, from a short-lived "Photo-History" series—a large sixty-five-page magazine-like booklet, rich in illustrations, entitled *Labor's Challenge.** In its pages, I first learned of Robber Baron Jay Gould saying "I can hire one half of the working class to kill the other half," and I saw the images of those men and women who stood up against such oppression and of some who gave their lives—the Mollie Maguires, the Haymarket Martyrs, Fannie Sellins—in labor's cause. I saw the determined faces of those who organized the Knights of Labor, of the American Federation of Labor (AFL), and of the rising dynamo that seemed to be changing everything, the Congress of Industrial Organizations. My great-grandfather,

---

* *Photo-History, Number 2: Labor's Challenge* (New York: Modern Age Books, 1937). The editors listed are Richard Storrs Childs, Ernest Galarza, and Sidney Pollatsek, and the associate editors Edward Levinson and John T. Bobbitt.

Harry Brodsky, had also been a pioneer activist in the International Ladies Garment Workers Union (ILGWU), and a gift he gave me on my thirteenth birthday was a more substantial left-wing account (with no pictures, alas!)— *Labor's Untold Story* (1955), written by Richard O. Boyer and Herbert M. Morais, and here I first read of the connection of Karl Marx—all fire and thunder and profundity, as interviewed by U.S. journalist John Swinton— with U.S. labor struggles.

As it turned out, some of my own work experience would connect with what some of the people in these pages are talking about. For a summer I was an agricultural worker; for several months I was a dish washer; for parts of my life I was a social-service employee; for a year or so I was a health care worker; over a several-year period I worked as a laborer, a ship-yard worker, and an auto worker. And, for many years, I have been a teacher. Some of these jobs also associated me with union membership.

In my years as a political activist, I have had opportunities to contribute my energies to labor's cause. The origins of this book are linked directly to that. In the 1990s, a political network of progressive labor activists, known as Labor Party Advocates (and its successor, an inaccurately labeled "Labor Party"), established a special lifetime membership category, involving special membership cards stamped with the portrait of one's choice from the following: Frederick Douglass, Eugene V. Debs, Mother Jones, John L. Lewis, or Cesar Chavez. I thought it might be a good idea to gather together the stories and the actual words of these people—perhaps as a pamphlet to help build that organization. Although the project was begun in a hopeful moment, this labor party effort soon declined and fell apart. But I never gave up on the idea of the book.

I have, over time, added more people to the list, and have also developed additional material that might be helpful in making sense of these remarkable people who committed themselves to the struggles of the working class in the United States. One might not agree with everything that one or another of these historical militants said or did. Not all of them would have fully agreed with the others, and some even came to disagree with their own earlier positions. At the same time, each reflects important aspects of the development of the U.S. working class and of the history of this country's labor struggles. I am particularly intrigued by the common elements and continuities—and feel that these especially have relevance to the experience, the hopes, and the efforts of present and future generations. Perhaps we can best comprehend the words of these fourteen people as arising from, and giving expression to, the deepest passions and insights of the working class over the generations, echoing the thoughts and voices of innumerable laboring men and women who have reached for "life, liberty, and the pursuit of happiness," struggling for liberty and justice for all.

Along with my father and his labor activist brother Adrian Le Blanc, the person I knew who gave me the greatest insights into the realities of the labor movement was Frank Lovell—all are very much missed, and yet for me they are present in these pages. I must also thank three labor historians—with different approaches and methodologies (and somewhat different politics as well)—who were teachers exercising significant influence over my own understanding: David Montgomery, the late Richard N. Hunt, and the late Philip S. Foner.

John Hinshaw, a fine labor historian in his own right, was a fellow Labor Party activist who helped to conceptualize this project in its very earliest stages. Much later, Kimberly Guinta and others at Routledge helped to flesh it out further and did all that was necessary to help make it a book. In particular, I would like to mention: Rebecca Novack, Brittany Yudkowsky, Siân Findlay, and Cheryl Vawdrey, as well as Sue Leaper, Fiona Isaac, Rosie White and Louise Smith from Florence Production Ltd.

Al Hart, long-time member of the United Electrical, Radio and Machine Workers of America (UE), and the present editor of the *UE News*, gave moral support and supplied me with materials from the late James Matles. I would also like to thank the following for supportive and/or critical feedback around one or another aspect of this project: Anthony Arnove, Sheila Cohen, Manny Ness, Kim Moody, Michael Yates, Bruce Levine, Fran Schor, Russell Pryor, Sharon Smith, Tom Twiss, and Nancy Ferrari.

Portions of the second chapter in the first part of this book first appeared in different form as entries in *The International Encyclopedia of Revolution and Protest*, a remarkable eight-volume entity edited by Immanuel Ness.

A wonderful secretary at La Roche College, Beth Waclawski, helped me out by typing the selections from Frances Wright, William Sylvis, and Terence Powderly. LaVerne Collins and others working at La Roche's Wright Library helped me secure important materials, as did the staff of the Tamiment Library at New York University, and of the Hillman Library at the University of Pittsburgh.

The writings provided in the "Voices of Labor Radicalism" section of this book have been edited for space reasons (three dots indicate passages not reproduced), with some adjustments also made in spelling, punctuation, and paragraph breaks.

ABBREVIATIONS

AFL	American Federation of Labor
AME	African Methodist Episcopal
ARU	American Railway Union
BSCP	Brotherhood of Sleeping Car Porters
CIO	Congress of Industrial Organizations
FOTLU	Federation of Organized Trades and Labor Unions of the United States and Canada
ILGWU	International Ladies Garment Workers Union
ILWU	International Longshore and Warehouse Union
IMIU	Iron Molders International Union
IUE	International Union of Electrical workers
IWA	International Workingmen's Association
IWPA	International Working People's Association
IWW	Industrial Workers of the World
NAACP	National Association for the Advancement of Colored People
NFWA	National Farm Workers Association
NLU	National Labor Union
NMU	National Maritime Union
PATCO	Professional Air Traffic Controllers' Organization
SDS	Students for a Democratic Society
SLP	Socialist Labor Party
SNCC	Student Nonviolent Coordinating Committee
TUEL	Trade Union Educational League
TUUL	Trade Union Unity League
UAW	United Auto Workers

UE	United Electrical, Radio and Machine Workers of America
UE	United Electrical workers
UMW	United Mine Workers of America
WPUS	Workingmen's Party of the United States

PART ONE

THE MEANING AND REALITY
OF LABOR RADICALISM

Some readers may want to skip over this portion of the book in order to engage with the actual words of the remarkable people whose voices can be heard in the second part of this volume. These brief comments are meant to tell such readers what they will be missing—and also to orient other readers who might choose to read this initial section of the book.

The first chapter tries to provide building blocks for understanding the reality of U.S. labor radicalism. Among other things, it defines and discusses the meaning of such basic concepts as: capitalism, culture, exploitation, labor movement, radical ideologies, and working class. It seeks to do this in clear language, drawing from the disciplines of sociology/anthropology and political science, also placing the U.S. labor movement in a global historical perspective. The chapter puts forward a distinctive notion—what I term a *labor–radical sub-culture*. This phenomenon is seen as important in the development of the U.S. labor movement, and also in the decline of the labor movement with the post-World War II erosion of that sub-culture.

The second chapter provides a general historical survey of revolutionary and radical currents and elements in the U.S. labor movement from 1776 to the early years of the twenty-first century. Subheadings of the chapter give a sense of its structure and content: Early Revolutionary Influences, Socialist Influences, Separation of Revolutionaries from Moderates, Twentieth-Century Challenges, From Great Depression to Cold War, From 1960s Radicalism to "Reaganism"—and "What Next". The emphasis is on radical currents that have been essential elements, not simply on the margins of the labor movement, but within its mainstream.

The terms "radical" and "revolutionary" tend to be used interchangeably in this book, with reference to three aspects of revolutionary influences in U.S. labor struggles: the influence of the tradition flowing from the American

Revolution, the influence of more explicitly left-wing (socialist, communist, anarchist) ideologies, and finally revolutionary challenges inherent in the nature of the labor movement, given the actual structure and dynamics of capitalist society. The working class (those who sell their ability to work for a paycheck, and those who are directly dependent on that paycheck) is the majority of people in the United States. Our living standards and enjoyment of certain democratic rights—it can be shown—have been advanced in large measure by mass struggles for a better life, initiated by "militant minorities" of activists within this working class. These activists have been animated by ideas that can be defined as *radical*—in the sense of favoring a deepening democracy and expansion of people's control over the conditions that shape their lives.

CHAPTER 1

UNDERSTANDING LABOR RADICALISM

At the core of all forms of labor radicalism is the belief that the working-class majority in our society—the great majority of people, without whose labor and life activity our society cannot run—is the group that should run society, ensuring that our economic resources will be used to provide genuine freedom, community, and creative self-development for each and every person.

This belief has often been labeled "socialism" and attributed to Karl Marx. In fact, there are many others, including some who came before Marx, who have argued the very same thing. It cannot be denied, however, that Marx was one of the most famous of these thinkers, and he freely acknowledged the radicalism of his approach. As he explained it, as a young philosopher in 1843, "to be radical is to grasp things by the root. But for man, the root is man himself," and he went on to insist upon "the categorical imperative to overthrow all conditions in which man is a degraded, enslaved, neglected, contemptible being."[1] In this volume, we will see some labor radicals who were influenced by Marx and others who were not. But all more or less shared the sensibilities expressed in these comments of 1843.

History has, in the eyes of many in the opening years of our century, rendered a cruel verdict on the socialist idea in general and on the ideas of Marx in particular—both being linked with actual experiences of oppressive bureaucracy, murderous dictatorship, and (far worse in the eyes of some) inefficiency and failure. Yet it can be argued:

1. that there is an unbridgeable chasm between the actual thought and political practice of Karl Marx and the crimes and tyrannies draped in his name (similar to the gap between the teachings of Jesus and the many vicious practices committed in his name);

2. that Marx's actual thought and political practice are deeply rooted in commitments to freedom and democracy; and

3. that Marx's thought can best be understood in the "social setting" (to draw on a notion developed by Michael Löwy) within which it developed —that of the working class, and particularly that of the rise and development of the labor movement.[2]

What this suggests is that labor radicalism, including—most certainly—that in the United States, is much broader and deeper than some are inclined to imagine. Karl Marx tirelessly labored to understand, strengthen, and articulate a consistent version of the labor radicalism of his time, employing the tools of social science in ways that transformed more than one academic discipline. Rather than Marx creating labor radicalism, however, it was an already-existing labor radicalism that "created" him as a radical thinker and activist. His own vitally important contributions, we can see from the voices of labor radicalism studied here, connect with broader streams related to radical Christian sensibilities, the Anglo-American Enlightenment, traditions of the American Revolution, utopian insights, and what might be called a "producerist" ethic.*

However, underlying such ideological interpretations are certain historical and structural realities associated with the origins, the nature, and the development of our economic life that seem naturally to have brought into being, time and again, variants of labor radicalism reflected in the voices we will examine in this volume.

Without labor, there cannot be life. Without human labor, there cannot be life-giving wealth—the things that we need (such as food, clothing, and shelter) and the things that we want (knowledge, multiple comforts and conveniences and entertainments, and creative outlets of many kinds). One could define the various economic systems that have provided the basis for the succession of human societies as the activities and relationships people enter into, and the resources they use, to get the things that they need and the things that they want.

For many thousands of years, the earliest humans were organized into relatively small groups—tribes, clans, kin groups, and so on.—in which people shared in the labor and shared in the fruits of their labor to provide some variant of life, liberty and the pursuit of happiness for all. These early cooperative economies combined the labor of human groups with primitive tools, connecting with the riches of nature, through hunting and gathering and

---

* Prevalent throughout nineteenth-century America, this "producerist" ethic gave primacy to those in society who actually *produce* the things that society needs—linking wage-workers with farmers, self-employed craftsmen, small shopkeepers, and even small-to-medium industrialists against bankers, financiers, Wall Street speculators, and other wealthy profiteers who were seen as becoming predominant in the economy.

finally early forms of agriculture (sometimes associated with "the Neolithic revolution"), to sustain humanity's existence and wonderous development.[3]

The success of such early economies created economic surpluses that made possible the rise of civilizations. The surplus has meant that the labor of many (especially through agriculture and manufacturing) has been able to sustain not only those who labor, but also some people not engaged in hunting, gathering, agricultural and industrial labor, and so on. There have been, down through the centuries, different forms of economy that have sustained a variety of civilizations, but all have shared one distinctive feature: powerful minorities who benefit—often enjoying lives of great wealth and luxury— from their control over laboring majorities. There may be slaves and masters, peasants and landed nobility, or modern wage-workers and capitalist employers. But, in each case, we find the exploited and the exploiter.

To exploit means to use. If I am an exploiter in this sense, I am using the wealth-creating labor of others in order to appropriate, for my own purposes, the economic surplus they can produce. The most dynamic of such economic systems happens to be our own—capitalism. This is a system in which the economy is privately owned, controlled by the owners, and utilized to maximize the profits of the owners. More than this, capitalism is a system of generalized commodity production. More and more aspects of life are drawn into the vortex of commodity production. A commodity is something that is produced for the purpose of being sold—and so increasingly, under capitalism, more and more things that we consider to be essential to our lives, the things that we need and want, become part of a buying and selling economy. Over time, the great majority of people get the money they need to buy such things by turning essential aspects of their lives (intelligence, life energy, strength, skills, etc.)—that is, their ability to work—into a commodity that they sell to a capitalist employer for a paycheck.[4]

The development of capitalism—accelerating since the fifteenth century— coincided with a number of other developments. The need to maximize profits helped to generate an increasingly rapid development of science and technology, and also the spread of education and critical thinking. Such things were essential for maximizing profits. There was a growing sense, among people from various social layers, that it was valid to question authority, and that it was possible to bring about positive change (the notion of progress). By the end of the eighteenth century, there were two transformative tides sweeping through the world—a powerful accumulation of democratic struggles and revolutions (with people seeking to have a meaningful say in the decisions affecting their lives) and the continually self-renewing Industrial Revolution.[5]

Such developments brought into being—through more and more of Europe, through more and more of the Americas, increasingly penetrating into Asia and Africa, and spilling over into Australia and the Pacific Islands as well—the modern, global, *working class*. It also brought about the rise of the *labor movement*.

Working Class, Labor Movement, Militant Minority

There has been enough confusion around these terms—*working class* and *labor movement*—that it is worth taking time to define them before we turn our attention to the development of U.S. labor radicalism.

The term *working class* is used here to refer to those who can make a living, or can hope to make a living, only through the sale of their ability to work (plus family members dependent on such "bread-winners") and includes both unemployed and retired workers.

The term *labor movement* refers to various organizations and struggles organized by and for workers to defend and advance their interests as workers. It includes:

- **trade unions** (focusing on improving wages and working conditions in the workplace);
- **reform groups** (seeking to bring about improvements, often through new laws, for example, that will result in limits on, or abolition of, child labor; limit the number of hours in the workday; enforce health and safety provisions at the workplace; extend the right to vote among those who labor, etc.);
- **self-help groups** (such as consumer cooperatives, health and burial societies, educational and cultural societies);
- **activist organizations** (engaging in a variety of activities for the working class, often guided by radical or revolutionary ideologies); and
- **political parties** (focusing on electoral and other activities designed to help the working class advance its political power and, ultimately, its control of the country's key governmental institutions).

The "working class" has meant, in the view of some, only manual wage-workers, especially factory workers—which excludes many others: various service employees (whether government workers, store clerks, social workers, maids, or laundry workers); so-called "white-collar" office workers; teachers, and, historically, artisans and craftsmen, indentured servants, and slaves. Some of the first labor organizations, however, were organized by artisans and craftsmen at the journeyman level, whose traditional route to evolve into master craftsmen (with the opportunity of owning their own establishments) was being blocked by the natural development of the capitalist economy.

For some labor radicals, an explicit link was made between the chattel slavery that exploited African–American laborers and the wage-slavery that exploited alleged "free labor." While some "white" labor radicals were inclined to adopt the racist argument that white workers deserved better treatment, the more revolutionary-minded labor radicals in the pre-Civil War period insisted that the abolition of black slavery was a precondition to overcoming the wage-slavery that oppressed all of "free labor." Similarly, many labor radicals of later years (for example, within the Knights of Labor in the 1880s and the Industrial Workers of the World of the early 1900s) had a more broadly inclusive definition of what constitutes the working class.

Nonetheless, the fragmentation of the working class—among different occupational, cultural, ethnic, racial, and gender groups, which have often rejected identification with each other—has been a factor nurtured by the complex development of the market economy and finding frequent reflection in the development of workers' consciousness and of the labor movement in the United States.

For example, the incredible waves of immigration (often from impoverished agricultural populations), drawn to the United States by the dynamism of a rapidly industrializing American capitalism, tended to flood the U.S. labor market in ways that were used by employers to bring down wages and also were detrimental to working conditions—often resulting in anti-immigrant sentiments among native-born workers (or even among earlier immigrants or their children). The use of women by employers to undercut wages and increase the rate of exploitation was similarly one of the factors contributing to male hostility to female labor. The fact that skilled workers could more easily be organized than unskilled workers contributed, among skilled workers who were organized into unions, to the prejudice that unskilled workers were "unorganizable" and not worth worrying about.

The most consistent revolutionary currents have labored to overcome divisions within the working class—generally insisting on "solidarity" among all who labor (production workers, service workers, "brain workers," unemployed workers, etc.), that "an injury to one is an injury to all," and in some cases arguing that the entire working class should be in "one big union." Often, these revolutionary impulses have—despite rhetorical pretenses to the contrary—been blunted or compromised by more conservative, more bigoted practices. But it has generally been from revolutionaries of one kind or another that effective efforts have been made for the labor movement to embrace all sectors of the working class.

It is important to recognize that the great majority of U.S. workers were at no time formally part of the labor movement. Union membership in the nineteenth and twentieth centuries was generally not greater (and often was much less) than 10 percent of the labor force—the high point being 36 percent in 1955. One could say that organized labor consisted of the working class's "vanguard," but often it was a militant minority with influence far beyond its numbers, helping to improve the working conditions and living conditions, not only of its own members, but also of the working class as a whole.

As already indicated, sometimes the majority elements of this labor vanguard turned inward to advance only the short-term interests of those who were organized, with a profoundly conciliatory attitude to the existing social realities and power relations. Our focus in this book, however, will be on the more revolutionary currents in the organized vanguard of the labor movement.

CONSCIOUSNESS AND CULTURE

Just as the development of the capitalist economy was a global phenomenon, so was the rise of the labor movement a worldwide development. Organizational expression of this reality can be found in the creation of several international organizations—the International Workingmen's Association (IWA), formed in 1864 and surviving until 1876; the Socialist International, established in 1889; and the Communist International of 1919–1943. These came to be known, respectively, as the First, Second, and Third Internationals.[6]

The First International, of which Karl Marx was one of the most prominent leaders, was a multi-tendency creation of working-class organizations—parties, trade unions, educational and reform groups, and so on—within which a variety of socialist, anarchist, and other radical labor ideologies coexisted. Predominantly European, with some affiliates also in the Americas, it was torn apart by growing internal differences plus repressive measures on the part of various governments after the revolutionary working-class uprising and bloody defeat of the Paris Commune in 1871.

The Second International—also predominantly European, with a few far-flung affiliates (including in the United States)—was ideologically more homogeneous, based on a number of mass socialist, social-democratic, and labor parties in which the influence of Marx's ideas prevailed (with some interpretations more revolutionary, and others—increasingly—more reformist).

In 1917, some of the most revolutionary of Russian socialists led a successful workers' and peasants' insurgency, establishing a government of democratic councils (soviets) that, under the extreme pressures of the succeeding years, crystallized into a one-party dictatorship that came to be known as the Soviet Union. In the full flush of revolutionary victory, Russia's revolutionary socialists renamed their organization the Communist Party and won masses of revolutionary workers and others to their uncompromisingly revolutionary Third International (which gradually declined under the influence of the bureaucratic dictatorship that became dominant in the Soviet Union). One of the distinctions of the new international was the fact that it became firmly rooted in all inhabited continents.

In each case, however, the internationals had life only because of the various working-class movements that crystallized, struggled, and grew in many different lands. These movements were, in turn, rooted in the specific economic, social, and political realities and were dependent on the development of what many revolutionaries, following Marx, referred to as *workers' class-consciousness*. In the 1890s, a young Marxist named Vladimir Ulyanov (later known as Lenin) explained this key concept in the same terms that his co-thinkers around the world would have used: "The workers' class-consciousness means the workers' understanding that the only way to improve their conditions and to achieve their emancipation is to conduct a struggle against the capitalist and factory-owner class created by the big factories."

In the spirit of *The Communist Manifesto*, Lenin added that "the workers' class-consciousness means their understanding that the interests of all the workers of any particular country are identical, that they constitute one class, separate from all the other classes in society." He concluded with the third point that "the class-consciousness of the workers means the workers' understanding that to achieve their aims they have to work to influence the affairs of the state, just as the landlords and capitalists did, and are continuing to do now."[7]

The fact remains that such revolutionary class-consciousness, while reflecting global developments, was necessarily rooted in and sustained by—and cannot be fully understood apart from—very specific cultures and subcultures. Raymond Williams has told us that the term *culture* is "one of the two or three most complicated words in the English language," noting that, "where culture meant a state or habit of mind, or the body of intellectual and moral activities, it means now, also, a whole way of life."

Most useful for our purposes is the way the concept has been developed by North American anthropologists—for example, Melville Herskovitz, who described culture as "a [conceptual] construct that describes the total body of belief, behavior, sanctions, values, and goals that mark the way of life of any people," adding that "in the final analysis it comprises the things that people have, the things that they do, and what they think." Ruth Benedict referred to it as involving "ideas and standards" people have in common—"learned behavior . . . learned anew from grown people by each new generation." Clyde Kluckhohn and W. H. Kelly elaborated that "culture in general as a descriptive concept means the accumulated treasury of human creation: books, paintings, buildings and the like; the knowledge of ways of adjusting to our surroundings, both human and physical; language, customs, and systems of etiquette, religion, morals . . ."[8]

Such things are built up over time—but one must realize that they are created by people to deal with the often-changing realities around them. In the face of social and economic transformations, new meanings are given to "traditional" customs, and sometimes-dramatic innovations are embraced. Eleanor Leacock indicated how this concept fits into historical materialism by stressing the importance of "analysis that rejects static a-historical views of culture, and transforms the concept into a tool for examining the role of ideology and consciousness in social process." Factors involved in culture, she suggested, include the way people conceptualize and express their relations with each other, which are related to the ties they develop with one another in the course of organizing both the labor of production and daily life—grounded in material conditions and social relations.[9]

Twentieth-century Marxism has offered insights that allow us to deepen our analysis. For revolutionary Marxists, of course, the conception of *class* is essential for making sense of culture. As Lenin put it in 1913, "there are two nations in every modern nation," and so "there are two national cultures in every national culture"—capitalist and working class. The dominant element in any modern national culture, he argued, was "the national culture of the bourgeoisie," which often intertwined with the even more reactionary orientations of the aristocratic landed proprietors and reactionary elements among the clergy. "Aggressive bourgeois nationalism," he warned, "which drugs the minds of the workers, stultifies and disunites them in order that the bourgeoisie may lead them by the halter—such is the fundamental fact of the times." Against this capitalist–reactionary culture, Lenin counterposed what he called "the international culture of democracy and the world working-class movement," which in turn is grounded in the specific experience of workers in all countries. "The *elements* of democratic and socialist culture are present," he insisted, "if only in rudimentary form, in *every* national culture, since in every nation there are toiling and exploited masses, whose conditions of life inevitably give rise to the ideology of democracy and socialism."[10]

Even greater complexity of the question was suggested, ten years later, by Leon Trotsky in *Problems of Everyday Life*: "The proletariat is a powerful social unity which manifests its strength fully during the periods of intense revolutionary struggle for the gains of the whole class. But within this unity we observe a great variety of types. Between the obtuse illiterate village shepherd and the highly qualified engine driver there lie a great many different states of culture and habits of life." Nor was this simply a problem of "backward Russia," in Trotsky's opinion. "One might say that the richer the history of a country, and at the same time of its working class, the greater within it the accumulation of memories, traditions, habits, the larger number of old groupings—the harder it is to achieve a revolutionary unity of the working class." For Marxists, this is one of the problems necessitating the creation of a revolutionary party—to help forge the unity in struggle of a multicultural working class by providing (as Marx and Engels put it in *The Communist Manifesto*) an understanding of "the common interests of the entire proletariat, independently of all nationality" and an "understanding [of] the line of march" that can lead to the triumph of the working-class movement.[11]

However, Marx never presumed that it would be possible for would-be revolutionaries to make history just as they pleased. Rather, they would have to make it "under circumstances directly encountered, given and transmitted from the past."[12] They must engage with the kinds of historically determined cultural reality alluded to by the anthropologists and revolutionaries we have been looking at. The specifics of how this actually works have been traced by some of the most perceptive labor historians. The cultural counterposition of capitalists and workers in England, according to E. P. Thompson, could be traced back to eighteenth-century social-cultural tensions of "the gentry" and "the laboring poor." Much of this evolving class divide, he tells us, opened wide in reaction against a "modernizing" capitalism: "We can read much eighteenth-century social history as a succession of confrontations between an innovative market economy and the customary moral economy of the plebs," Thompson tells us. He continues: "In one sense the plebian culture is the people's own; it is a defense against the intrusions of gentry or clergy; it consolidates those customs which serve their interests; the taverns are their own, the fairs are their own, rough music is among their own means of self-regulation." This harmonizes with Lenin's view, as does Thompson's 1963 generalization, which has become a classic statement:

> Class happens when some men [and women], as a result of common experiences (inherited or shared), feel and articulate the identity of their interests as between themselves, and as against other men whose interests are different from (and usually opposed to) theirs. The class experience is largely determined by the productive relations into which ... [people] are born—or enter involuntarily. Class-consciousness is the way in which these experiences are handled in cultural terms: embodied in traditions, value-systems, ideas, and institutional forms.[13]

LABOR–RADICAL SUB-CULTURE

Following in Thompson's footsteps (and also concerning himself with the sort of issues Trotsky pointed to), U.S. labor historian Herbert Gutman observed: "Men and women who sell their labor to an employer bring more to a new or changing work situation than their physical presence. What they bring to a factory depends, in good part, on their culture of origin, and how they behave is shaped by the interaction between that culture and the particular society into which they enter." Surveying the evolving U.S. working class from 1815 to 1919, he noted that it "was constantly altered in its composition by infusions, from within and without the nation, of peasants, farmers, skilled artisans, and casual day laborers who brought into industrial society ways of work and other habits and values not associated with industrial necessities and the industrial ethos."

The response to capitalist exploitation and oppression varied: "Some shed these older ways to conform to new imperatives. Others fell victim or fled, moving from place to place. Some sought to extend and adapt older patterns of work and life to a new society. Others challenged the social system through varieties of collective associations."

This last grouping—those involved in organized challenges to the social system—represented what might be called a "vanguard" layer of the working class reflecting a radical labor sub-culture. According to Gutman, by the middle of the nineteenth century a proletarian recasting of democratic–republican ideology had become an essential element within U.S. working-class culture, adding: "Their beliefs went beyond the redefinition of eighteenth-century republicanism, and sparked and sustained recurrent collective efforts—in the form of trade unions, strikes, cooperatives, a tart labor press, and local politics—to check the increasing power of the industrial capitalist."[14]

In the late 1880s, Karl Marx's bright and perceptive daughter Eleanor, along with her companion Edward Aveling, toured the United States for fifteen weeks and then wrote a fascinating account of *The Working-Class Movement in America*. The book begins with their listing of close to a hundred genuine working-class newspapers published throughout the United States, reflecting and impacting upon a vibrant sub-culture. In discussing the objective socio-economic factors of working-class experience, they noted that the United States, in contrast to Europe, had "no remnants of old systems, no surviving classes that belonged to these"—instead, "the capitalist system came here as a ready-made article, and with all the force of its inherent, uncompromising brutality." The condition of the working class in the United States, they argued, was certainly no better than in England.

While the overwhelming majority of the people they met had no idea what socialism was, the Marx-Avelings concluded that there was in fact "the prevalence of what we call unconscious Socialism," as, when the actual meaning of socialism was explained (*not* equal division of property, *not* blowing up capitalists with dynamite, *not* anarchy—but social ownership and democratic control of the major economic resources), "in town after town, by hundred upon hundred, [people] declared, 'Well, if that is Socialism, we are Socialists.'" In fact, hundreds of thousands had flocked to the Knights of Labor, which the couple saw as "the first expression by the American working people of their consciousness of themselves as a class." In addition, there were the trade unions associated with AFL—as they put it, "the result of many years of evolution" and benefitting from "the practical experience especially of the German[–American] Socialists." The Knights of Labor, the trade unionists, and various labor-radicals (including socialists) were joined together, in various cities, in what seemed to be promising labor party efforts, which (the two optimists speculated) would "pass through several preliminary stages" that would eventually culminate in the adoption of a socialist program, with "the attainment of supreme political, and then of supreme economic power."[15]

The work of Gutman and other U.S. labor historians identifies reasons why the Marx-Aveling forecast was seriously off-target. While providing a snapshot of U.S. realities in the late 1880s, the two revolutionary visitors could not adequately factor in enough of the complex and fluid realities, not to mention the dramatic transformations, that would engulf and fragment the U.S. working-class movement. As Lenin warned, disunity of workers along the lines of culture and consciousness (and also the de-radicalizing impact, for some of the more "privileged" skilled workers, due to U.S. capitalism's economic upswings) meant that—more than Eleanor Marx anticipated—the bourgeoisie was able to lead many workers "by the halter." One can certainly find brutal ethnic hostility, especially a poisonous racism toward non-white peoples, permeating much white working-class life throughout the nineteenth and twentieth centuries. One or another racial or ethnic group was all too often found to be unworthy to be in one's union, and would be excluded from one's workplace—and consequently could be used as a source of scabs during a strike, generating deepened hatred among workers toward each other. There were debilitating fissures along gender lines as well. Sometimes, these tainted much of the radical labor sub-culture—although ultimately the balance tipped increasingly in a more radical, inclusive direction. This was so particularly as various sections of the ethnically and racially diverse U.S. working class experienced, within themselves, the crystallization of radical-proletarian sub-cultures and consciousness developing in confrontation to aspects of the bourgeois-dominated "national culture."

In the United States, from the period spanning the end of the Civil War in 1865 down through the Depression decade of the 1930s, a vibrant working-class sub-culture had developed throughout much of the United States. Often, this "sub-culture" was more like a network of sub-cultures having very distinctive ethnic attributes, but these different ethnic currents were, at various times, connected by left-wing political structures (such as the old Knights of Labor, the Socialist Party of Eugene V. Debs, the Industrial Workers of the World, the Communist Party, various groups of socialist militants, Trotsky-ists, anarchists, and others) and also, to an extent, by trade union frameworks —culminating in the 1930s in the remarkable Congress of Industrial Organizations (CIO). We see it being both reflected in, and nourished by, such class-struggle battles as the mass uprising of 1877; the eight-hour upsurge of 1886; the Homestead steel strike of 1892; the 1909 rising of the 20,000 in New York City; the Lawrence Textile strike of 1912; the momentous 1919 strike wave; the 1934 general strikes in Minneapolis, Toledo, and San Francisco; the innumerable sit-down strikes of the 1930s; and the nationwide explosion of victorious strikes in 1945–1946. Within this context of struggle and organization, inseparable from the radical workers' sub-culture, flourished the widespread class-consciousness that is essential to the creation of a revolutionary party.[16]

If we examine the decade of what has been called "Labor's Giant Step"— the 1930s—we see a variety of intersecting struggles that were inseparable from, reflected in, and nourished by, a broad, amazingly rich and vibrant, left-wing sub-culture. In addition to several significant socialist and communist formations, there was an array of organizations formed around a variety of issues—groups and coalitions for labor rights and democracy; against war and militarism; against racism and fascism; against poverty and unemploy-ment, and so on. Related to such things were an incredible number of conferences, educational classes and forums; books and pamphlets; newspapers and magazines; novels and short stories; songs and poems; plays and paintings; picnics and socials, marches and rallies—all blending together to create an expanding and deepening pool of ideas and sensibilities, of human relationships and a sense of solidarity, of insight and understanding. It was, in fact, a sub-culture (involving what the anthropologist Herskovits called a "total body of belief, behavior, sanctions, values, and goals") that generated and nourished the kind of consciousness necessary for the sustained struggles that brought about a genuine power shift in U.S. society, to the benefit of the working-class majority.[17]

A historical survey of working-class movements in other countries reveals the same reality. Perhaps the best-known example is provided by the German labor movement, which involved such a rich alternative culture in Germany that sociologist Max Weber referred to it as a "state within a state."[18]

Based on Italian experience, Antonio Gramsci outlined the creation of a working-class "intellectual–moral bloc," as he put it (and which appears to be the same thing as the radical working-class sub-culture), "which can make politically possible the intellectual progress of the mass and not only of small intellectual groups." While acknowledging the importance of "traditional intellectuals" who had been won to Marxism, Gramsci stressed the importance of developing "organic intellectuals" who were (and remained) part of the working class, and he emphasized the importance of working "incessantly to raise the intellectual level of the ever-growing strata of the populace, to give a personality [a "class-consciousness"] to the amorphous mass element," seeking to "stimulate the formation of homogeneous, compact social blocs, which will give birth to their own intellectuals, their own commanders, their own vanguard—who will in turn react upon those blocs in order to develop them."[19]

The Russian revolutionary Marxist Leon Trotsky, drawing on decades of rich experience, offered a description and theorization in the early 1930s, as he sought to persuade Social-Democratic and Communist workers to join together in preventing the imminent Nazi victory in Germany:

> Within the framework of bourgeois democracy and parallel to the incessant struggle against it, the elements of proletarian democracy have formed themselves in the course of many decades: political parties, labor press, trade unions, factory committees, clubs, coopera-tives, sports societies, etc. The mission of fascism is not so much to complete the destruction of bourgeois democracy as to crush the first outlines of proletarian democracy. As for our mission, it consists in placing those elements of proletarian democracy, already created, at the foundation of the soviet system of the workers' state. To this end, it is necessary to break the husk of bourgeois democracy and free from it the kernel of workers' democracy. Therein lies the essence of the proletarian revolution.[20]

Onslaughts and Erosions

Of course, one of the highest priorities of the Nazi movement was the thorough destruction of this subversive counter-culture of the German working class, which was quickly and brutally accomplished when Hitler came to power. This is why the Nazis were embraced by Germany's big-business interests, and initially by the upper classes throughout Europe. It is worth noting how Gramsci described the similar, earlier fascist onslaught on what he saw as radical-labor organizational "links" in 1920s Italy:

> It set out to destroy even that minimum to which the democratic system was reduced in Italy—i.e., the concrete possibility to create an organizational link at the base between workers, and to extend this link gradually until it embraced the great masses in movement ... The strength and capacity for struggle of the workers for the most part derive from the existence of these links, even if they are not in themselves apparent. What is involved is the possibility of meeting, of discussing; of giving these meetings and discussions some regularity; of choosing leaders through them; of laying the basis for an elementary organic formation, a league, a cooperative or a party section. What is involved is the possibility of giving these organic formations a continuous functionality; of making them into the basic framework of an organized movement ... After three years of this kind of [fascist] action, the working class has lost all form and all organicity; it has been reduced to a disconnected, fragmented, scattered mass.[21]

Fascist onslaughts and repression have not been the only means by which such sub-cultures are destroyed. There was a dramatic break in the continuity of this labor–radical tradition in the United States after 1945, owing to the realities that resulted from World War II, and the social, economic, political, and cultural transformations of the 1950s and 1960s.

Labor radical Frank Lovell once emphasized that, in the history of the twentieth century, "World War II was the great divide, like a chasm caused by an earthquake of unimaginable force." This global holocaust—which really was a convergence of holocausts that destroyed 80 million human beings in both combat and non-combat contexts—was a combination of several wars. Underlying them all was a set of inter-imperialist rivalries between Germany, Britain, France, Italy, Japan, and the United States for global hegemony (which was absolutely won by the United States, setting the stage for what was called "the American Century"). But also very much coming to the fore was a set of what might be called "people's wars," involving populations of Europe and Asia fighting against the invasion of their homelands by brutal, racist military machines, in some cases also involving anti-colonial struggles in Asia and Africa. There was also the massive defense of the Soviet Union (in which more than 20 million people in the USSR died, and the back of the Nazi war machine was broken). This, combined with the impending triumph of the Chinese Revolution and the expansion of Soviet dominance in Eastern Europe, set the stage for the decades of Cold War rivalry between the so-called "Free World" coalition led by the United States and the Communist bloc.[22]

"The war changed the world," Lovell reflected. "It changed almost everything about the world that we had known. It changed class relations among people around the world. And of course it left vast destruction and devastation in its wake." He goes on to make a key point: "But this was the very condition needed for the recovery and expansion of the capitalist system. Capitalism as a world system gained renewed strength from the process of rebuilding." Michael Yates describes the impact of the war on his mother's Western Pennsylvania coal-mining community: "The Second World War brought the mining village out of the Depression. It also helped to assimilate many Italian-Americans into the more conservative American mainstream. After the war, nationalism and anti-communism became much stronger, and individual acquisitiveness began to replace the more communal life of the pre-war era."[23] The reminiscences of Communist stalwart Steve Nelson, who had experience organizing among foreign-born workers, touch on dimensions of the same reality:

> It was a fact of life—the older generation was not pulling the younger into the movement. Increasingly, first and second generations [among the immigrant groups originating from southern and eastern Europe] not only spoke different languages but opted for different lifestyles . . . World War II was a watershed. Sons who went to high school and then served in the armed forces thought in far different terms than their fathers. Daughters who worked in the shipyards and electrical plants were a world away from their mothers' experiences with domestic service and boarders. Industrial workers after the war were no longer pick and shovel men. Machine tenders who enjoyed the security provided by unions with established channels for collective bargaining could not appreciate the chronic insecurity of the pre-CIO era . . . Participation in the labor movement and especially the war effort . . . eased the process of acceptance [into the "mainstream" of U.S. culture] of the foreign-born and their children.[24]

Essential specifics of workers' occupations and workday experience underwent fundamental changes. Related to this was the transformation of the global economy (and the dominant U.S. role within that economy), as capitalism profitably rebuilt itself after the devastation of war, at the same time bringing about remarkable innovations in economic organization and productivity, enhanced by a lucrative economic expansionism securing raw materials, markets, and investment opportunities throughout the world. This combined with the victories of unionization and social reforms in the 1930s, which helped fuel not only economic prosperity but also an unprecedented upward swing in working-class living standards. There were virtual revolutions in transportation, and in the communication and entertainment industries, plus new lifestyles generated by suburbanization and consumerism. At the same time, the long stretch of Cold War confrontation between the United States and the Soviet Union placed a pervasive and conservatizing anti-Communism at the very center of the dominant political culture.

The organizations associated with the labor movement were similarly transformed—impacted by a complex combination of assaults, co-optations, corruptions, and erosions. The communities, culture, and consciousness of the working class became so different from the mid-1940s to the 1960s that only faded shreds of the old, radical labor sub-culture remained.[25] Even in 1953, as he tried to make sense of the decline of radicalism among U.S. workers, the veteran revolutionary socialist James P. Cannon commented:

> It is now sixteen years since the sit-down strikes made the new CIO unions secure by the seniority clause. These sixteen years of union security, and thirteen years of uninterrupted war and postwar prosperity, have wrought a great transformation in the unprivileged workers who made the CIO ... The pioneer militants of the CIO unions are sixteen years older than they were in 1937. They are better off than the ragged and hungry sit-down strikers of 1937; and many of them are sixteen times softer and more conservative. This privileged section of the unions, formerly the backbone of the left wing, is today the main social base of the conservative Reuther bureaucracy [in the UAW union].[26]

Studying the de-radicalization process of the 1950s and 1960s, sociologist John C. Leggett wrote that "a new middle class arose which included a large number of young people of working-class background," noting that many prospering working people had moved out of traditional working-class communities to become home owners in the suburbs. "The class struggle abated with the end of the post-World War II strikes, although repeated flare-ups between management and workers occurred during and after the Korean War," he added, in his description of the same auto workers discussed by Cannon. "At the same time, another trend pointed up this harmony. Governmental boards and labor unions often helped minimize class conflict as unions grew more friendly toward companies which were willing to bargain with, and make major concessions to, labor organizations. Prosperity reached almost everyone. Even working-class minority groups [that is, some African–Americans and Hispanics] improved their standard of living and sent sons and daughters into the middle class."[27]

According to Stanley Aronowitz, such realities also involved tendencies, in his words, "toward the replacement of all the traditional forms of proletarian culture and everyday life—which gave working-class communities their coherence and provided the underpinnings for the traditional forms of proletarian class consciousness—with a new, manipulated consumer culture which for convenience's sake we can call mass culture." In 1963, black autoworker James Boggs commented that, "today the working class is so dispersed and transformed by the very nature of the changes in production that it is almost impossible to select out any single bloc of workers as working-class in the old sense." By this "old sense," he meant class-conscious workers. "The working class is growing, as Marx predicted," acknowledged Boggs, "but it is not the old working class which the radicals persist in believing will create the revolution and establish control over production. That old working class is the vanishing herd."[28] As Boggs makes clear, it was hardly the working class that was vanishing—but rather the class-consciousness that had been essential to building the labor and socialist movements.

All of this was just fine with the bureaucratic leadership of organized labor. "I believe in free, democratic, competitive capitalism," explained the president of the once-socialist ILGWU, Sol Chaikin, in 1979. He elaborated that, "managers should manage and then workers should sit down with them to collectively bargain for their share of the results of management efficiency and worker productivity." Earlier in the decade, George Meany, President of the AFL-CIO, put things this way: "Our members are basically Americans. They basically believe in the American system, and they have a greater stake in the system now than they had fifteen or twenty years ago, because under the system and under our trade union policy, they have become 'middle class.' They have a greater stake."[29]

Such views were not inconsistent with the consciousness prevalent among a majority of union members in the post-World War II decades. When the radical upsurge of the 1960s shifted the political center of gravity leftward— with the massive civil rights struggles, the student and youth insurgencies, the profound opposition to the U.S. war in Vietnam, the early stirrings of a new wave of feminism, and more—it was all far less connected to any genuine working-class movement than had been the case with radical upsurges in the 1880s and 1890s, the early 1900s, and certainly the 1930s and 1940s. This was so even though a majority of the activists came from backgrounds (and were destined for occupations) in which one made one's living by selling an ability to work for a paycheck, which is the classical Marxist definition of what it means to be working class. But the activists tended to see themselves—and were certainly portrayed—as "middle class," not as part of a self-conscious working class. To a very large extent, the organized labor movement of the 1960s and 1970s—with very honorable yet modest exceptions—held itself aloof from the buoyant movements for social change in that period.

In the twentieth century's final decades, the "mature" labor movement, shorn of its radicalism, stagnated—and then began a precipitous decline. George Meany's successor as President of the AFL-CIO, Lane Kirkland, vainly sought to advance a National Accord "between business, labor, and government to join together in the rebuilding of the country's core industrial base," according to his biographer, but instead (as big-business conservatives were able to put their own champion, Ronald Reagan, into the White House), "unions . . . found themselves on the defensive in dealings with the corporate world, as the social contract that had governed relations between trade unions and business unraveled in an environment of intense global competitiveness." Aggressive and relentless demands were made by the big corporations, backed by the government (and most Democrats and Republicans), that unions offer concessions—giving back the gains of previous decades. This was followed by *de-industrialization*, "a euphemism for the closing of hundreds of factories that made automobiles, steel, machine tools, and other core products, with the resulting loss of millions of jobs and the decimation of some of America's largest and most fabled unions." Kirkland remained cautiously optimistic, remarking that "we're not going to start on the assumption that what might turn out to be bad already has," and he was determined to continue policies dedicated to "the transformation of relations between labor and management [away] from the traditional adversarial model."[30]

Yet the conciliatory approach hardly meant a reversal of declining living standards for U.S. workers, and this was accompanied by declining union membership, from 35 percent of the labor force in 1955, to 23 percent in 1980, to 12 percent in 2007. "Workers can see you don't need a union card to hold up a white flag," quipped left-wing union leader Tony Mazzocchi of the Oil, Chemical, and Atomic Workers. In the mid 1990s, Mazzocchi was emphasizing the need for "the rejuvenation of a working-class culture that once existed in this country," scoffing at the notion that workers were "middle class." He recalled: "When I grew up [in the 1930s], working class meant anyone who worked for a wage and wasn't a manager or a small-business person, whether you're a white-collar or a blue-collar person. In a culture that existed when I came into this workforce, you understood the value of organization, of unions. You supported unions." He added that, "in those days, if you lived in a neighborhood, it was a working-class neighborhood," and that "People understood the nature of their class, and they knew the nature of those who were benefitting at their expense."[31]

It remains to be seen whether the twenty-first century will see the recreation of the consciousness and sub-culture to which Mazzocchi referred, which are essential for the vitality and even the existence of any meaningful labor movement. Without that, however, it seems unlikely that decent living conditions and working conditions can be secured by the great majority of people who depend for their livelihood on the sale of labor power for wages and salaries.

CHAPTER 2

REVOLUTIONARY CURRENTS IN THE U.S. LABOR MOVEMENT

We have seen in the previous chapter that the labor movement does not simply mean *trade unions*, but actually refers to a more multifaceted reality. The twentieth century saw powerful pressures in the United States to narrow down the "legitimate" labor movement into only one of its components, trade unions. This is the way many Americans have come to understand the term. However, the legitimacy of even this narrowed conception of the labor movement was increasingly and powerfully challenged by the final decades of the twentieth century, and the U.S. labor movement seemed to dwindle as an effective force for the economic betterment of the working class.

The power of the labor movement historically has been related to its expansiveness and its inclination to be radical (to go to the root). This has been essential for its ability to animate masses of people with the sense of a "cause" or a "crusade" that would embrace the highest ideals, connect multiple issues, give participants a sense of purpose, and at the same time hold the promise of a better life for themselves and their children. The necessity of the practical element—maintaining a cohesive organization and pursuing achievable goals—has often obscured the revolutionary element (*revolutionary* in the sense of pushing in the direction of a fundamental shift in society, giving political and economic power to the laboring majority). The triumph of the "practical" over the "revolutionary" is associated with what has been called, in various contexts, "bread and butter unionism" or "pure and simple unionism" or "economism" or "business unionism."[1]

Historically, such tilts toward the "practical" have often been accompanied by the growth of authoritarian and bureaucratic structures in the labor movement, and have also been accompanied by a loss of vitality, a fall-off in worker activism and participation, a decline in the movement's influence and power. The exclusive emphasis on the "practical" seems related to a growing inability to achieve the truly practical goals of defending and advancing the working conditions and living conditions of union members and of the working class in general.

This suggests that organized labor is able to have a powerful impact, and to achieve practical goals beneficial to the working class, primarily when the maintenance of cohesive organizations and pursuit of winnable goals are interwoven with revolutionary commitments. This combination, the interweaving of practical with revolutionary, is essential to the meaning of the term *labor radical*. Such dynamics can, in fact, be traced in the history of the U.S. labor movement.[2]

Those considered "moderates" in the labor movement*—even many who have done fierce battle with labor radicals—have often shown elements of labor radicalism in their own outlooks. While it can be persuasively argued that, for some labor moderates, such "labor radicalism" adds up simply to hypocritical and self-serving rhetorical flourishes, the fact remains that (a) it is unlikely that *all* such expressions of labor radicalism have nothing to do with what the labor moderate actually thinks or feels, and (b) the fact that even an opportunistic labor moderate feels compelled, at least sometimes, to offer expressions of labor radicalism means that there is something compelling him or her to do this. Sometimes, it may be the radicalism of those to whom the labor moderate is speaking, but it also has something to do with the deepest historical roots, and perhaps even the very logic, of the labor movement.

What we will find, in the contributions offered in the latter part of this volume, is that there are definite revolutionary currents that are an integral part of the history of the U.S. labor movement:

1. There are strong influences flowing from the American Revolution and the Second American Revolution (the Civil War).
2. There have been self-consciously revolutionary currents—led by various socialist, communist, and anarchist elements—which at times played an essential role in the struggles to advance the interests of the working class in the United States.
3. There are also, it can be argued, revolutionary challenges inherent in the nature of the labor movement, which sometimes find reflection even in some of the more conservative elements of organized labor.

---

* The reference to "labor moderate" is not meant to indicate moderation in all things—only in regard to the revolutionary goals, which they reject. Some labor moderates (though hardly all) have demonstrated immoderate capacities for authoritarian methods, corruption, use of violence, etc.

The survey provided in this chapter is not meant to constitute even a summary history of the U.S. working class or of the labor movement. It simply seeks to provide a coherent account (with some contextualization) of the development and ongoing expression of labor radicalism—even on the part of many considered to be labor moderates—in the history of the U.S. labor movement.

EARLY REVOLUTIONARY INFLUENCES

The United States of America was established through the American Revolution (1775–1783), which proclaimed that governments should not be ruled by powerful kings but should be based on "the consent of the governed" and exist to provide "life, liberty and the pursuit of happiness" for the people who live here. The merchants, plantation owners and lawyers who were the nation's "Founding Fathers" *were* able to prosper after independence was won from Britain—but many of them prospered at the expense of poor, laboring people and slaves. In fact, the anti-democratic, immoral, inhuman institution of slavery became an essential component of U.S. economic development and was written into the U.S. Constitution. The Native-American peoples, the Indians, were systematically driven off their land and destroyed. A dirty war was initiated against Mexico that stole half of that country and absorbed it into our own, turning Mexican-Americans from Colorado to Arizona and from Texas to California into second-class citizens. All such things were justified by a racism that stressed the Manifest Destiny of the United States as a "white man's republic." Bigotry was also used against many millions of immigrants—from Ireland and Germany, from China and Japan, from Italy and Poland, and many other parts of the world—who were drawn to this country for the purpose of exploiting their much-needed labor, even as they were put down by various forms of violent prejudice and pervasive discrimination.[3]

However, a powerful countervailing tendency also existed, particularly within sectors of the laboring population. There were some people who took certain Judeo-Christian values so seriously that they insisted on the humanity and dignity and rights of all people, regardless of race, creed, or color. There were some who completely and consistently embraced the radical democratic principles of the 1776 Declaration of Independence:

> We hold these truths to be self-evident, that all men are created equal, that they are endowed by their Creator with certain unalienable rights, that among these are life, liberty and the pursuit of happiness, that to secure these rights, governments are instituted among men, deriving their just powers from the consent of the governed, that whenever any form of government becomes destructive of these ends, it is the right of the people to alter or abolish it, and to institute a

new government, laying its foundation on such principles and organizing its powers in such form as to them shall seem most likely to effect their safety and happiness.[4]

Consistent reference was made—in a variety of reform struggles in succeeding decades—to this document, and to the heroic example of revolutionary struggle waged by modest farmers, small shopkeepers, and both skilled and unskilled laborers in creating a republic in which there was to be liberty and justice for all. Some people fought to implement the proposition that everyone—regardless of race, creed, color, gender, or income level—is included in the notion that "all are created equal" and deserving of equal rights. Such influences could be found among those engaged in struggles against slavery, for women's rights, against racial and ethnic discrimination, and for the dignity of labor.

One of the most radical of the spokesmen for the American Revolution, Tom Paine, whose 1775 classic *Common Sense* powerfully influenced the Declaration of Independence, in 1797 expressed concerns that would become essential themes of the early labor movement: "The accumulation of personal property is, in many instances, the effect of paying too little for the labor that produced it; the consequence of which is, that the working hand perishes in old age [a category, at that time, which might embrace people in their late 40s and 50s], and the employer abounds in affluence." While by no means an opponent of the growing market economy, the old revolutionary (aged 60) nonetheless believed that "the contrast of affluence and wretchedness is like dead and living bodies chained together."[5]

By the early nineteenth century, as the impact of industrial capitalism was beginning to make itself felt in the new republic, workers who organized unions for their mutual protection were often arrested for "unlawful combination." In response, a Boston carpenter and labor agitator named Seth Luther, in the spirit of Paine, scoffed that "the Declaration of Independence was the work of a combination, and was as hateful to the traitors and tories of those days as combinations among workingmen are now to the avaricious monopolist and purse proud aristocrat." In contrast to some male labor activists, Luther insisted that, "unless we have the female sex on our side, we cannot hope to accomplish the object we have in view." In fact, striking factory girls in Lowell, Massachusetts, sounded the same revolutionary note as that articulated by the Boston agitator: "As our fathers resisted unto blood the lordly avarice of the British ministry, so we, their daughters, never will wear the yoke that has been prepared for us."[6]

Such sentiments as these found expression among many engaged in union-organizing efforts: carpenters, typographical workers, masons, shoe workers, textile workers, cigar makers, and more. There were also impressive efforts, in the 1820s, to organize independent workers' parties. Organizers of such efforts won significant support, for a time, as they called for a check on business monopolies and for the expansion of public education, at the same time thundering against the polarization of the American republic into "two distinct classes, the rich and the poor; the oppressor and the oppressed; those that live by their own labor, and they that live upon the labor of others." Such efforts were soon drawn into (and ultimately frustrated by) the Democratic Party, which was reorganized under the rags-to-riches slave owner Andrew Jackson. Yet non-electoral reform struggles (such as that for the ten-hour workday) continued to attract working-class support. "Our cause is the cause of truth—of justice and humanity," in the words of Seth Luther, who added: "Let us be determined no longer to be deceived by the cry of those who produce nothing and who enjoy all, and who insultingly term us—the farmers, the mechanics, and the laborers—the lower orders—and exultingly claim our homage for themselves as the *higher* orders—while the Declaration of Independence asserts that 'All men are created equal.'"[7]

Much of the organized labor movement in the United States failed to rise in support of the abolition of slavery. In some cases, representatives of that movement were inclined to make common cause with agricultural pro-slavery forces against the increasing hegemony of industrial capitalism. A skilled black wage-worker who had been a slave and later became a leader of the abolitionist movement, Frederick Douglass, perceptively analyzed this problem in a manner consistent with revolutionary–democratic principles:

> The slaveholders, with a craftiness peculiar to themselves, by encouraging the enmity of the poor, laboring white man against the blacks, succeeds in making the said white man almost as much a slave as the black slave himself. The difference between the white slave and the black slave is this: the latter belongs to *one* slaveholder, and the former belongs to *all* the slaveholders collectively. The white slave has taken from him by indirection what the black slave has taken from him directly, and without ceremony. Both are plundered, and by the same plunderers. The slave is robbed by his master of all his earnings, above what is required for his bare physical necessities; and the white man is robbed by the slave system, of the just results of his labor, because he is flung into competition with a class of laborers who work without wages . . . They appeal to their pride, often denouncing emancipation as tending to place the white working man on an equality with negroes, and by this means they succeed in drawing off the minds of the poor whites from the real fact that, by the rich slave-master, they are already regarded as but a single remove from equality with the slave.[8]

On the other hand, a radical critique of slavery did find expression among some labor activists, particularly in New England. One 1848 resolution from a convention of workingmen deplored the fact that, "there are at the present time three millions of our brethren and sisters groaning in chains on Southern plantations," and, two years later, a similar convention resolution asserted that, "we regret the despotic attitude of the Slave Power at the South, and the domineering ascendancy of the Money Oligarchy are equally hostile to the interests of labor and incompatible with the preservation of popular rights."[9]

By the late 1850s, a substantial number of Northern workers were drawn into the newly formed Republican Party, in part because they agreed with that party's commitment to the ultimate triumph of the free-labor system predominant in the North over the slave-labor system on which the South's plantation economy was based. The Republicans represented a broad alliance in which pro-industrial business interests were interwoven with small business and farming interests in the North, as well as certain radical sectors of the labor movement and various other reform movements, such as abolitionists and feminists.[10]

Elements of Republican ideology that attracted, reflected, and influenced labor activists can be found in various comments by its most effective early leader, Abraham Lincoln. Most fundamental was his commitment to the revolutionary–democratic ideals of the Declaration of Independence that heralded "a new nation, conceived in liberty, and dedicated to the proposition that all men are created equal," and that would establish "government of the people, by the people, and for the people." Commenting in 1860 about a shoe-workers' strike in New England, he said: "I am glad to see that a system of labor prevails in New England under which laborers can strike when they want to, where they are not obliged to work under all circumstances, and are not tied down and obliged to labor whether you pay them or not."

This defense of the free-labor system was by no means antagonistic to capitalism—Lincoln emphasized that "we do not propose any war on capital," but simply to "allow the humblest man an equal chance to get rich with everybody else . . . in the race for life." At the same time, influenced by the labor theory of value advanced by such classical economists as Adam Smith, he reflected: "Labor is prior to and independent of capital. In fact, capital is the fruit of labor, and could not have existed if labor had not first existed. Labor can exist without capital, but capital could never have existed without labor. Hence, labor is the superior—greatly superior to capital."[11]

Such notions, hardly unique to Lincoln, represented an extension of the revolutionary ideology of 1776 and permeated the ranks of organized labor in the years before and after the Second American Revolution, the Civil War of 1861–1865.

SOCIALIST INFLUENCES

There were other revolutionary influences in the ranks of organized labor, particularly those associated with modern socialist, communist, and anarchist ideologies.

Among the most dramatic of these was Frances (or Fanny) Wright, who first came to the United States from Scotland in 1818 as an enthusiast of the democratic ideals inherent in the American Revolution. Along with Robert Dale Owen (the eldest son of British utopian socialist Robert Owen), she played a major role in the agitation for workingmen's parties in the United States during the 1820s and early 1830s, enjoying a substantial following in New York and beyond. Wright was a prominent writer, editor, and spokesperson for a number of reforms related to public education for all, women's rights, the anti-slavery cause, equal rights for African–Americans, utopian socialist experiments, and the cause of labor. In Wright's opinion, there was now (1830) "a war of class" in which "now and everywhere the oppressed millions are making common cause against oppression," with "labor rising up against idleness, industry against money; justice against law and against privilege." Regarding the 1827 founding of the interracial utopian community of Nashoba in Tennessee, she emphasized the labor theory of value, associated with the pro-capitalist Adam Smith economist, but from which—as in her case—anti-capitalist conclusions could be drawn: "Labor is wealth; its reward should be enjoyment."[12]

While the Nashoba experiment soon collapsed, the term "Fanny Wright-ism" for some time was synonymous with the term radicalism among labor reformers and their enemies. The development of the U.S. economy, however, provided little support for the development of rural utopian communities—the wave of the future was with the rising factory system brought into being by the relentless spread of the Industrial Revolution—in which machine power replaced muscle power in the production of commodities, and the muscles of more and more workers were hitched (now as unskilled laborers) to tending new, wealth-enhancing technologies for lower wages. More and more of the labor force in the United States, soon the majority, was reduced to what labor radicals referred to as "wage-slavery."[13]

An influx of German–American immigrants in the wake of the failed Revolution of 1848 resulted in important new, radical influences on the American scene. Among these were small but vibrant currents that identified with the theoretical perspectives developed by such intellectuals as Wilhelm Weitling, Ferdinand Lassalle, and Karl Marx. Marx's influence would prove especially durable, because it combined a comprehensive orientation rooted in the social sciences with a practical-minded commitment to the actually existing movements and struggles of the working class. In the 1850s, the handful of Marxist partisans, such as Joseph Weydemeyer, sought to strengthen the sporadically growing labor movement, and—organized into such small groups as the New York Communist Club—to help the American workers to realize that "the laboring class is the foundation stone upon which must rest the main reliance of all movements for general and special reforms," and that it was "up to the proletariat" to replace capitalism with "the rule of its own class—the class that no longer has any other class below it," in order to bring about "the abolition of all class privileges."[14]

Yet these revolutionaries found themselves in an incredibly contradictory and fluid reality that created far too many obstacles for the consistent development of such working-class consciousness. In touch with these comrades, Marx was alert to countervailing tendencies in the United States that blocked the realization of the revolutionary socialist scenario. In analyses from the 1840s through the 1850s, he suggested that the radicalism inherent in the early working-class movement of capitalist America had little hope of being triumphant as long as slavery continued to exist and as long as the "safety-valve" of Western lands remained available—which was consistent with the experiences of such German–American communists as Weydemeyer. They consequently threw themselves into the anti-slavery struggle, constituting a dynamic left fringe of the new Republican Party, and did not hesitate to enlist in the ranks of the Union Army with the outbreak of the Civil War. Weydemeyer himself became a colonel leading a regiment of German–Americans, rose to the rank of brigadier-general, and was assigned by Lincoln to serve as commander of the military district of St. Louis, Missouri. Although Weydemeyer himself died a year after the Civil War's end, a significant current of German–Americans, similarly influenced by Marx's ideas, went on to play an essential role in the U.S. labor movement, which grew dramatically (as Marx had suggested it would) after the abolition of the slave system.[15]

In the post-Civil War period, a significant interplay can be observed between the evolution of two of the most prominent "home-grown" labor radicals—William Sylvis and Ira Steward—and Marxist-influenced immigrant workers.

A Pennsylvania iron molder who identified with the radical–democratic currents that had been absorbed into the Democratic Party, Sylvis was a supporter of the Democratic presidential candidate Stephen A. Douglas (who, in turn, was a supporter of the continuation of the slave system), but, as soon as the Civil War broke out, Sylvis's allegiance was with the North, committed to the preservation of the United States, and "from the day the first gun was fired, it was my earnest hope that the war might not end until slavery ended with it." Nonetheless, far from rallying to the ranks of the Republican Party, Sylvis and some like-minded Northern workers hoped to organize a new political party that would place "in positions of public trust men of known honesty and ability; men who know the real wants of the people and who will represent us according to our wishes; men who . . . will not become mere tools of rotten corporations and aristocratic monopolies . . ." After being elected president of the National Molders' Union, Sylvis presented an unabashedly revolutionary orientation:

> I believe that all men are "endowed by their creator with certain inalienable rights" among which is the divine right to labor, the right

to an interest in the soil, the right to free homes, the right to limit the hours of toil to suit our physical capacities, the right to place a valuation upon our own labor proportionate to our social and corporeal wants, the right to be in the first social position in the land, the right to a voice in the councils of the nation, the right to control and direct legislation for the good of the majority, the right to compel the drones of society to seek useful employment . . . and the right to adopt whatever means we please within the pale of reason and law to secure these rights.[16]

With this motivation, he helped to organize and lead the first federation of trade unions after the close of the Civil War, the National Labor Union (NLU). His militancy did not diminish, as he noted that, "to work, to slave, and suffer, for the simple reward of what will keep body and soul together, with no hope of a respite in old age, is the real condition of millions at this hour." According to Sylvis, "the cause of all these evils is the wages system. So long as we continue to work for wages, so long will we be imposed upon by those who buy our labor, so long will we be subjected to small pay, poverty, and all the evils of which we complain . . . We must adopt a system that will divide the profits of labor among those who produce them." With such an orientation, it is not surprising that he welcomed the 1864 formation of the IWA led by Karl Marx, welcomed activists associated with Marx into the NLU, and just before his premature death in 1869 sent the International a warm message:

Our cause is a common one. It is a war between poverty and wealth: labor occupies the same low condition, and capital is the same tyrant in all parts of the world . . . Go ahead in the good work you have undertaken, until the most glorious success crowns your efforts. That is our determination. Our late war resulted in the building up of the most infamous monied aristocracy on the face of the earth. This monied power is fast eating up the substance of the people. We have made war upon it, and we mean to win.[17]

While the NLU failed to survive Sylvis's death (in part owing to the pull of divergent electoral strategies), his ideas were absorbed by what remained of the labor movement, which in fact was spreading and deepening in the years that followed—in the mushrooming Knights of Labor, in a dramatically growing independent labor press, and in the trade unions that were proliferating, especially among skilled workers, and that would soon culminate in the AFL.

Perhaps the most influential labor intellectual to arise in the post-Civil War period was a Boston mechanic named Ira Steward, the foremost figure in the movement for the eight-hour workday. Like Sylvis, who supported his efforts, Steward was an uncompromising foe of the "wages system." Emerging from the milieu of antebellum reformism and labor-radicalism, he independently crafted a revolutionary critique of political economy and capitalism that in many ways paralleled that of Karl Marx.

Steward argued that, just as the reason for "making a man a slave was to get his labor, or its results, for nothing," so "the motive for employing wage-labor is to secure *some* of its results for nothing; and in point of fact, larger fortunes are made out of the profits of wage-labor than out of the products of slavery." In his view, the struggle for the eight-hour workday without a reduction in the worker's income would be possible and desirable, because it would bring about a rise in workers' living standards and freedom while driving down the capitalist's profits. This would mean an end to the wage system, and the capitalist would "pass away with the kings and royalty of the past," giving way to a cooperative economy and a true working-class democracy, or, in Steward's terms, "a republicanization of labor, as well as a republicanization of government."

While Marxist-influenced socialists such as Friedrich Sorge inclined toward a different terminology, they saw in Steward a kindred spirit. They shared with him an English translation of excerpts from Marx's *Das Kapital* (Steward was positively impressed and wrote that he would "help introduce and make his name more common to our readers"), and made common cause with him in organizing a nationwide struggle for the eight-hour workday.[18]

The Workingmen's Party of the United States (WPUS), organized July 19–22, 1876, was the first nationwide socialist organization in the United States. While it did not last even for two years before splitting into irreconcilable factions, it was an important seed-bed for future developments of the American labor movement—embracing trade unionism, labor journalism, workers' education, struggles for social reforms, socialism, and electoral activity.

The WPUS was formed through a merger of several groupings. This included the North American remnants of the IWA (the First International of which Karl Marx had been a primary leader), which included Friedrich Sorge, Carl Speyer, and Otto Weydemeyer. There was the Social-Democratic Workingmen's Party of North America, which included Adolph Strasser, Peter J. McGuire, George Schilling, Thomas J. Morgan, and Albert Parsons. In addition, there were two smaller groups—the Workingmen's Party of Illinois and the Social Political Workingmen's Party of Cincinnati (Ohio). The influence of Marx was obvious within the WPUS, but there were other influences as well, including ideas of the late German socialist leader Ferdinand Lassalle, and the analyses and agitation for the eight-hour workday by Ira Steward.

The fact that the United States was a multicultural "nation of nations" was reflected in the WPUS. The party had two official weekly German-language papers—the Chicago *Verbote* (Herald) edited by Conrad Conzett and the New York *Arbeiter-Stimme* (Labor's Voice) edited by Otto Walster—reflecting the large number of German–American members (Germans were the largest immigrant group in the U.S. at this time, followed by the Irish.) The party's official English-language weekly, the *Labor Standard*, was edited by J. P. McDonnell, a former Irish Fenian and later, for a time, a secretary to Karl Marx in the First International). In addition to this, no fewer than twenty-one other newspapers were published, in various languages, around the country, supporting the WPUS. By the following summer, the WPUS had doubled its membership to 7,000, with eighty-two sections (of which twenty-three were English-language).

The WPUS favored working-class unity, transcending racial and ethnic divisions. Yet there is evidence of prejudice among some of the members in California toward imported Chinese laborers and in Missouri toward black workers. Nor was there an appreciation in the organization of the catastrophe wrought by the Republican Party's final betrayal of Reconstruction and black rights in the South. There were also differences over whether women workers should be organized into trade unions or instead be driven back to their "rightful place" in the home, so as not to compete with male labor. On the other hand, the WPUS did have a small number of black members (most prominently Peter H. Clark of Cincinnati) and women members (generally concentrated in "women's clubs" or, in German, *Frauenverein*), and one of its founding documents proclaimed the organization's adherence to "perfect equality of rights of both sexes."[19]

The decisive event in the short life of the WPUS was what has been appropriately tagged "the great labor uprising," a wave of militant labor insurgencies that swept through many cities as part of a nationwide strike of railway workers. This explosion of working-class protest rocked the United States in the summer of 1877. Initiated as a more or less spontaneous railway workers' strike, it became generalized into a nationwide crescendo of street protests and pitched battles. Millions of dollars' worth of property was destroyed, and well over a hundred lives were lost, with many more injuries. Pittsburgh was at the volatile center of this historic upsurge, but similar confrontations and struggles wracked cities throughout the eastern and mid-western portions of the country. Strikers in Martinsburg, West Virginia, issued a manifesto capturing the sentiments of many:

> Strike and live! Bread we must have! Remain and perish! ... A company that has from time to time so unmercifully cut our wages and finally has reduced us to starvation ... has lost all sympathy ... The merchants and community at large all along the line of the road are on our side, and the working classes of every State in the Union are in our favor, and we feel confident that the God of the poor and the oppressed of the earth is with us. Therefore let the

clashing of arms be heard, let the fiery elements be poured out if they think it right, but in heed to our right and in defense of our families, we shall conquer or we shall die![20]

In many cities, WPUS members seem to have played no visible part in the upsurge. Support meetings and rallies were organized in others—most notably in Boston, Cincinnati, Louisville, Newark, New York City, Paterson, and San Francisco. In Chicago's general strike, WPUS leaders Philip Van Patten, George Schilling, and Albert Parsons were arrested for their efforts to draw the spontaneous outburst into more organized channels, and in St. Louis such WPUS stalwarts as Albert Currlin and Peter Lofgreen (who later assumed prominence as a writer under the name of Laurence Gronlund) played a central role in a general strike that, for a brief period, put workers in control of that city—being dubbed by newspapers "the St. Louis Commune."

The uprising was systematically repressed by Federal troops, but its powerful impact helped to generate future labor struggles, and it also brought a flood of new members into the WPUS, determined to help advance the struggle of labor against capital.

Many of the new members responded to the determination of some WPUS leaders—in contradiction to the organization's more cautious founding documents—to accelerate the efforts to field candidates in elections. In the autumn of 1877, the working-class ferment in many U.S. cities encouraged WPUS sections to run candidates, and rewarded them with amazingly high vote totals. They refused to turn back from this path, and would soon seek alliances and joint efforts with a massive but fuzzy-minded Greenback Labor Party effort that, within a few years, collapsed, leaving the socialist electoralists in disarray. By the 1890s, the organization came under the sway of a doctrinaire interpretation of Marxism associated with Daniel De Leon, which limited its influence in the broader labor movement.[21]

Reacting against the electoralist impulse, a substantial minority in 1877— including Friedrich Sorge, Otto Weydemeyer, Carl Speyer, J. P. McDonnell, Adolph Strasser, a young Samuel Gompers, and others—left the WPUS in order to concentrate on trade union organizing that began with the International Labor Union and eventually evolved into the Federation of Organized Trades and Labor Unions, later renamed the American Federation of Labor. The WPUS majority renamed the organization the Socialistic Labor Party, later simply the Socialist Labor Party (SLP).

Another split occurred in 1881, in the wake of the Greenback-Labor debacle, when more revolutionary elements—disillusioned with electoralism —bolted from the SLP in order to help create the anarchist-influenced International Working People's Association (IWPA). The Chicago wing of this organization (which tended toward a revolutionary, anti-statist interpretation of Marx's ideas more than toward traditional anarchist theory) gained an especially large following and foothold in the labor movement.[22]

Also in 1881, the Federation of Organized Trades and Labor Unions of the United States and Canada (FOTLU) was formed in Pittsburgh, Pennsylvania, largely guided by the trade unionist current among early socialists associated with Adolph Strasser, Friedrich Sorge, Samuel Gompers, and others. In large measure through the efforts of an indefatigable socialist organizer among the carpenters, P. J. McGuire, the Federation called in 1882 for the celebration of Labor Day on the first Monday in September, and also called for nationwide work stoppages and demonstrations on May 1, 1886 in favor of the eight-hour workday (initiating May Day, the international workers' holiday). The influence of Karl Marx was evident in the organization's preamble—which was retained in 1886 when the group was reorganized as the AFL:

> A struggle is going on in the nations of the civilized world between the oppressors and the oppressed of all countries, a struggle between capital and labor, which must grow in intensity from year to year and work disastrous results to the toiling millions of all nations if not combined for mutual protection and benefit. This history of the wage-workers of all countries is but the history of constant struggle and misery engendered by ignorance and disunion; whereas the history of the non-producers of all ages proves that a minority, thoroughly organized, may work wonders for good or evil . . . Conforming to the old adage, "In union there is strength," the formation of a Federation embracing every trade and labor organization in North America, a union founded upon a basis as broad as the land we live in, is our only hope.[23]

Samuel Gompers of the Cigar Makers Union was nominated to be president of the Federation, but so was Richard Powers of the Lake Seaman's Union. The *Pittsburgh Commercial-Gazette* ran an article explaining the contest in this way: "It is thought that an attempt will be made to capture the organization for Gompers as the representative of the Socialists, and if such an attempt is made, whether it succeeds or not, there will likely be some lively work, as the delegates opposed to Socialism are determined not to be controlled by it." In fact, such internal conflict was side-stepped by adept compromises, and Gompers later explained in his autobiography:

> In those early days not more than half a dozen people had grasped the concept that economic organization and control over economic power were the fulcrum which made possible influence and power in all other fields. Control over the basic things of life gives power that may be used for good in every relationship of life. This fundamental concept on which the AFL was later founded was at that time

not formulated in men's minds, and the lines between Socialists and trade unionists were very blurred.[24]

At the founding convention, a controversy also arose around whether the new Federation should consist exclusively of people who were already members of labor unions. In this period, and for many years afterward, only skilled workers were able to build and sustain trade unions organized on a specific craft basis. A decision to make the Federation an exclusively union organization would restrict it to skilled workers. Many delegates agreed with the comments of one that, "I wish this Federation broad enough to encompass all working people in its folds," and an African–American delegate from Pittsburgh explained: "We have in the city of Pittsburgh many men in our organization who have no particular trade, but should not be excluded from the Federation . . . I speak more particularly of my own people and declare to you that it would be dangerous to skilled mechanics to exclude from this organization the common laborers, who might, in an emergency, be employed in positions they could readily qualify them to fill."[25]

This inclusiveness was consistent with the orientation of the Knights of Labor, by far the largest labor organization at the time, some of whose members were present in force at the FOTLU founding. The Knights organized workers into reform struggles, social events, and educational efforts as well as trade union activities. FOTLU included members and some unions that were affiliated with the expansively reformist Knights of Labor, and it was formally on record as favoring close relations with the larger organization. But it represented in the minds of many trade unionists "a broad and enduring basis," as FOTLU secretary Frank Foster put it, for organization because—in contrast to the Knights—it drew members together along "the trade line," providing "greater feasibility and . . . economic soundness" in facing "the growing power of associated capital." Rather than relying on lobbying and elections to secure gains, "in the world of economic reform the working classes must depend upon themselves for the enforcement of measures as well as for their conception," as Foster put it. Eventually, the two groups became rivals, and in the late nineteenth century the reformed AFL would eclipse the then-disintegrating Knights.[26]

SEPARATION OF REVOLUTIONARIES FROM MODERATES

During the 1880s, Gompers became known not as an advocate of socialism but as an advocate of what became known as "pure and simple trade unionism." This meant organizing workers into unions that would focus on struggles at the workplace around issues of higher wages, fewer hours of work, and improved working conditions—to the exclusion of radical social causes, whether socialism or anything else. When asked what the labor movement wanted, Gompers once replied simply: "More." Yet Pennsylvania Federation of Labor president James Maurer (himself a dedicated socialist) has left this record of one of Gompers's many "pure and simple" union speeches:

> If a workingman gets a dollar and a half for ten hours' work, he lives up to that standard of a dollar and a half, and he knows that a dollar seventy-five would improve his standard of living and he naturally strives to get that dollar and seventy-five. After that he wants two dollars and more time for leisure, and he struggles to get it. Not satisfied with two dollars he wants more; not only two and a quarter, but a nine-hour workday. And so he will keep on getting more and more until he gets it all or the full value of all he produces.[27]

Despite rhetoric that retained something of the ardor and implications associated with the old revolutionary orientation, however, a growing number of labor radicals in and around the AFL—including Gompers himself—began to pull in a different direction that enabled them to adapt to the prejudices of some skilled workers (against the unskilled, against new immigrants, against blacks and Asians and other people of color, against female wage-workers) and also to reach far-reaching compromises with some of the more astute ("liberal-minded") representatives of the capitalist system. By the early 1900s, Gompers (while still defending the memory of Karl Marx and the German–American Marxists who had been his teachers and comrades) became an explicit and uncompromising foe of socialism.[28]

In the same period that Gompers was beginning to de-radicalize, however, some of the most vibrant representatives of revolutionary labor were coming to the fore. This was especially true in Chicago, where such figures as August Spies and Michael Schwab among German–Americans, as well as Albert and Lucy Parsons among English-speaking Americans, rose to the leadership of the IWPA, which blended an uncompromisingly revolutionary interpretation of Marx's ideas (which had been moderated and diluted among some of their former SLP comrades) with libertarian and anarchist ideas.

The IWPA was founded at an 1883 conference in Pittsburgh, and it produced a "Pittsburgh Manifesto," which blended ideas from the Declaration of Independence, *The Communist Manifesto*, and anti-centralist conceptions of Russian anarchist Mikhail Bakunin, all in an intransigently revolutionary tone. Some of the Chicago participants were uneasy with this, and (according to one of them), "one time the Pittsburgh program with which many were unsatisfied was discussed. Spies explained: 'The Pittsburgh program is secondary, our program is the *Communist Manifesto*!' . . . Spies had Parsons, Gorsuch and other Americans around him in the office of the *Arbeiter-Zeitung* [Workers Journal, the left-wing daily which he edited] on whom he impressed the basic teachings of the booklet." Parsons himself went out of his way to emphasize that, "the IWPA was not founded by Bakunin" and that, "the IWPA is not in opposition to Marx ... The first publication ever issued by the IWPA was written by Marx and Engels." This was the *Communist Manifesto* (in the first English translation by Helen Macfarlane), of which 25,000 copies were distributed in one year.[29]

Parsons (editor of a lively weekly paper issued by the English-language section of the Chicago IWPA, *The Alarm*, with a weekly circulation of 2,000), noted: "We are called by some Communists, or Socialists or Anarchists. We accept all three of the terms."[30] The ideal society for which Parsons and his comrades were fighting, however, was one in which there would be no government ruling over the laboring majority, not even a paternalistic one dedicated to their well-being, but instead a system of self-government embedded in democratic organizations of the workers themselves, in which the free development of each person would be the condition for the free development of all. Of all the IWPA groupings, only those around Spies and Parsons had the sympathies of the German–American Marxist stalwart Friedrich Sorge, whose description gives a sense of the movement there:

> It is undeniably the meritorious accomplishment of the Chicago anarchists to have brought into this marvelous mixture of workers of all nationalities and languages a certain order, to have created affinity, and to have given the movement at that time unity and goals ... Only the Chicagoans maintained a certain agreement of views and tactics, stayed in close touch with the trade unions and other organizations, and secured themselves great respect and importance among the working population of the city. This they took advantage of on various occasions and made the bourgeois authorities very uncomfortable ... At the head of the Chicago anarchists, indeed of the Chicago workers at that time, stood intelligent and energetic people ... To the aforementioned characteristics must also be added great courage, loyalty of conviction, and untouchable personal honor.[31]

The IWPA leaders were at the head of the massive movement for the eight-hour workday on the first May Day, in 1886, but shortly thereafter were victimized and falsely condemned for murder in the wake of the violent Haymarket Affair, in which someone threw a bomb at police who were breaking up a workers' rally. The subsequent repression destroyed the IWPA and threw the labor movement into disarray. Eight IWPA leaders were arrested for murder, and four (including Spies and Parsons) were executed —although it was widely acknowledged, in the years following their deaths, that they had been innocent of the crimes for which they had been convicted.

A later governor of Illinois provided a posthumous exoneration of the martyrs who had, to a large extent, been killed because of their practical commitment to revolutionary ideas. Those ideas, the speeches and writings of the Haymarket martyrs, were circulated widely within much of the labor movement in future years. Future leaders of the American Railway Union (ARU) and the Western Federation of Miners, Eugene V. Debs and William D. Haywood, are two among many who later personally attested to their profound influence.

In carrying on the revolutionary tradition represented by the Haymarket martyrs, activists such as Debs and Haywood diverged from the path followed by Samuel Gompers and others guiding the AFL. Gompers and his co-thinkers were going in the opposite direction. Increasingly, they veered away from revolutionary principles, on to a path marked by reformist moderation, narrowing "pure and simple" unionism, and partnership with political representatives of the capitalist status quo.

By 1894, when Debs's ARU was engaged in a life-and-death struggle with the railroad industry through the Pullman Strike, with Federal troops coming in on the side of the corporations, Gompers and the AFL leadership gave a rhetorical salute to the "impulsive, vigorous protest against the gathering, growing forces of plutocratic power and corporation rule." But, considering it "folly" to join the ARU in its confrontation with corporate power, the AFL leadership headed off a movement for a general strike in Chicago, the storm center of the Pullman dispute, which was the last best hope for the ARU. The AFL leadership—unsympathetic with the ARU's industrial union structure (at variance with the more exclusive craft union structures and skilled-worker base of most of its own member organizations)—was also less and less inclined to accept the expansive militancy and combative commitment to major social change evident in Debs's own evolution.

By 1901, Debs and others had formed the Socialist Party of America, which enjoyed considerable support among radicalized workers and intellectuals, with a base that soon gave them control of an estimated one-third of the AFL unions. Some unions, such as the locals of the ILGWU, but also miners, machinists, and many others, could not have come into being without the dedication and energy of socialist activists. But they now found themselves at loggerheads with Gompers, who declaimed:

> I want to tell you, Socialists, that I have studied your philosophy; read your works upon economics, and not the meanest of them; studied your standard works . . . And I want to say that I am entirely at variance with your philosophy. I declare it to you. I am not only at variance with your doctrines, but with your philosophy. Economically, you are unsound; socially, you are wrong; industrially, you are an impossibility.[32]

Debs, addressing a state convention of the AFL in Kansas, advanced the other side of the question. He called for trade union organization on an industrial basis, not a craft basis, and for the working class to organize politically as well as economically. "We have now no revolutionary organization of the workers along the lines of this class struggle, and that is the demand of this time," he argued. "The pure and simple trade union will no longer answer. I would not take from it the least credit that belongs to it. I have fought under its banner for thirty years. I have followed it through victory and defeat, generally defeat." It had served a useful function once, but it was being made obsolete by the development of industrial capitalism and the intertwining of big-business corporations with the government. "The tool you worked with twenty-five years ago will no longer do. It would do then; it will not do now." Workers were being organized economically in a union but then being divided in support of one or another pro-capitalist party. This was a recipe for defeat. "You have got to unify your forces," he insisted. "You have got to stand together shoulder to shoulder on the economic and political fields and then you will make substantial progress toward emancipation."[33]

In Debs's view, "the labor question, which is really the question of all humanity, will never be solved until it is solved by the working class. It will never be solved for you by the capitalists. It will never be solved for you by the politicians. It will remain unsolved until you yourselves solve it." The key was consciousness, will, and organized struggle: "As long as you can stand and are willing to stand for these conditions, these conditions will remain; but when you unite all over the land, when you present a solid class-conscious phalanx, economically and politically, there is no power on this earth that can stand between you and complete emancipation." That was the purpose of the political organization to which he had now committed his life: "The Socialist party as the party of the exploited workers in the mills and mines, on the railways and on the farms, the workers of both sexes and all races and colors, the working class in a word, constituting a great majority of the people and in fact THE PEOPLE, demands that the nation's industries shall be taken over by the nation and that the nation's workers shall operate them for the benefit of the whole people."[34]

By 1905, Debs and other (but hardly all) Socialist Party members joined with other socialists, anarchists, and labor radicals to form a new revolutionary union—the Industrial Workers of the World (IWW). It pledged to organize the entire working class on an industrial basis, regardless of race, ethnicity, sex, or occupation, into "One Big Union." The "Wobblies," as they were nicknamed, envisioned their organization as a revolutionary union that would fight for immediate gains as steps designed to lead, hopefully sooner rather than later, to a general strike by the entire working class, capable of bringing the functioning of the entire capitalist economy and government to a standstill. With power in the hands of the working-class majority, the economy would then be owned, organized, and run by the working class. One of the clearest statements of "What We Want" was expressed clearly in one of the many popular songs of Joe Hill, the Swedish immigrant worker who became a U.S. labor martyr in 1915:

> We want all the workers in the world to organize
> Into a great union grand,
> And when we all united stand
> The world for workers we'll demand.
> If the working class could only see and realize
> What mighty power labor has,
> Then the exploiting master class
> Would soon fade away.
>
> Come all ye toilers that work for wages,
>   Come from every land,
>   Join the fighting band,
>   In one union grand,
> Then for the workers we'll make upon this earth a paradise
> When the slaves get wise and organize.[35]

Fired by this vision, the Wobblies reached out to timber workers on the West Coast, harvest hands on the Great Plains, textile workers in New England, steelworkers in the Midwest, and more. The IWW organized black and white timber workers in a united struggle in Louisiana. The organization proved willing and able to organize what many in the AFL had dismissed as "unorganizable," such as the thousands of immigrant workers—men, women, and children laboring in the textile mills—who joined together in what came to be called "the bread and roses strike" in Lawrence, Massachusetts, in 1912. As James Oppenheim put it in his song, dedicated to women workers:

> As we come marching, marching, we bring the greater days.
> The rising of the women means the rising of the race.
> No more the drudge and idler—ten that toil while one reposes.
> But a sharing of life's glories: Bread and roses! Bread and roses![36]

In this strike, the eloquent Wobbly orator Elizabeth Gurley Flynn joined with other skilled organizers such as Arturo Giovannitti and Carlo Tresca to mobilize workers and their families, leading them to victory. Flynn explained the IWW conception of "a labor victory" by insisting that strikes must help workers "gain economic advantage, but must also gain revolutionary spirit, in order to achieve a complete victory." She elaborated:

> For workers to gain few more cents a day, a few more minutes less
> a day, and go back to work with the same psychology, the same

attitude toward society is to have achieved a temporary gain and not a lasting victory. For workers to go back with a class-conscious spirit, with an organized and determined attitude toward society means that even if they made no economic gain they have the possibility of gaining in the future. In other words, a labor victory must be economic and it must be revolutionizing.[37]

In his opening remarks at the founding convention of the IWW, proclaiming the intention of "emancipation of the working class from the slave bondage of capitalism," militant leader "Big Bill" Haywood had denounced the AFL for failing to live up to its own class-struggle preamble, noting that "there are organizations affiliated . . . with the A. F. of L. which in their constitution and by-laws prohibit the initiation or conferring of the obligation [of union membership] on a colored man; that prohibit the conferring of the obligation on foreigners. What we want to establish at this time is a labor organization that will open wide its doors to every man that earns his livelihood either by brain or muscle." What Haywood did, for example during the Lawrence strike, was consistent with these words. "He actually loved to spend time with the workers, to talk with their women and children," recalled tough-minded anarchist Carlo Tresca of the hulking, battle-scarred organizer. "He went to supper with strikers every night . . . He would sleep in the houses of Italians, Syrians, Irish, Poles, Letts. People were all brothers to him."[38]

This approach was translated into practical organizational realities. From 1913 to the early 1920s, for example, a largely immigrant and African–American local of the IWW controlled Philadelphia's docks, led by the black Wobbly, Ben Fletcher. "The organized labor movement has not begun to become a contender for its place in the sun until every man, woman and child in industry is eligible to be identified with its cause, regardless of race, color or creed," Fletcher explained. Noting that "organized labor for the most part, be it radical or conservative, thinks in terms of the white race," he emphasized that this would be changed only when black workers themselves organized "to generate a force which when necessary could have rendered low the dragon of race prejudice whenever and wherever it raised its head." His militant union showed how this could be done, leading to black–white unity and consequent gains for all workers.[39]

The labor radicals *assumed* that the big-business employers would be dedicated to dividing and cheating the workers and using violence against them—and IWW organizers became adept at militant and intelligent mass mobilizations to push back such attacks. Even more serious was the IWW goal of replacing the capitalist economic system with what some of them called "the commonwealth of toil," an economic system that would be owned by all of society and democratically controlled by the working-class majority. The spirit and ideals of the IWW were captured in the great labor anthem

composed by Ralph Chaplin, "Solidarity Forever," which has inspired idealistic activists in the labor movement ever since. Its last verse says:

> In our hands is placed a power greater than their hoarded gold,
> Greater than the might of armies magnified a thousandfold.
> We can bring to birth a new world from the ashes of the old,
> For the union makes us strong.[40]

Fear of this revolutionary labor union caused many mainstream politicians
and some of the smarter employers to develop a more generous attitude
toward reforms that would improve the living conditions and working
conditions of the working class, and even the toleration of more moderate
trade unions. In order to save the existing capitalist system, it would become
necessary to make growing numbers of people feel that the system—while
imperfect—works well enough for enough of the people, enough of the time.
This opened up more space for the more moderate mainstream of the
American labor movement, under the banner of Samuel Gompers's AFL.

TWENTIETH-CENTURY CHALLENGES

The failure of the IWW to replace the increasingly conservatized AFL
highlights challenges faced by revolutionary-minded labor activists in the face
of twentieth-century capitalism in the United States.

The IWW was primarily an organization of working-class revolutionaries
who believed, in the words of its 1908 constitutional preamble, that, "the
working class and the employing class have nothing in common" and that,
"between these two classes a struggle must go on until workers of the
world organize as a class, take possession of the earth and the machinery
of production, and abolish the wage system." Yet this represents the view of
revolutionary workers, not all workers, and under normal circumstances most
workers will not be prepared to risk all that they have for the purpose of
abolishing the wages system. They are dependent on wages for their livelihood
and their very survival. In fact, a function of the trade union is to increase
the income and improve the conditions associated with jobs that are an
integral part of the wages system.

While revolutionaries can help to build strong, effective unions to advance
workers' interests, it is not the case that an organization of revolutionaries can itself function as a trade union, which must include masses of
workers, many of whom may not understand or agree with the revolutionary
program.[41]

One of the clearest revolutionary critiques of the IWW orientation was
developed by someone who had been active in both the IWW and the Socialist
Party, William Z. Foster, who helped develop and lead the small Syndicalist

League of North America and what later became the more substantial Trade Union Educational League (TUEL). Foster rejected the notion of breaking away from non-revolutionary trade unions in order to form revolutionary ones. "The truth is that the trade union movement acts always upon the revolutionary policy of utilizing its power to the utmost in forcing the employer to grant concessions." He insisted that, because of their very nature, "in all trade union movements, conservative as well as radical, there is going on a double-phased process of strengthening their forces and increasing their demands accordingly, and that this process of building constantly greater power and making bigger demands inevitably pushes the unions on . . . to overthrow capitalism." He believed that, in addition to the dynamics inherent in capitalism, the class struggle, and the nature of unions, there was a need for what he called the *militant minority*, comparable with the leaven necessary to cause a loaf of bread to rise. "The militant minority is the thinking and acting part of the working class," Foster asserted. "It works out the fighting programs and takes the lead in putting them into execution."[42]

Foster and a small circle of co-thinkers immersed themselves in organizing activity with the AFL (a strategy they termed "boring from within"), finding strong allies in such people as John Fitzpatrick, president of the Chicago Federation of Labor, in a successful organizing drive among packinghouse workers, and more vacillating support from Samuel Gompers himself and the entire AFL in the effort to organize steelworkers that culminated in the momentous 1919 steel strike. The strike took place during the "Red Scare" repression of radical labor in the United States during and after World War I and in the wake of the 1917 Russian Revolution, from which V. I. Lenin, Leon Trotsky, and others called for global working-class insurgencies to overthrow capitalism. The primary targets of the repression had been the Socialist Party, the IWW, and the anarchists, but the steel strike was also tarred with the same brush. The strike was smashed by the combination of intransigent steel corporations, a viciously hostile press, and brutal assaults from local, state, and national authorities, with the AFL leadership backing away, once again, as it had done at the time of the Pullman Strike.[43]

Inspired by the Russian Revolution's establishment of a soviet republic, and the subsequent founding of the Communist International, segments of the Socialist Party and IWW, even some anarchists, as well as Foster and others from the TUEL, came together to establish a U.S. branch of the Communist Party. In the early 1920s, under Foster's leadership, the TUEL became a significant force in many of the unions affiliated to the AFL. The promising beginnings of this labor left wing were shattered by the combined effects of an anti-communist offensive orchestrated by the Gompers leadership and sectarian blunders of the Communists themselves.[44]

By the late 1920s and early 1930s, the Communists' consequent isolation from labor's mainstream intertwined with a sectarian policy emanating from the Stalin dictatorship in the Soviet Union that called for the formation of "revolutionary trade unions," which caused American Communists to build rival unions to those of the AFL. Despite some heroic efforts under the banner of the Trade Union Unity League, Communist Party efforts yielded few positive results.

Some left-wing socialists and dissident communists sought to maintain the "boring from within" strategy that would enable radical organizers to build up a dynamic left wing in the mainstream of the labor movement. One of the most influential figures to advance this perspective was Rev. A. J. Muste, who served as the director of Brookwood Labor College from 1921 to 1933. Hundreds of labor activists were trained at Brookwood, which was largely funded and supported by AFL unions, but within which there were strong left-wing influences—symbolized by a May Day celebration in which there were portraits of Samuel Gompers, Eugene V. Debs, Karl Marx, and Vladimir Ilyich Lenin. The tensions inherent in this situation culminated in the ejection of Muste and others, who went on to form their own left-wing American Workers Party.[45]

From Great Depression to Cold War

When the U.S. and global economies took a disastrous downturn with the Great Depression of the 1930s, an increasing number of radicalizing young workers began organizing militant struggles and industrial unions more in the spirit of the old IWW, and the AFL proved completely incapable of overcoming its ingrained conservatism and narrowness. In 1934, there were signs that the workers could win if they had capable leaders. In Minneapolis, Vincent Raymond Dunne and other dissident-communist followers of Leon Trotsky (who opposed the Stalin dictatorship that had taken over in the decade following the Russian Revolution) led thousands of teamsters and others to victory through a militant general strike that used bold new tactics. In San Francisco, mainstream communists allied with Harry Bridges led West Coast longshoremen to a partial victory after a hard-fought general strike. In Ohio, Toledo Auto-Lite workers, led by militants from A. J. Muste's American Workers Party, won a similar victory.[46]

These three victories rocked the labor movement, particularly owing to the revolutionary orientation of the strikes' leadership. "Our policy was to organize and build strong unions so workers could have something to say about their own lives and assist in changing the present order into a socialist society," Dunne matter-of-factly commented. On the West Coast, Bridges offered the view that, "the capitalistic form of society . . . means the exploitation of a lot of people for a profit and a complete disregard of their interests for that profit, [and] I haven't much use for that." In "every strike situation," Muste commented, "the policy of drawing in the broadest forces—all the unions, unemployed organizations, political parties and groups—must be carried out in order to break down trade union provincialism; to politicalize the struggle; develop class consciousness; face the workers with the problems of conflict with capitalist governmental agencies, etc."[47]

The revolutionary challenge transformed the American labor movement. This is dramatically illustrated in the evolution of John L. Lewis of the United Mine Workers of America (UMW). Lewis had never been a labor–radical or a socialist—he had been a Republican and an advocate of the Gompers "pure and simple unionism" line. But he was convinced, along with several other top union leaders in the AFL, that the time had come to organize the mass of unskilled and semi-skilled mass-production workers in the steel, auto, electrical, rubber, textile, and other industries, as well as transit workers, longshoremen and maritime workers, white collar workers, and others. In order to do that, it would be necessary to overcome many of the racial, ethnic, and gender barriers of the AFL, to work with idealistic left-wing political radicals shunned by the traditional AFL leaders, and to organize on a more inclusive industrial-union basis. This could only be done, in the 1930s, by breaking with the AFL and starting a new, more radical and socially conscious labor federation—the CIO.[48]

The CIO was built by thousands of men and women who organized their co-workers into new industrial unions, went on strike and maintained picket lines, and conducted sit-down actions that took over factories, winning over and mobilizing communities, facing and defying company goons, and battling anti-union vigilantes and sometimes pro-company police forces and National Guard units. None of this would have been possible without the involvement of a "militant minority" of revolutionary activists—from the Communist and Socialist Parties, from Trotskyist and other dissident–communist groups, and from various independent socialist and anarchist currents.[49]

Nonetheless, Lewis, with his stern face, his bushy eyebrows, and his militant labor oratory, which resonated with Shakespearean and Biblical tones, became a powerful symbol of the new unionism that was transforming and revitalizing the American labor movement. Echoes from the revolutionary rhetoric of more than a century could be heard in his pronouncements:

> This movement of labor will go on until there is a more equitable and just distribution of our national wealth. This movement will go on until the social order is reconstructed on a basis that will be fair, decent, and honest. This movement will go on until the guarantees of the Declaration of Independence and of the Constitution are enjoyed by all the people, and not by a privileged few.[50]

The radical editor of the CIO News, Len DeCaux, later described the early CIO as "a mass movement with a message, revivalistic in fervor, militant in mood, joined together by class solidarity." The CIO's expansive and radical idealism was captured by DeCaux in this description:

As it gained momentum, this movement brought with it new political attitudes—toward the corporations, toward police and troops, toward local, state, national government. Now we're a movement, many workers asked, why can't we move on to more and more? Today we've forced almighty General Motors to terms by sitting down and defying all the powers at its command, why can't we go on tomorrow, with our numbers, our solidarity, our determination, to transform city and state, the Washington government itself? Why can't we go on to create a new society with the workers on top, to end age-old injustices, to banish poverty and war.[51]

In the mid-to-late 1930s, however, Lewis and other CIO leaders (including those associated with the Communist Party) turned away from the notion of launching an independent labor party in order to support, instead, the social–liberal presidency of Franklin D. Roosevelt and the New Deal reform program of the Democratic Party. As James Matles, left-wing leader of the UE, commented, in the difficult years of the Great Depression, "Roosevelt knew that this [capitalist] system had to make concessions in order to save itself, and he proceeded on a course to do just that, to save the corporate system in America . . . Under the pressure of the millions, he gave ground. He put through some of the outstanding labor and social legislation of our time . . ." In doing this, he helped to nurture a dependence of the growing labor movement, both CIO and AFL, on the Democratic Party and on institutions of the state (such as the National Labor Relations Board). When someone even as influential in labor's ranks as John L. Lewis resisted this trend, he was forced out of the leadership of the CIO. Those inclined toward revolutionary perspectives, no less than those inclined toward trade union moderation, would feel the resulting constraints in future years, particularly as the political climate in the United States tilted in a more conservative direction.[52]

Another complication for would-be revolutionaries in the U.S. labor movement involved the contradictions that developed in the Communist movement with the consolidation of the vicious bureaucratic regime over Soviet communism of Josef Stalin. Those loyal to the Communist mainstream, whatever their noble and idealistic intentions or their substantial and positive contributions to the labor movement, became associated with one of the worst dictatorships in human history, and with policies sometimes more in tune with foreign policy preferences of Soviet leaders than with actual revolutionary principles or the best interests of the working class. During World War II, when the United States and the Soviet Union were allies against Nazi Germany, this seemed unproblematical. But, in the late 1940s, a Cold War confrontation developed between the two countries, lasting for half a century. This helped generate a new, anti-communist "red scare," and the deepened dependence of labor on government supportiveness caused leaders of both the AFL and the CIO to launch fierce assaults on Communists, but also on other radicals and revolutionaries in their own ranks.[53]

The expulsion of eleven "left-wing" unions from the CIO was part of a de-radicalization that enabled the two labor federations to unite into the AFL–CIO in 1955, with the consequent marginalization of the revolutionary influences that had played such an important role in the labor movement in earlier times. This was reinforced by dramatic changes in the U.S. economy and social reality that would erode the conditions which had provided the base for labor radicalism in earlier decades—an unprecedented, long-term prosperity embracing a majority of the working class until the 1970s and 1980s; the spread of consumerism and suburbanization; the transformation of the workplace through technological innovation; a dramatic increase in the percentage of white-collar occupations in the working class; and early developments in what would eventually explode into what would later be called "globalization."

This led to a long-term decline, not only of revolutionary currents in the labor movement, but of the labor movement's social vision and old idealism that had made it such an attractive force for many working people. It could be argued that AFL–CIO President George Meany, a tough-talking, cigar-chomping plumber, had an outlook in many ways no broader than that of Sam Gompers in his twilight years. A counter-argument—a variation of William Z. Foster's old notion that the trade union movement was inherently more revolutionary than the excessively moderate stance of its leaders—was advanced by a popular Socialist Party spokesperson of the 1960s and 1970s, Michael Harrington, who argued that the "progressive" social policies of ostensibly pro-capitalist labor leaders such as Meany and ex-socialist Walter Reuther of the United Auto Workers (UAW) added up to the creation of new "socialist definitions of capitalism" that could pull the United States beyond the oppressive limitations of the market economy.[54]

One person who represented a genuinely expansive social vision in the AFL–CIO, and who never renounced his earlier socialist commitments, was the head of the Brotherhood of Sleeping Car Porters (BSCP), A. Philip Randolph. Randolph had pioneered in forming a strong, all-black union—no mean trick in the racist climate of the 1920s—a union that pushed its way into a reluctant AFL and stayed there, fighting both for black–white unity in labor struggles and for racial equality within the labor movement. An early pioneer and highly respected leader of the modern civil rights movement, Randolph's crowning achievement was to conceive of and oversee the organization of the 1963 March on Washington—the massive march where Martin Luther King, Jr. gave his "I Have a Dream" speech. Randolph proclaimed to the gathering that this massive demonstration represented "the advance guard of a massive moral revolution for jobs and freedom."[55]

In 1966, Randolph issued *A "Freedom Budget" for All Americans*, endorsed by over 200 prominent civil rights, trade union, social activist, and academic figures. He described the Freedom Budget's meaning:

> The "Freedom Budget" spells out a specific and factual course of action, step by step, to start in early 1967 toward the practical liquidation of poverty in the United States by 1975. The programs urged in the "Freedom Budget" attack *all* of the major causes of poverty—unemployment and underemployment; substandard pay, inadequate social insurance and welfare payments to those who cannot or should not be employed; bad housing; deficiencies in health services, education, and training; and fiscal and monetary policies which tend to redistribute income regressively rather than pro-gressively. The "Freedom Budget" leaves no room for discrimination in any form, because its programs are addressed to *all* who need more opportunity and improved incomes and living standards—not just to some of them.

Randolph explained that such programs "are essential to the Negro and other minority groups striving for dignity and economic security in our society," but that "the abolition of poverty (almost three-quarters of whose victims are white) can be accomplished only through action which embraces the totality of the victims of poverty, neglect, and injustice." He added that, "in the process everyone will benefit, for poverty is not an isolated circumstance affecting only those entrapped by it. It reflects—and affects—the performance of our national economy, our rate of economic growth, our ability to produce and consume, the condition of our cities, the levels of our social services and needs, the very quality of our lives." In Randolph's opinion, the success of this effort would depend on "a mighty coalition among the civil rights and labor movements, liberal and religious forces, students and intellectuals—the coalition expressed in the historic 1963 March on Washington for Jobs and Freedom."[56]

However, the Freedom Budget was too radical for most of the Democratic and Republican politicians—and it "didn't sell" under the Lyndon Johnson presidency, not to mention that of his conservative successor, Richard Nixon. As labor didn't have a political party of its own, this closed the door on such proposals as the "Freedom Budget." A bitter Randolph commented that the persistence of poverty and racism is rooted in "fundamentally economic problems which are caused by the nature of the system in which we live. This system is a market economy in which investment and production are determined more by the anticipation of profits than by the desire to achieve social justice." This suggested, despite Randolph's desire to appeal to moderate labor and political elements, the revolutionary implications of the Randolph's far-reaching goals.

His ally, Martin Luther King, Jr.—less inclined than Randolph to compromise with Democratic Party politicians who (at the time) prioritized the Vietnam War over any wars on poverty—argued, before he was killed, that "revitalized sectors of the labor movement" must join together with other social movements to (in his words) "reshape economic relationships and usher in a breakthrough to a new level of social reform."[57]

FROM 1960S RADICALISM TO "REAGANISM"

Such developments failed to take shape in the final decades of the twentieth century. With the dramatic and relentless decline in the power, influence, and membership of the organized labor movement in the United States, those defending the "pure and simple" approach of Gompers and the relatively conservative "business unionism" of Meany increasingly lost credibility. More radical rhetoric once again found expression within labor's leadership, and some in labor's ranks began to look for inspiration to the movement's revolutionary traditions.

There were vital pockets of left-wing influence that survived from the labor–radicalism of the 1930s—some of which were rooted in what remained of the communist-influenced unions expelled at the end of the 1940s. Two major unions, the UE and the West Coast International Longshore and Warehouse Union (ILWU), survived—battered, smaller, but tough and resilient. Others passed out of existence, but with elements absorbed by other unions, in some cases those with leaderships still relating to left-of-center and even socialist traditions. Among the most notable were the United Packinghouse Workers of America, the Amalgamated Meat Cutters and Butcher Workmen of North America, and Retail, Wholesale and Department Store Employees—which fostered the Hospital Workers Union Local 1199.

Especially in the 1960s, Local 1199 (soon to become a full-scale union in its own right) played an outstanding role in drawing together a variety of militant workers—with large percentages of Jewish–American workers joining with rapidly growing numbers of African–American and Puerto Rican workers, and others, to form a militant, multicultural union suffused with the traditions of labor militancy, the idealism characteristic of the civil rights movement, and a radical social vision going far beyond the modernized "pure and simple" unionism that characterized the Meany leadership of the AFL–CIO and the bulk of the unions affiliated to it.[58]

The organization of health care workers was part of a larger trend that saw service workers of various kinds, and public employees, flock into unions in increasing numbers—such as the American Federation of Teachers (competing with the National Education Association, which was in the process of shifting from being a "professional organization" to a union orientation), the Service Employees International Union, and the American Federation of

State, Municipal, and County Employees. The U.S. labor movement consisted of increasing numbers of women and people of color, who also represented a substantial percentage of the influx of members in the service and public sector unions—qualitatively changing a movement that had historically been dominated by white males and introducing a radical challenge to racist and sexist tendencies in the ranks of organized labor.

Another sector of the labor force brought into the union movement in the 1960s and 1970s involved agricultural workers, organized by the United Farm Workers of America under the leadership of Cesar Chavez, and later involving such groups as the Farm Labor Organizing Committee. Here, too, explicitly radical ideals and values were an integral part of the crusading fervor that it took to carry out and build nationwide solidarity for the organizing efforts.[59]

All of this was taking place within a larger context of resurgent social protest that swept through the country, and became increasingly prevalent, from the late 1950s into the 1970s. A variety of issues—ranging from foreign policy to multiple domestic social ills—gave rise to protests and social movements. Within this broadening and diverse mixture of activism, one could find many motivated by the radical and revolutionary perspectives of bygone decades—different variants of socialism (some insistently revolutionary; others strongly reformist, often blended with a strong Cold War anticommunism) and communism (including the old-line Communist Party, Trotskyists of different blends, and a new current inspired by Mao Zedong Thought from China). There was a strong leaven of social radicalism more independent of Marxist influence (including a sprinkling of anarchist ideas), and quite powerful doses of religious radicalism. Evolving in contradictory interrelation with all of this was the rise of a very youthful "new left," whose most influential organizations were initially the Student Nonviolent Coordinating Committee (SNCC), on the left wing of the civil rights movement, and Students for a Democratic Society (SDS).[60]

Most of this was flourishing outside of the organized labor movement. Indeed, the mainstream of that movement—the AFL–CIO under George Meany—tended, in its great majority, to be stand-offish, suspicious, or openly hostile to such radicalism. This caused many of the younger radical activists (and some older ones as well) to be dismissive of unions, and in some cases of the working class itself as a force that would ever be capable of bringing about meaningful social change. Both appeared to have become pillars of the capitalist status quo (although some perceptive social critics with experience in labor struggles—Harvey Swados, C. L. R. James, and Harry Braverman, among others—sharply challenged "the myth of the happy worker").[61] On the other hand, many pro-labor ideologists (especially those tied in with the Meany leadership) dismissed most of the social protests and radical critics as "middle class," having nothing to do with America's working-class majority and peripheral to the concerns of the majority of people dealing with everyday economic realities in the actual workplaces of America. This notion found expression among some organizations of the "old left."

Middle class is a notoriously fuzzy, ambiguous, sometimes almost mindlessly derogatory term that can have multiple and divergent meanings.[62] Its value in characterizing the social protests of the 1960s was challenged by left-wing analyst George Breitman, with rich labor experience of his own, who responded: "It is idiotic and insulting to think that the worker responds only to economic issues." He elaborated:

> The radicalization of the worker can begin off the job as well as on. It can begin from the fact that the worker is a woman as well as a man; that the worker is black or Chicano or a member of some other oppressed minority as well as white; that the worker is a father or mother whose son can be drafted [into the military]; that the worker is young as well as middle aged or about to retire. If we grasp the fact that the working class is stratified and divided in many ways—the capitalists prefer it that way—then we will be better able to understand how the radicalization will develop among workers and how to intervene more effectively. Those who haven't already learned important lessons from the radicalization of oppressed minorities, youth, and women had better hurry up and learn them, because most of the people involved in these radicalizations are workers or come from working-class families.[63]

Despite the validity of these insights, the facts remain that:

1. the radicalization of the 1960s for the most part developed independently of the organized labor movement;
2. the consciousness animating the various movements and struggles of that period simply did not, in most instances, involve a clear *class* consciousness;
3. increasingly, owing to the realities noted by Breitman, it would be the case that the relative conservatism prevalent in many unions would increasingly be altered by the influence of various social movements—civil rights, anti-war, student radical, feminist, environmental, gay rights, and so on.

A proliferation of caucuses and committees arose in various unions in the late 1960s and 1970s and, in some cases, across union lines, as with the Coalition of Black Trade Unionists and the Coalition of Labor Union Women (both reflecting the fact that African–Americans and women represented dramatically rising percentages of union membership). In the late 1960s, a number of left-leaning union officers, staffers, and members created an organization called Labor for Peace that, by 1970, breaking sharply with the AFL–CIO position of support for the Vietnam War, called the conflict "A Rich Man's War and a Poor Man's Fight," explaining:

> The greatest horror of Vietnam is its cost in lives . . . 40,000 young Americans so far, and hundreds of thousands of Vietnamese. No amount of American money, or material, or good intentions can buy back the lives lost. Nor assuage the agony of thousands of our families. This is horror enough. But Vietnam creates a second horror: The disfigurement of our society and our economy. . .
>
> Compelling economic facts convince us that the Vietnam War is a threat to the American people and to the kind of society we, as trade unionists, are trying to establish. Vietnam eats up workers' wages. Vietnam causes inflation. As long as we are in Vietnam, we will not achieve tax justice. As long as we are in Vietnam, we will have insufficient housing, education and health care; our cities will rot.[64]

In some cases, younger radicalized activists coming into the workforce were able to connect with seasoned veterans of radical struggles who were already there—but, in some cases, there were tensions and conflicts between one-time radical union leaders and younger rank-and-file militants. One of the most dramatic instances of this involved a confrontation in the UAW between the Black Revolutionary Union Movement (many of whose members were animated by a blend of black nationalism and Maoism) and the UAW leadership around Walter Reuther. In other cases, younger radicals were able to join with more experienced trade unionists to help bring about significant changes. This was the case, to a considerable degree, within the UMW and also within the International Brotherhood of Teamsters—both unions that had been built up through surges of class-conscious militancy; both unions in which earlier left-wing dissidents had been dealt overwhelming defeats by autocratic leaders; both unions in which corrupted bureaucracies were now effectively challenged by rank-and-file insurgencies partially inspired by the rich traditions of labor radicalism—with Miners for Democracy and Teamsters for a Democratic Union bringing about significant transformations, with major victories followed by some (but not all) hopes being disappointed.[65]

It was a militant campaign in the United Steelworkers of America in 1976–1977, however, that seemed like it could tilt labor's mainstream far to the left. Denouncing the bureaucratic conservatism represented by George Meany's AFL–CIO, which had long permeated the United Steelworkers, Ed Sadlowski called—in his presidential challenge to the union's established leadership—for "a tough, democratic unionism" that would emphasize broad social ideals and a militant class-consciousness reminiscent of the radicalism of the 1930s. It seemed that the nature of the U.S. labor movement could change dramatically if members of the powerful United Steelworkers responded to Sadlowski's message. One reporter took down this piece of that message:

> Guys who work in the mill, they'd give their right arm to get outta there. But they want something more than that paycheck. They know this country can't do without their labor. Instead, these companies treat 'em like animals or throw 'em away when they find some machine to replace them. Everybody needs some cause to identify with. So you don't give up and let 'em run over you. The present labor leadership's failed in that. The CIO—now that didn't stand [just for] for pensions and vacations—that stood for a vision of social justice and people's dignity.

Time magazine sniffed that such stuff might appeal to "limousine liberals" more than to the average steelworker: "Basic Steelworkers average about $8 an hour, hardly a depressed wage; many live in the suburbs, and few are disposed to left-leaning politics." In fact, Sadlowski went down to defeat—but he got 200,000 votes, against 300,000 for the incumbent machine, suggesting that there was indeed some resonance to his message among many "average Steelworkers." In the shifting economic climate that had given rise to the Sadlowski challenge (and to radical-democratic insurgencies in other unions), a future left-shift among a majority of workers in the highly unionized industrial sector of the labor force was not inconceivable.[66]

The wages, benefits, and "middle-class" lifestyle of many steelworkers—and other workers in "America's industrial heartland"—would soon be in jeopardy as an increasing number of industrial corporations began shifting operations and investments away from areas with high levels of union membership. Greater profits could be made in other parts of the world and other sectors of the economy. The United Steelworker leadership's much-vaunted harmonious relationship with the steel companies' top executives proved worthless in stopping this trend—though it is not clear that the militancy represented by radical union insurgents would have been able to prevent the *de-industrialization* strategy of the United States-based multinational corporations that dominated the national economy.

This by no means meant the immediate collapse either of organized labor or of the labor radicalism that sought to revitalize it. In the Oil, Chemical, and Atomic Workers union, for example, Tony Mazzocchi played an outstanding role in helping connect health and safety concerns in his union (related to the case of martyred union militant Karen Silkwood) with larger environmental struggles.[67] He went on to press for a militant, socially conscious unionism in his own organization and the larger labor movement, among other things arguing that big business has two parties (Democrats as well as Republicans) but there should be one that is of, by, and for the working class—initiating Labor Party Advocates with a number of other left-of-center forces in the labor movement. In addressing the members of his own union, he emphasized:

> The labor movement should be a crusade. It's a commitment for tomorrow . . . Brothers and sisters, black and brown and white, I'm urging you to join me in a new crusade. I'm urging you to join me to find that rededication that once moved this labor movement— that speaks to the best of the Joe Hills and the Karen Silkwoods and the Martin Luther Kings . . . We can build a new movement and a new movement can build a new America. And in the words of the song we sang at the beginning of the convention, "We *do* have a power mightier than the gold, and we *will* build a new world from the ashes of the old."[68]

In organizations as diverse as the International Association of Machinists and the Screen Actors Guild, radical themes were also sounded—with their respective presidents, William Winpisinger and Ed Asner, explicitly identifying themselves as socialists. This was reflective of a growing sense of militancy within labor's ranks—particularly with the increasingly perceptible erosion of working conditions and living standards, and employer "get-tough" attitudes toward unions in general.

Such ferment was also reflected in the unprecedented Solidarity Day march and rally drawing over 250,000 union members and supporters to Washington, DC, on September 19, 1981, organized under the leadership of labor moderate Lane Kirkland, the new President of the AFL–CIO. Mobilizing for labor rights and working-class interests, and especially targeting the conservative anti-labor policies of the recently elected president, Ronald Reagan, the action seemed to represent a dramatic shift away from the modernized "pure and simple" union approach represented by the recently deceased George Meany. "Virtually every significant union brought members from around the country," according to Kirkland's biographer, Arch Puddington, "as did organizations representing blacks, Hispanics, women, environmentalists, the disabled, the elderly, and various organizations of the political left."[69]

What the modestly leftish tilt did not represent, however, was either (1) a break from traditional union support for the Democratic Party (many saw Solidarity Day as representing an effort to influence the pro-capitalist Democrats to do battle for labor's cause), or (2) the harbinger of any kind of left-wing class struggle strategy on the part of labor's leadership. No effective resistance was mounted to prevent President Reagan's strike-breaking destruction of the Professional Air Traffic Controllers' Organization (PATCO), nor to stop the vicious use of replacement workers to break strikes at Continental Airlines, Eastern Airlines, Hormel, Greyhound, Phelps-Dodge, and Danley Machine Corporation.[70]

Militant strikes influenced by older radical traditions and tactics were conducted by the United Mineworkers against the Pittston Coal Corporation and, to a somewhat lesser extent, by the United Steelworkers against the Ravenswood Aluminum Company. These two strikes were among the few union victories in the 1980s. Union strength continued to be eroded, thanks to the resurgence of aggressively anti-union policies within the business community, thanks to the unrelentingly pro-business policies of what came to be dubbed "Reaganism" (continued in varying ways by the presidencies of George H. W. Bush, Bill Clinton, and George W. Bush), and thanks to the far-reaching economic restructuring carried out by United States-based multinational corporations associated with "globalization." Largely in reaction to labor's declining situation, a "New Voices" slate headed by John Sweeney, accompanied by the militant young leader of the Mineworkers, Rich Trumka (destined to succeed him in 2009), and other labor progressives, was swept into the leadership of the AFL–CIO in 1995.[71]

Sweeny's self-identification as a socialist, along with his openness to more socially expansive rhetoric and experiments, excited hopes among many who believed that labor could only survive by applying traditional radical perspectives to the new realities facing U.S. workers. But the continued failure of the AFL–CIO to grow and to reverse the downward slide of working-class living standards was to generate controversy, crisis, and fragmentation within labor's ranks.

WHAT NEXT?

Historian Warren Van Tine once suggested that the U.S. labor movement has variously been characterized by four different images—"the union as a fraternity, a democracy, an army, and a business." By the 1920s, he tells us, "the concepts of the union as an army and the union as a business were far more prominent and influential," with hierarchy, elitism, and bureaucracy displacing notions of the union as a band of brothers and sisters or as representing rule by the people.[72] This was especially so with the triumph of the dramatically conservatized and corrupted AFL over the idealistic militants of the IWW. In the 1930s, with the rise of the left-wing-influenced CIO, this trend was temporarily reversed. By the 1950s and 1960s, as we have seen, the model of "business unionism"—encouraged by the general prosperity and working-class gains—became predominant. But this much-lauded "realistic" and "mature" approach would prove woefully inadequate in the face of new challenges that were about to arise.

Through a social compromise forged with big business and big government during and after World War II, the leadership of the organized labor movement in the United States embraced the rights of the capitalist elite to control the economy, as well as an essentially imperialist foreign policy, in order to secure "the American Dream" for a majority of the U.S. working class. But, by the late 1970s, the most powerful of the capitalists—driven by the profit-maximizing dynamics of their own system—had decided on a different approach. The great revolutionary Rosa Luxemburg once spoke of trade union struggles as "the labor of Sisyphus"—referring to the mythical being who kept rolling an immense boulder up a hill, only to have powerful oppressors roll it back down again. That is how capitalism works, and the dynamic reasserted itself with a vengeance.

While the bureaucratic–conservative leadership of organized labor had little interest in maintaining in "their" unions the popular-democratic idealism that had mobilized millions of workers to win the victories of the 1930s and 1940s, it had been these victories that caused important elements among the capitalist power elite to accept a dramatic power shift in the economy. The economic regulations and social programs imposed by a liberal government and acceptance of organized labor's existence and influence constituted President Franklin D. Roosevelt's New Deal, which (with modifications) was more or less accepted by both the Democratic and Republican parties for three decades. But there had always been a financially powerful conservative faction in the business community that refused to accept this. It would spend considerable time, resources, and energies to build what would soon prove to be a triumphant counter-attack.

With the electoral sweep of Ronald Reagan in 1980, the once-marginal perspectives of the business conservatives of the late 1940s and 1950s became the new political and economic orthodoxy of the United States in the final decades of the twentieth century. The demolition of the assumptions and programmatic vestiges of the New Deal, and of the once-powerful labor movement, seemed to have been largely a "mission accomplished," even before George W. Bush took office.[73] Kim Moody's summary cannot be improved upon:

> The industrial centerpieces of the US economy shrank or reorganized, and the cities, towns, and unions based on them went into decline and/or dramatic changes in make-up. The industrial "heartland" became the rust belt. The "industries" that appeared to replace them were low-wage and mostly nonunion. Technology, "deployed with ferocity" in a more competitive world, as one economist put it, eliminated some jobs and intensified others. The loss of union density turned into an absolute loss of union members. The institution of collective bargaining was turned from a phalanx of advance to a line

of retreat. The upward trend in real wages of the previous thirty years reversed into a prolonged downward spiral. The decline in economic inequality that began during World War II stopped, and inequality accelerated with each decade. The New Deal liberal consensus that had dominated politics for over three decades was drowned in a sea of money and replaced by an aggressive neoliberalism that called itself conservative. The underpinnings of American labor ideology were invalidated, though union leaders clung tenaciously to the old tenets. Greed became good. Business values took center field. What had been national became global. Globalization, in turn, became the reason or excuse for every move against the working-class majority.[74]

Since World War II, the U.S. working class has decomposed and recomposed—capitalism is continually doing that—through the workings of the never-ending economic restructuring designed to maximize employer control over the labor process and the profits they are able to extract.[75]

Such recomposition of the working class, however, is not accompanied by an automatic resurrection of the old radical labor sub-culture of years gone by. Yet the accumulating humiliations and injuries and disappointments, generating widespread reactions among layers of the working class, have opened *possibilities* in our own time for the recomposition of a radical labor sub-culture that could be the basis for a widespread class-consciousness. Michael Yates has referred to this as "a labor-centered way of thinking and acting based upon the understanding that a capitalist society is not and cannot be a just one." The necessity of this way of thinking and acting, Yates suggests, is related to the fact that "what might motivate workers to become part of a movement is the possibility that the current system can be transcended and a new, democratic, egalitarian society built."[76]

This intersects with insights of labor activists whose focus has been riveted to the radical revitalization of trade unions. In their rich "how-to" book, *Democracy is Power: Rebuilding Unions From the Bottom Up*, Mike Parker and Martha Gruelle emphasize the necessity of developing what they call "a democratic culture" within reform caucuses in unions (which they envision becoming the culture within the reformed union itself), involving "how members taking initiative can generate creative strategies, how active inclusion of racial or gender minorities can strengthen the whole group, how encouraging new leadership can also encourage new activism." British labor educator Sheila Cohen, whose thinking runs along similar lines, speaks of an "activist layer" within the union that must have a sharp "focus on issues of ideology and consciousness," helping to develop "an explicit awareness on the part of many of the most militant activists of the need for independence from the objectives of capital, and attention to member-led democracy."[77]

Some might argue, however, that the revitalization Parker, Gruelle, and Cohen are reaching for cannot be realized within an exclusively trade union context. Dan Clawson makes the point quite effectively:

> In the 1960s, the labor movement was largely missing when a set of new movements arose to fight for racial equality, women's liberation, student empowerment, anti-intervention [in Vietnam and else-where], environmental protection, gay and lesbian liberation, and much more. The failure of labor and those movements to connect weakened *both* labor *and* those movements. Labor lost a chance to reinvigorate itself and to make advances on issues that are central to workers' lives; as a consequence, it tended to become narrow, bureaucratic, and insular.

He concludes that, "unless there is a new period of mass social movements, labor is likely to continue to lose ground." Clawson's vision involves insurgencies embracing trade unions, workers' centers, community organizations, social movements, and more.[78]

The question is: how could such a vision become a reality? "A left wing in the unions is not a spontaneous development, any more than strikes and strike-support actions are spontaneous," observed the seasoned labor radical Frank Lovell. "They have to be organized." Noting that a radicalization process had been working its way through growing sectors of the U.S. working class in the course of the 1980s and 1990s, he warned against the fallacy of "identifying radicalization with class warfare. They are not the same. Mass radicalization is a condition of changing attitudes, shifting beliefs, rejecting previously accepted values. It is the subjective responses to social crises." Lovell emphasized: "The radicalization prepares the ground for the success of such [class-struggle] actions, but they do not occur automatically out of the radicalizing process." The same can be said of the ambitious labor–community alliances and elaborate movement combinations projected by Clawson and others. As Bill Fletcher, Jr. and Fernando Gapasin note, in reviewing the history of U.S. labor struggles, "leftist parties and groupings were essential players in developing a class-conscious militant core within a variety of unions"—and, one might add, in a variety of social movements.[79]

To the extent that the combination of these components might be achieved, a mass labor radicalism might crystallize once again. Something akin to a molecular transformation could shift political realities far to the left—with a revolutionary class-consciousness connected with the interplay of organizations, movements, and creative struggles. But such consciousness assumes, at the same time, the existence of a radical labor sub-culture—ranging, one would imagine, from picnics and social gatherings to marches and rallies; from concerts and plays to speeches and forums, various forms of literature (leaflets, pamphlets, poems, and novels) and films (hard-hitting documentaries, well-funded blockbusters, etc.); educational conferences; independent news media; encyclopedias; paintings and drawings; music; multiple Internet outlets, and more.

Elements for such sub-culture and consciousness certainly exist, at least in embryonic form. But, if such a recomposition actually takes place, it will be within a very different economic, social, and cultural reality than existed in the late-nineteenth and early-twentieth centuries. Many of the specifics would necessarily have a different shape and flavor from the sub-culture of earlier years. Yet, regardless of the specifics, the fact that revolutionary and radical labor traditions reach back to the very beginnings of the American Republic would seem to give greater strength and resonance to manifestations of alternative and oppositional cultures among those who labor in the twenty-first century.

CONCLUSION

One purpose of this brief and necessarily incomplete survey has been to demonstrate the centrality of revolutionary currents in the broad stream of U.S. labor history. These currents have not always predominated within that mainstream, but they have never been—and really could never have been—absent. They have historically been a defining element within that mainstream. Given the actual structure and logic of our socio-economic reality, this would seem to be necessarily true. This could explain why they are recurrent, and why they are reflected in the words and actions, not only of labor radicals, but also, time and again, of many considered to be labor moderates.

The history of U.S. labor indicates that, given the extent to which revolutionary currents have been marginalized in the labor movement, the stage has been set for the marginalization of the labor movement as such. We have seen that its strongest partisans have been convinced that, for the labor movement to be triumphant, the revolutionary element—*in the sense of pushing in the direction of a fundamental shift in society giving political and economic power to the laboring majority*—must become predominant.

We concluded this survey with a number of labor analysts suggesting that, to survive and grow, the labor movement must expand well beyond "pure and simple" trade unionism—and must involve far more than simple trade unionism. They believe it must become expansive, generating a rich, affirming, oppositional culture capable of embracing the great majority of the working class, capable of bringing to birth a new world from the ashes of the old. It has yet to be demonstrated, however, how practical this vision actually is.

In his epic poem from the Great Depression of the 1930s, Carl Sandburg wanted to end with optimistic affirmations, but was forced instead to speak in question marks appropriate for today:

Time is a great teacher.
Who can live without hope?

In the darkness with a great bundle of grief
The people march.

In the night, and overhead a shovel of stars for
keeps, the people march:

"Where to? what next?"[80]

PART TWO

VOICES OF U.S. LABOR RADICALISM

The following section of this book is *not* meant to be a Pantheon of Labor Heroes, although each of the people considered did play a heroic role, at least at some point in their lives. But that is true of many thousands, perhaps millions, of others who have been associated with working-class movements and labor struggles since the coming into being of the United States of America.

Nor should there be any notion that these are "perfect" models of what one should be or do in the struggles of labor. All did set examples worth emulating, for longer or shorter periods of their lives. But these are human beings, and none is free from the limitations of the human condition. Some —Terence Powderly, John L. Lewis, Cesar Chavez—became leaders of organizations that were extremely beneficial to the lives of large numbers of men and women of the working class. Yet each has been legitimately criticized for high-handed and authoritarian practices contradicting the democratic essence of labor's cause.

Contradictions in some of these people can also be found in the way they deal with the key identities of class, race, and gender, which are complex in their evolution and interaction. Some of the people presented here did not have an opportunity to overcome the limitations and biases absorbed in the contexts within which they had developed. For example, William Sylvis —impressive and admirable in his capacity to broaden and deepen his perspectives—was able to come to an understanding of the possibility and need for racial unity in the struggle for workers' dignity, and to defend the participation in the congresses of the NLU of such "notorious" feminists as Susan B. Anthony and Elizabeth Cady Stanton. But one can also find in his writings criticisms of interracial socializing and the notion that the woman's place in society is as "queen of the household." On the other hand, the first three people presented here—Tom Paine, Frances Wright, Frederick Douglass—were never in a position to develop the incredibly vibrant understanding of working-class experience that comes through in the speeches and writings of Sylvis.

It can be interesting and instructive to consider such differences. On the other hand, taking all of these people—Chavez, Douglass, Lewis, Paine, Powderly, Sylvis, Wright, and the others—we can see that the ideas animating them, the ideals and perspectives to which they gave voice, reflected the broad, multifaceted stream of thought and sensibility associated with what we have identified as the revolutionary dimension in U.S. labor history.

It is hardly the case that they all saw themselves as the same kind of "revolutionary." Powderly, who demonstrated an inclination toward "enlightened" class collaboration reminiscent of some of Frances Wright's utopian idealism, was, on multiple issues, at the opposite pole from the uncompromising anarcho-communist Albert Parsons. Eugene V. Debs was a frequent presidential candidate of the Socialist Party, while John L. Lewis was a registered Republican. Whereas Fannia Cohn was a loyal (if sometimes frustrated) fixture in the de-radicalizing bureaucracy of socialists and ex-socialists in the ILGWU, Genora Dollinger was a rank-and-file militant who openly challenged such tendencies in the UAW. On the left end of the spectrum, socialist A. Philip Randolph was unyieldingly anti-communist, while the UE led by James Matles was expelled from the CIO on charges of being associated with the Communist Party. Considering differences within the communist tradition, it is likely that, in 1940 (for example), Genora Dollinger and James Matles had fiercely opposing assessments of Leon Trotsky and Joseph Stalin.

However, the differences, in a sense, highlight the significance of the commonalities. Reflected in the excerpts of writings and speeches presented here are essential elements of the language, imagery, perceptions, values, insights, and aspirations permeating the labor movement down to our own time. These have inspired and mobilized millions of working people throughout the history of the United States. To the extent that such things are forgotten or repressed, the labor movement is weakened or destroyed—and to the extent to which they flourish, the labor movement is revitalized and becomes vibrant.

An obvious problem with this selection is that it includes only fourteen people. No less valuable would be the selection of fourteen others: Seth Luther; Peter J. McGuire; Leonora O'Reilly; "Big Bill" Haywood; Ben Fletcher; Arturo Giovanetti; William Z. Foster; Rose Pesotta; Farrell Dobbs; Maida Springer; Walter Reuther; Moe Foner; Philip Vera Cruz, and Tony Mazzocchi.

Or one could put forward a different fourteen: Thomas Skidmore; Isaac Myers; August Spies; Rose Schneiderman; James Maurer; Elizabeth Gurley Flynn; Ben Gold; John Brophy; Vincent Raymond Dunne; Victor Reuther; Mike Quill; Cleveland Robinson; Dow Wilson, and Dolores Huerta. Another list might include Sarah Bagley; Ira Steward; J. P. McDonnell; Lucy Gonzales

Parsons; Vincent St. John; Carlo Tresca; Sidney Hillman; Pauline Newman; Charles Zimmerman; Robert Travis; Abner Berry; E. D. Nixon; Joseph Yablonski, and Ed Mann.

Lists of fourteen could be multiplied for pages and pages—because there have been so many vitally important people in the ranks of labor. One is reminded of the line in Shelley's revolutionary poem, contrasting laboring masses with wealthy elites—"we are many, they are few."

Thomas Paine.

CHAPTER 3

THOMAS PAINE

Tom Paine (1737–1809) was a hero among the early working classes of Britain and the United States, and his ideas helped to nourish the early currents of labor radicalism on both sides of the Atlantic. Paine himself arose from the layer of artisans and craftsmen, the majority of whom would soon evolve into the modern working class.

Born in England, Paine was the son of a stay-maker (or corset maker), a trade that, after some modest schooling, he himself entered for a time. Before coming to America in 1774, he also worked, at various times, as a seaman, an excise-man (tax collector), teacher, and, for a short time before its failure, the owner of a small tobacco shop. His humble and sometimes impoverished circumstances possibly impacted on his two marriages—his first wife dying in childbirth, his second wife separating from him after three years. But, increasingly, he was drawn into the world of ideas—with a keen interest in science and a bent for poetry, a passing engagement with dissenting religious thought (he was the son of a mixed-religion household, Quaker and Anglican, and had a brush with radical Methodism), and a growing concern for social issues and politics. Before leaving England, he had been drawn into radical circles in which critical attitudes toward the wealthy and powerful aristocracy combined with strong democratic–republican inclinations.

The quintessential "self-made man," Benjamin Franklin, facilitated Paine's emigration to Britain's North American colonies on the eve of the American Revolution. Franklin—whose interests, like Paine's, also embraced science and politics and books of all kinds, with a keen interest in writing and publishing—had risen from artisan to entrepreneur and would evolve from being a loyal, if critical-minded, subject of the King to one of the foremost American revolutionaries. Paine connected with similar circles upon his arrival in Philadelphia, and soon became editor of *Pennsylvania Magazine*, which became the best-selling magazine in North America. The journal carried articles and poetry (some of each authored by Paine) dealing especially with various social and political questions. One of Paine's earliest articles was an attack on the institution of slavery. But the publication initially shied away from taking a position on the deepening rift between Britain and her North American colonies.

Military conflicts between colonists and British troops at the 1775 battles of Lexington and Concord propelled Paine to become one of the most radical spokesmen among the insurgent colonists—his best-selling pamphlet *Common Sense* attacked the very principle of monarchy, insisting that the thirteen colonies should join together in establishing a new democratic republic entirely independent of Britain. With its plain and pungent rhetoric, it became especially popular among people from the laboring and "middling" classes—artisans and craftsmen, unskilled laborers, shopkeepers, and small farmers, many of whom were mobilized to support the cause of independence thanks to the radical–democratic spin offered by Paine. It was one of the key influences in the writing of the Declaration of Independence. Its conceptions also influenced the writing of the 1776 Pennsylvania state constitution, which provided for universal suffrage, democratic representation, complete religious freedom, and a unicameral legislature elected annually. More than this, Paine threw himself into the military struggle as a volunteer in the Continental Army, becoming an aide-de-camp to General Nathaniel Greene. In this period, however, the Continental Army was suffering devastating defeats at the hands of the powerful and professional military forces of Great Britain, and the fortunes of the revolutionaries seemed bleak. Paine composed an inspiring short pamphlet, entitled *The Crisis*— noting that "these are the times that try men's souls"—which General George Washington, commander of the Continental Army, ordered be read to his troops and was commonly held to be an important factor in raising their morale as they fought their way to victory at the Battle of Trenton.

During the revolutionary struggle, Paine issued more than a dozen more special *Crisis* pamphlets dealing with various issues of concern to the patriots. He also assumed various positions in the revolutionary governments, nationally and in Pennsylvania. As the war came to an end, he could be found inclining strongly toward the more radical and democratic elements in the revolutionary coalition, but also toward those that favored a governmental structure that would make the United States a cohesive nation with a more centralized government—which he saw as fully consistent with his belief in a democratic republic. After the conflict, he was given modest compensations —£500 in cash from the state of Pennsylvania and a small farm by the state of New York—and turned his attention to science and inventions. But he was soon drawn to France in 1789, where masses of people were following the example of the American Revolution in challenging the right of kings and hereditary aristocrats to rule over them.

Beginning in 1790, Paine participated in the French revolutionary movement, becoming a member of the National Assembly, the governing body of revolutionary France, which was soon renamed the Convention. When the great British conservative Edmund Burke attacked the revolution and democratic principles in general, Paine responded with a two-part classic, *The Rights of Man*, which more thoroughly and radically developed the ideas he had put forward during the American Revolution. He soon found himself at odds, however, with the radical Jacobin faction, opposing the execution of King Louis XVI and the so-called Reign of Terror. He himself was arrested, along with many other oppositionists, and was on the list to be executed. While in prison, Paine began the composition of his controversial tract, *The Age of Reason*, powerfully reaffirming his belief in a Supreme Being, but just as powerfully attacking all forms of organized religion. With the overthrow of the Jacobins by more moderate (and corrupt) groupings in the Convention, Paine was freed and returned to the United States.

For most of his life, Paine embraced the developing market economy—his perceptions were, in many ways, similar to those of Adam Smith, whose 1776 study, *The Wealth of Nations,* presented an insightful and positive vision of the emerging capitalist order. Initially, he was confident that a democratic republic would be sufficient to provide liberty and justice for all. His revolutionary–democratic sensibilities were jolted, however, by the persistence and dramatic growth of economic inequality. Paine strongly protested against this development and, in his final years, he advocated reforms to help ensure a decent life for all—with radical implications seeming to challenge the capitalist order. This was presented in his last great work, *Agrarian Justice*, in which he called for a tax on all land ownership for the purpose of creating a fund that would eliminate poverty.

Taken together, *Common Sense*, *The Crisis*, *The Rights of Man*, and *Agrarian Justice* provided ideas and inspiration for future generations of labor radicals.

Sources for Biographical Sketch

Moncure Daniel Conway, *Life of Thomas Paine* (New York: G. P. Putnam's Sons, 1909).

Eric Foner, *Tom Paine and Revolutionary America* (New York: Oxford University Press, 1977).

Philip S. Foner, ed., *The Complete Writings of Thomas Paine*, 2 vols. (New York: Citadel Press, 1969).

Harvey J. Kaye, *Thomas Paine and the Promise of America* (New York: Hill and Wang, 2005).

John Keane, *Tom Paine, A Political Life* (New York: Grove Press, 1995).

Sources for Selections

All can be found in Philip S. Foner, ed., *The Complete Writings of Thomas Paine*, 2 vols. (New York: Citadel Press, 1969), vol. 1, page numbers indicated in the following: selection 1—*Common Sense*, pp. 9–10, 13, 30–31; selection 2—*The American Crisis*, p. 50; selection 3—*The Rights of Man*, pp. 251–252, 256; selection 4—*The Rights of Man*, pp. 265–266, 267; selection 5—pp. 357–358; selection 6 —*The Rights of Man*, pp. 370, 371–372, 375; selection 7—*The Rights of Man*, pp. 397, 404–405; selection 8—*Agrarian Justice*, pp. 609–613, 617–619, 620, 621–622.

SELECTION 1:
EQUALITY, FREEDOM, AND A DEMOCRATIC REPUBLIC

Mankind being originally equals in the order of creation, the equality could only be destroyed by some subsequent circumstance; the distinctions of rich, and poor, may in a great measure be accounted for, and that without having recourse to the harsh, ill-sounding names of oppression and avarice. Oppression is often the CONSEQUENCE, but seldom or never the MEANS of riches; and though avarice will preserve a man from being necessitously poor, it generally makes him too timorous to be wealthy . . .

In the early ages of the world, according to the scripture chronology, there were no kings; the consequence of which was, there were no wars; it is the pride of kings which throws mankind into confusion. Holland without a king hath enjoyed more peace for this last century than any of the monarchial governments in Europe. Antiquity favors the same remark; for the quiet and rural lives of the first patriarchs hath a happy something in them, which vanishes away when we come to the history of Jewish royalty . . .

To the evil of monarchy we have added that of hereditary succession; and as the first is a degradation and lessening of ourselves, so the second, claimed as a matter of right, is an insult and an imposition on posterity. For all men being originally equals, no ONE by BIRTH could have a right to set up his own family in perpetual preference to all others for ever, and though himself might deserve SOME decent degree of honors of his contemporaries, yet his descendants might be far too unworthy to inherit them . . .

[A]s no man at first could possess any other public honors than were bestowed upon him, so the givers of those honors could have no power to give away the right of posterity. And though they might say, "We choose you for OUR head," they could not, without manifest injustice to their children, say, "that your children and your children's children shall reign over OURS for ever." Because such an unwise, unjust, unnatural compact might (perhaps) in the next succession put them under the government of a rogue or a fool. Most wise men, in their private sentiments, have ever treated hereditary right with contempt; yet it is one of those evils, which when once established is not easily removed; many submit from fear, others from superstition, and the more powerful part shares with the king the plunder of the rest ...

O ye that love mankind! Ye that dare oppose, not only the tyranny, but the tyrant, stand forth! Every spot of the old world is overrun with oppression. Freedom hath been hunted round the globe. Asia, and Africa, have long expelled her—Europe regards her like a stranger, and England hath given her warning to depart. O! receive the fugitive, and prepare in time an asylum for mankind.

SELECTION 2:
FREEDOM MEANS STRUGGLE

These are the times that try men's souls. The summer soldier and the sunshine patriot will, in this crisis, shrink from the service of their country; but he that stands it now, deserves the love and thanks of man and woman. Tyranny, like hell, is not easily conquered; yet we have this consolation with us, that the harder the conflict, the more glorious the triumph. What we obtain too cheap, we esteem too lightly: it is dearness only that gives every thing its value. Heaven knows how to put a proper price upon its goods; and it would be strange indeed if so celestial an article as FREEDOM should not be highly rated.

SELECTION 3:
SELF-DETERMINATION AND REVOLUTION

There never did, there never will, and there never can, exist a Parliament, or any description of men, or any generation of men, in any country, possessed of the right or the power of binding and controlling posterity to the "end of time," or of commanding for ever how the world shall be governed, or who shall govern it; and therefore all such clauses, acts or declarations by which the makers of them attempt to do what they have neither the right nor the power to do, nor the power to execute, are in themselves null and void.

I am not contending for nor against any form of government, nor for nor against any party, here or elsewhere. That which a whole nation chooses to do, it has a right to do. Mr. Burke says, No. Where, then, does the right exist? I am contending for the rights of the living, and against their being willed away and controlled and contracted for by the manuscript assumed authority of the dead, and Mr. Burke is contending for the authority of the dead over the rights and freedom of the living ...

It was not against Louis XVI, but against the despotic principles of the Government, that the nation revolted. These principles had not their origin in him, but in the original establishment, many centuries back: and they were become too deeply rooted to be removed, and the Augean stables of parasites and plunderers too abominably filthy to be cleansed by anything short of a complete and universal Revolution. When it becomes necessary to do anything, the whole heart and soul should go into the measure, or not attempt it. That crisis was then arrived, and there remained no choice but to act with determined vigor, or not to act at all.

When despotism has established itself for ages in a country, as in France, it is not in the person of the king only that it resides. It has the appearance of being so in show, and in nominal authority; but it is not so in practice and in fact. It has its standard everywhere. Every office and department has its despotism, founded upon custom and usage. Every place has its Bastille, and every Bastille its despot. The original hereditary despotism resident in the person of the king, divides and sub-divides itself into a thousand shapes and forms, till at last the whole of it is acted by deputation. This was the case in France; and against this species of despotism, proceeding on through an endless labyrinth of office till the source of it is scarcely perceptible, there is no mode of redress. It strengthens itself by assuming the appearance of duty, and tyrannies under the pretence of obeying.

When a man reflects on the condition which France was in from the nature of her government, he will see other causes for revolt than those which immediately connect themselves with the person or character of Louis XVI. There were, if I may so express it, a thousand despotisms to be reformed in France, which had grown up under the hereditary despotism of the monarchy, and became so rooted as to be in a great measure independent of it. Between the Monarchy, the Parliament, and the Church there was a rivalship of despotism; besides the feudal despotism operating locally, and the ministerial despotism operating everywhere . . .

SELECTION 4:
REFLECTIONS ON REVOLUTIONARY VIOLENCE

More of the citizens fell in this struggle than of their opponents: but four or five persons were seized by the populace, and instantly put to death; the Governor of the Bastille, and the Mayor of Paris, who was detected in the act of betraying them; and afterwards Foulon, one of the new ministry, and Berthier, his son-in-law, who had accepted the office of intendant of Paris. Their heads were stuck upon spikes, and carried about the city; and it is upon this mode of punishment that Mr. Burke builds a great part of his tragic scene. Let us therefore examine how men came by the idea of punishing in this manner.

They learn it from the governments they live under; and retaliate the punishments they have been accustomed to behold. The heads stuck upon spikes, which remained for years upon Temple Bar, differed nothing in the horror of the scene from those carried about upon spikes at Paris; yet this was done by the English Government. It may perhaps be said that it signifies nothing to a man what is done to him after he is dead; but it signifies much to the living; it either tortures their feelings or hardens their hearts, and in either case it instructs them how to punish when power falls into their hands.

Lay then the axe to the root, and teach governments humanity. It is their sanguinary punishments which corrupt mankind. In England the punishment in certain cases is by hanging, drawing and quartering; the heart of the sufferer is cut out and held up to the view of the populace. In France, under the former Government, the punishments were not less barbarous. Who does not remember the execution of Damien, torn to pieces by horses? The effect of those cruel spectacles exhibited to the populace is to destroy tenderness or excite revenge; and by the base and false idea of governing men by terror, instead of reason, they become precedents. It is over the lowest class of mankind that government by terror is intended to operate, and it is on them that it operates to the worst effect. They have sense enough to feel they are the objects aimed at; and they inflict in their turn the examples of terror they have been instructed to practice . . .

I give to Mr. Burke all his theatrical exaggerations for facts, and I then ask him if they do not establish the certainty of what I here lay down? Admitting them to be true, they show the necessity of the French Revolution, as much as any one thing he could have asserted. These outrages were not the effect of the principles of the Revolution, but of the degraded mind that existed before the Revolution, and which the Revolution is calculated to reform. Place them then to their proper cause, and take the reproach of them to your own side . . .

SELECTION 5:
GOVERNMENT, SOCIETY, AND DEMOCRATIC REPUBLIC

To understand the nature and quantity of government proper for man, it is necessary to attend to his character. As Nature created him for social life, she fitted him for the station she intended. In all cases she made his natural wants greater than his individual powers. No one man is capable, without the aid of society, of supplying his own wants, and those wants, acting upon every individual, impel the whole of them into society, as naturally as gravitation acts to a centre.

But she has gone further. She has not only forced man into society by a diversity of wants which the reciprocal aid of each other can supply, but she has implanted in him a system of social affections, which, though not necessary to his existence, are essential to his happiness. There is no period in life when this love for society ceases to act. It begins and ends with our being.

If we examine with attention into the composition and constitution of man, the diversity of his wants, and the diversity of talents in different men for reciprocally accommodating the wants of each other, his propensity to society, and consequently to preserve the advantages resulting from it, we shall easily discover, that a great part of what is called government is mere imposition.

Government is no farther necessary than to supply the few cases to which society and civilization are not conveniently competent; and instances are not wanting to show, that everything which government can usefully add thereto, has been performed by the common consent of society, without government . . .

Every government that does not act on the principle of a Republic, or in other words, that does not make the res-publica its whole and sole object, is not a good government. Republican government is no other than government established and conducted for the interest of the public, as well individually as collectively. It is not necessarily connected with any particular form, but it most naturally associates with the representative form, as being best calculated to secure the end for which a nation is at the expense of supporting it . . .

[T]he government of America, which is wholly on the system of representation, is the only real Republic, in character and in practice, that now exists. Its government has no other object than the public business of the nation, and therefore it is properly a republic; and the Americans have taken care that *this*, and no other, shall always be the object of their government, by their rejecting everything hereditary, and establishing governments on the system of representation only. Those who have said that a republic is not a form of government calculated for countries of great extent, mistook, in the first place, the business of a government, for a form of government; for the res-publica equally appertains to every extent of territory and population. And, in the second place, if they meant anything with respect to form, it was the simple democratical form, such as was the mode of government in the ancient democracies, in which there was no representation. The case, therefore, is not, that a republic cannot be extensive, but that it cannot be extensive on the simple democratical form; and the question naturally presents itself, What is the best form of government for conducting the *Res-Publica*, or the *Public Business* of a nation, after it becomes too extensive and populous for the simple democratical form? It cannot be monarchy, because monarchy is subject to an objection of the same amount to which the simple democratical form was subject . . .

Retaining, then, democracy as the ground, and rejecting the corrupt systems of monarchy and aristocracy, the representative system naturally presents itself; remedying at once the defects of the simple democracy as to form, and the incapacity of the other two with respect to knowledge.

Simple democracy was society governing itself without the aid of secondary means. By ingrafting representation upon democracy, we arrive at a system of government capable of embracing and confederating all the various interests and every extent of territory and population; and that also with advantages as much superior to hereditary government, as the republic of letters is to hereditary literature.

It is on this system that the American government is founded. It is representation ingrafted upon democracy. It has fixed the form by a scale parallel in all cases to the extent of the principle. What Athens was in miniature America will be in magnitude. The one was the wonder of the ancient world; the other is becoming the admiration of the present. It is the easiest of all the forms of government to be understood and the most eligible in practice; and excludes at once the ignorance and insecurity of the hereditary mode, and the inconvenience of the simple democracy . . .

In the representative system, the reason for everything must publicly appear. Every man is a proprietor in government, and considers it a necessary part of his business to understand. It concerns his interest, because it affects his property. He examines the cost, and compares it with the advantages; and above all, he does not adopt the slavish custom of following what in other governments are called *Leaders* . . .

SELECTION 6:
RULE BY TRADITION OR RULE BY THE PEOPLE?

Almost every case must now be determined by some precedent, be that precedent good or bad, or whether it properly applies or not; and the practice is become so general as to suggest a suspicion, that it proceeds from a deeper policy than at first sight appears.

Since the revolution of America, and more so since that of France, this preaching up the doctrines of precedents, drawn from times and circumstances antecedent to those events, has been the studied practice of the English government. The generality of those precedents are founded on principles and opinions, the reverse of what they ought; and the greater distance of time they are drawn from, the more they are to be suspected. But by associating those precedents with a superstitious reverence for ancient things, as monks show relics and call them holy, the generality of mankind are deceived into the design. Governments now act as if they were afraid to awaken a single reflection in man. They are softly leading him to the sepulcher of precedents, to deaden his faculties and call attention from the scene of revolutions. They feel that he is arriving at knowledge faster than they wish, and their policy of precedents is the barometer of their fears. This political popery, like the ecclesiastical popery of old, has had its day, and is hastening to its exit. The ragged relic and the antiquated precedent, the monk and the monarch, will molder together.

Government by precedent, without any regard to the principle of the precedent, is one of the vilest systems that can be set up. In numerous instances, the precedent ought to operate as a warning, and not as an example, and requires to be shunned instead of imitated; but instead of this, precedents are taken in the lump, and put at once for constitution and for law . . .

The Rights of Man are the rights of all generations of men, and cannot be monopolized by any. That which is worth following, will be followed for the sake of its worth, and it is in this that its security lies, and not in any conditions with which it may be encumbered . . .

SELECTION 7:
RULE BY THE PEOPLE AND SOCIAL JUSTICE

Government ought to be as much open to improvement as anything which appertains to man, instead of which it has been monopolized from age to age, by the most ignorant and vicious of the human race. Need we any other proof of their wretched management, than the excess of debts and taxes with which every nation groans, and the quarrels into which they have precipitated the world? Just emerging from such a barbarous condition, it is too soon to determine to what extent of improvement government may yet be carried. For what we can foresee, all Europe may form but one great Republic, and man be free of the whole . . .

When, in countries that are called civilized, we see age going to the workhouse and youth to the gallows, something must be wrong in the system of government. It would seem, by the exterior appearance of such countries, that all was happiness; but there lies hidden from the eye of common observation, a mass of wretchedness, that has scarcely any other chance, than to expire in poverty or infamy. Its entrance into life is marked with the presage of its fate; and until this is remedied, it is in vain to punish.

Civil government does not exist in executions; but in making such provision for the instruction of youth and the support of age, as to exclude, as much as possible, profligacy from the one and despair from the other. Instead of this, the resources of a country are lavished upon kings, upon courts, upon hirelings, impostors and prostitutes; and even the poor themselves, with all their wants upon them, are compelled to support the fraud that oppresses them.

Why is it that scarcely any are executed but the poor? The fact is a proof, among other things, of a wretchedness in their condition. Bred up without morals, and cast upon the world without a prospect, they are the exposed sacrifice of vice and legal barbarity. The millions that are superfluously wasted upon governments are more than sufficient to reform those evils, and to benefit the condition of every man in a nation, not included within the purlieus of a court. This I hope to make appear in the progress of this work.

It is the nature of compassion to associate with misfortune. In taking up this subject I seek no recompense—I fear no consequence. Fortified with that proud integrity, that disdains to triumph or to yield, I will advocate the Rights of Man . . .

SELECTION 8:
OVERCOMING THE DIVISION BETWEEN RICH AND POOR

To preserve the benefits of what is called civilized life, and to remedy at the same time the evil which it has produced, ought to be considered as one of the first objects of reformed legislation.

Whether that state that is proudly, perhaps erroneously, called civilization, has most promoted or most injured the general happiness of man is a question that may be strongly contested. On one side, the spectator is dazzled by splendid appearances; on the other, he is shocked by extremes of wretchedness; both of which it has erected. The most affluent and the most miserable of the human race are to be found in the countries that are called civilized.

To understand what the state of society ought to be, it is necessary to have some idea of the natural and primitive state of man; such as it is at this day among the Indians of North America. There is not, in that state, any of those spectacles of human misery which poverty and want present to our eyes in all the towns and streets in Europe.

Poverty, therefore, is a thing created by that which is called civilized life. It exists not in the natural state. On the other hand, the natural state is without those advantages which flow from agriculture, arts, science and manufactures.

The life of an Indian is a continual holiday, compared with the poor of Europe; and, on the other hand it appears to be abject when compared to the rich. Civilization, therefore, or that which is so-called, has operated two ways: to make one part of society more affluent, and the other more wretched, than would have been the lot of either in a natural state.

It is always possible to go from the natural to the civilized state, but it is never possible to go from the civilized to the natural state. The reason is that man in a natural state, subsisting by hunting, requires ten times the quantity of land to range over to procure himself sustenance, than would support him in a civilized state, where the earth is cultivated.

When, therefore, a country becomes populous by the additional aids of cultivation, art and science, there is a necessity of preserving things in that state; because without it there cannot be sustenance for more, perhaps, than a tenth part of its inhabitants. The thing, therefore, now to be done is to remedy the evils and preserve the benefits that have arisen to society by passing from the natural to that which is called the civilized state.

In taking the matter upon this ground, the first principle of civilization ought to have been, and ought still to be, that the condition of every person born into the world, after a state of civilization commences, ought not to be worse than if he had been born before that period.

But the fact is that the condition of millions, in every country in Europe, is far worse than if they had been born before civilization began, had been born among the Indians of North America at the present. I will show how this fact has happened.

It is a position not to be controverted that the earth, in its natural, cultivated state was, and ever would have continued to be, *the common property of the human race*. In that state every man would have been born to property. He would have been a joint life proprietor with the rest in the property of the soil, and in all its natural productions, vegetable and animal.

But the earth in its natural state, as before said, is capable of supporting but a small number of inhabitants compared with what it is capable of doing in a cultivated state. And as it is impossible to separate the improvement made by cultivation from the earth itself, upon which that improvement is made, the idea of landed property arose from that parable connection; but it is nevertheless true, that it is the value of the improvement, only, and not the earth itself, that is individual property . . .

There could be no such thing as landed property originally. Man did not make the earth, and, though he had a natural right to *occupy* it, he had no right to *locate as his property* in perpetuity any part of it; neither did the Creator of the earth open a land-office, from whence the first title-deeds should issue. Whence then, arose the idea of landed property? I answer as before, that when cultivation began the idea of landed property began with it, from the impossibility of separating the improvement made by cultivation from the earth itself, upon which that improvement was made . . .

To create a national fund, out of which there shall be paid to every person, when arrived at the age of twenty-one years, the sum of fifteen pounds sterling, as a compensation in part, for the loss of his or her natural inheritance, by the introduction of the system of landed property:

And also, the sum of ten pounds per annum, during life, to every person now living, of the age of fifty years, and to all others as they shall arrive at that age . . .

It is not charity but a right, not bounty but justice, that I am pleading for. The present state of civilization is as odious as it is unjust. It is absolutely the opposite of what it should be, and it is necessary that a revolution should be made in it. The contrast of affluence and wretchedness continually meeting and offending the eye, is like dead and living bodies chained together. Though I care as little about riches as any man, I am a friend to riches because they are capable of good.

I care not how affluent some may be, provided that none be miserable in consequence of it. But it is impossible to enjoy affluence with the felicity it is capable of being enjoyed, while so much misery is mingled in the scene. The sight of the misery, and the unpleasant sensations it suggests, which, though they may be suffocated cannot be extinguished, are a greater drawback upon the felicity of affluence than the proposed ten per cent upon property is worth. He that would not give the one to get rid of the other has no charity, even for himself.

There are, in every country, some magnificent charities established by individuals. It is, however, but little that any individual can do, when the whole extent of the misery to be relieved is considered. He may satisfy his conscience, but not his heart. He may give all that he has, and that all will relieve but little. It is only by organizing civilization upon such principles as to act like a system of pulleys, that the whole weight of misery can be removed . . .

It is the practice of what has unjustly obtained the name of civilization (and the practice merits not to be called either charity or policy) to make some provision for persons becoming poor and wretched only at the time they become so. Would it not, even as a matter of economy, be far better to adopt means to prevent their becoming poor? This can best be done by making every person when arrived at the age of twenty-one years an inheritor of something to begin with.

The rugged face of society, checkered with the extremes of affluence and want, proves that some extraordinary violence has been committed upon it, and calls on justice for redress. The great mass of the poor in countries are become an hereditary race, and it is next to impossible for them to get out of that state of themselves. It ought also to be observed that this mass increases in all countries that are called civilized. More persons fall annually into it than get out of it . . .

The plan here proposed will benefit all, without injuring any. It will consolidate the interest of the republic with that of the individual. To the numerous class dispossessed of their natural inheritance by the system of landed property it will be an act of national justice . . .

Separate an individual from society, and give him an island or a continent to possess, and he cannot acquire personal property. He cannot be rich. So inseparably are the means connected with the end, in all cases, that where the former do not exist the latter cannot be obtained. All accumulation, therefore, of personal property, beyond what a man's own hands produce, is derived to him by living in society; and he owes on every principle of justice, of gratitude, and of civilization, a part of that accumulation back again to society from whence the whole came . . .

A revolution in the state of civilization is the necessary companion of revolutions in the system of government. If a revolution in any country be from bad to good, or from good to bad, the state of what is called civilization in that country must be made conformable thereto, to give that revolution effect . . .

It is a revolution in the state of civilization that will give perfection to the Revolution of France. Already the conviction that government by representation is the true system of government is spreading itself fast in the world.

The reasonableness of it can be seen by all. The justness of it makes itself felt even by its opposers. But when a system of civilization (growing out of that system of government) shall be so organized that not a man or woman born in the Republic but shall inherit some means of beginning the world, and see before them the certainty of escaping the miseries that under other governments accompany old age, the Revolution of France will have an advocate and an ally in the heart of all nations.

Frances Wright.

Courtesy of National Portrait Gallery, Smithsonian
Institution, ART2487.

CHAPTER 4

FRANCES WRIGHT

Fanny Wright (1795–1852) was born in Dundee, Scotland, but orphaned at the age of three. Her father had become a well-to-do linen merchant before his death and left his daughter a substantial estate, enhanced by bequests from other relatives. Undoubtedly influenced by the fact that her father had been a fervent admirer of Tom Paine, she was drawn to the revolutionary–democratic ideology associated with Paine and his comrades. While in their teens, she and her younger sister Camilla joined the household of her uncle, James Mylne, who taught at the University of Glasgow and was part of a liberal and radical intellectual and political milieu. This powerfully contributed to her own intellectual development, which was deepened as she educated herself in the libraries of Glasgow.

Drawn to what appeared to be an increasingly democratic republic, consistent with her own radical ideals, Wright visited the United States in 1818 and again in 1825—this time in the company of George Washington's one-time aide-de-camp the Marquis de Lafayette, who introduced her to Thomas Jefferson, James Madison, and other leading lights of the new republic.

Shocked by the contradiction between slavery and democratic promise, she purchased land in Tennessee in order to establish an experimental community called Nashoba. Influenced by several utopian socialist experiments she had visited in the United States, and by the radical ideas of Robert Owen, Wright and several friends drew together a dozen slaves in order to create an interracial community of shared labor and shared wealth that was meant to be a training ground for freedom and a model for racial equality and economic harmony, which she hoped would positively influence the larger society.

Poor harvests, illness, and extreme public hostility brought an end to the experiment within three years. The slaves were freed and eventually given passage to Haiti, but Wright stayed in the United States—working with Robert Dale Owen (son of Britain's pioneering socialist, Robert Owen) in educational efforts and political organizing, increasingly within urban working-class circles, in the late 1820s and early 1830s. She edited the influential radical papers *New Harmony Gazette* (associated with the Owenite utopian community in New Harmony, Indiana) and *The Free Enquirer*. Wright wrote and lectured on such topics as the need for public education; opposition to slavery; women's rights; criticisms of organized religion; the oppression of labor, and the need for far-reaching economic and social reforms in the United States.

Becoming deeply involved in the early labor movement, she threw her energies into the Workingmen's Party of New York; the term "Fanny Wrightism" (much to her dismay) became an often-derogatory synonym for working-class radicalism. While John Stuart Mill remembered her as "one of the most important women of her day," she became a target for increasingly hostile and vicious attacks by defenders of the status quo. However, to working-class radical activists such as the future poet Walt Whitman, "she was a brilliant woman, of beauty and estate who was never satisfied unless she was busy doing good—public good and private good ... We all loved her; fell down before her; her very appearance seemed to enthrall us." Scornful of her many critics, Whitman added that she was "a woman of the noblest make-up whose orbit was a great deal larger than theirs—too large to be tolerated for long by them: a most maligned, lied-about character—one of the best in history though also one of the least understood."

In many ways far ahead of her time, Wright was soon marginalized, and she fled into the safety of what soon became a horrendous and stifling marriage to a husband who sought to take control of her life and wealth (after several years of struggle, she succeeded in divorcing him in 1850) and who succeeded in turning their daughter against her and all that she stood for. Yet, even in her final, unhappy years, Wright never abandoned the ideals that had animated her. Later historians tend to see her as having made important contributions to efforts on behalf of social reform, women's rights, opposition to slavery, anti-racism—and to the cause of labor.

Sources for Biographical Sketch

Susan S. Adams, "Introduction," in Frances Wright, *Reason, Religion, and Morals* (New York: Humanity Books, 2004), pp. 9–26.

Richard Goff, "Francis Wright," in Immanuel Ness et al., ed., *The International Encyclopedia of Revolution and Protest, 1500 to the Present*, vol. VII (Malden, MA/Oxford, UK: Wiley-Blackwell, 2009), pp. 3666–3667.

Celia Morris, *Fanny Wright, Rebel in America* (Urbana, IL: University of Illinois Press, 1992).

Sean Wilentz, *Chants Democratic: New York and the Rise of the American Working Class, 1788–1850* (New York: Oxford University Press, 1984).

Sources for Selections

Selection 1: Frances Wright, "Statement on Nashoba (1826)," in Albert Fried, ed., *Socialism in America: From the Shakers to the Third International, A Documentary History* (Garden City, NY: Anchor Books, 1970), pp. 112, 114, 115–116.

Selections 2–6: Frances Wright, *Reason, Religion, and Morals* (New York: Humanity Books, 2004; originally published in 1829), pp. 197–201, 205–211, 318–319, 320–322, 368–371, 374–375.

SELECTION 1:
SOCIALIST VISION OF NASHOBA—INTERRACIAL COMMUNITY
OF LABOR

In attempting an institution in the United States, for the benefit of the negro race, I was fully aware that much assistance would be necessary, before anything of importance could be effected . . . Every part of the United States feels, more or less, the contamination of slavery. The negro race is everywhere, more or less, held by the great majority of the population in contempt and suspicion. Its very color is an object of disgust. And in the speeches and votes of congress we find evidence that the most northern sections of the country harbor prejudices equal in strength of those of the extreme south . . .

In facing the subject of slavery, it is necessary to bear in mind the position of the master, equally with that of the slave—bred in the prejudices of color and authority, untaught to labor and viewing it as a degradation . . . We should come to the slaveholder, therefore, not in anger but in kindness, and when we ask him to change his whole mode of life, we must show him the means by which he may do so, without the complete compromise of his ease and interests . . .

It will be seen that this establishment [of the community of Nashoba] is founded on the principle of community of property and labor; presenting every advantage to those desirous not of accumulating money, but of enjoying life, rendering services to their fellow creatures—these fellow creatures, that is, the blacks here admitted, requiting these services, by services equal or greater, by filling occupations, which their habits render easy, and which, to their guides and assistance, might be difficult or unpleasing. No life of idleness, however, is proposed to the whites. Those who cannot work must give an equivalent in property. Gardening or other cultivation of the soil, useful trades practiced in society, or taught in the school; the teaching of every branch of knowledge; tending the children; and nursing the sick—with present a choice of employments sufficiently extensive.

Labor is wealth; its reward should be enjoyment. Those who feel and admit this truth will see that it needs not to be rich, in the now received sense of the word, to contribute towards the building up of an institution, which, however small in its infancy, may be made, with their cooperation, to open the way to a great national reform. Deeds are better than words. After all that has been said, let something at least be attempted. An experiment, that has such an end in view, is surely worth the trial . . . Let us dare to express our feelings and to act in accordance with them . . .

SELECTION 2:
SECULAR EDUCATION AND SOCIAL REFORM

I shall now present a few observations on the necessity of commencing, and gradually perfecting, a radical reform in your existing outlays of time and money . . .

Of substituting for your present cumbrous, expensive, useless, or rather pernicious, system of partial, opinionative, and dogmatical instruction, one at once national, rational, and republican; one which shall take for its study, our own world and our own nature; for its object, the improvement of man; and for its means, the practical development of truth, the removal of temptations to evil, and the gradual equalization of human condition, human duties, and human enjoyments, by the equal diffusion of knowledge without distinction of class or sect—both of which distinctions are inconsistent with republican institutions as they are with reason and with common sense, with virtue and with happiness.

Time is it in this land to commence this reform. Time is it to check the ambition of an organized clergy, the demoralizing effects of a false system of law; to heal the strife fomented by sectarian religion and legal disputes; to bring down the pride of ideal wealth, and to raise honest industry to honor. Time is it to search out the misery in the land, and to heal it at the source. Time is it to remember the poor and the afflicted, ay! and the vicious and the depraved. Time is it to perceive that every sorrow which corrodes the human heart, every vice which diseases the body and the mind, every crime which startles the ear and sends back the blood affrighted to the heart—is the product of one evil, the foul growth from one root, the distorted progeny of one corrupt parent—IGNORANCE.

Time is it to perceive this truth; to proclaim it on the housetop, in the market place, in city and forest, throughout the land; to acknowledge it in the depths of our hearts, and to apply all our energies to the adoption of those salutary measures which this salutary truth spontaneously suggests. Time is it, I say, to turn our churches into halls of science, our schools of faith into schools of knowledge, our privileged colleges into state institutions for all the youth of the land. Time is it to arrest our speculations respecting unseen worlds and inconceivable mysteries, and to address our inquiries to the improvement of our human condition, and our efforts to the practical illustration of those beautiful principles of liberty and equality enshrined in the political institutions, and, first and chief, in the national declaration of independence.

And by whom and how, are these changes to be effected? By whom! And do a free people ask the question! By themselves. By themselves—*the people.*

I am addressing the people of Philadelphia—the people of a city where Jefferson penned the glorious declaration which awoke this nation and the world—the city, where the alarm so astounding to tyranny, so fraught with hope, and joy, and exulting triumph to humankind, was first sounded in the ears of Americans. I speak to the descendants of those men who heard from the steps of their old state house the principles of liberty and equality first proclaimed to man. I speak to the inhabitants of a city founded by the most peaceful, the most humane, and the most practical of all Christian sects. I speak to mechanics who are uniting for the discovery of their interests and the protection of their rights. I speak to a public whose benevolence has been long harrowed by increasing pauperism and whose social order and social happiness are threatened by increasing vice. I speak to sectarians who are weary of sectarianism. I speak to honest men who tremble for their honesty. I speak to the *dis*honest whose integrity has fallen before the discouragements waiting upon industry; and who, by slow degrees, or in moments of desperation, have forsaken honest labor, because without a reward, for fraudulent speculation, because it promised one chance of success to a thousand chances of ruin. I speak to parents anxious for their offspring—to husbands who, while shortening their existence by excess of labor, foresee, at their death, not sorrow alone, but unrequited industry and hopeless penury, involving shame, and perhaps infamy, for their oppressed widows and unprotected children. I speak to human beings surrounded by human suffering—to fellow citizens pledged to fellow feeling—to republicans pledged to equal rights and, as a consequent, to equal condition and equal enjoyments; and I call them—oh, would that my voice were loud to reach every ear, and persuasive to reach every heart!—I call them to UNITE; and to unite for the consideration of the evils around us—for the discovery and application of their remedy.

SELECTION 3:
THE RIGHTS OF LABOR

Hitherto, my friends, in government as in every branch of morals, we have but too much mistaken words for truths, and forms for principles. To render men free, it sufficeth not to proclaim their liberty, to make them equal, it sufficeth not to call them so. True, the 4th of July, '76, commenced a new era for our race. True, the sun of promise then rose upon the world. But let us not mistake for the fullness of light what was but its harbinger. Let us not conceive that man in signing the declaration of his rights secured their possession; that having framed the theory, he had not, and hath not still, the practice to seek.

Your fathers, indeed, on the day from which dates your existence as a nation, opened the gates of the temple of human liberty. But think not they entered, nor that you have entered the sanctuary. They passed not, nor have you passed, even the threshold.

Who speaks of liberty while the human mind is in chains? Who of equality while the thousands are in squalid wretchedness, the millions harassed with health-destroying labor, the few afflicted with health-destroying idleness, and all tormented by health-destroying idleness, and all tormented by health-destroying solicitude? Look abroad on the misery which is gaining on the land! Mark the strife, and the discord, and the jealousies, the shock of interests and opinions, the hatreds of sect, the estrangements of class, the pride of wealth, the debasement of poverty, the helplessness of youth unprotected, of age uncomforted, of industry unrewarded, of ignorance unenlightened, of vice unreclaimed, of misery unpitied, of sickness, hunger, and nakedness unsatisfied, unalleviated, and unheeded. Go! mark all the wrongs and the wretchedness with which the eye and the ear and the heart are familiar, and then echo in triumph and celebrate in jubilee the insulting declaration—*all men are free and equal!*

That evils exist, none that have eyes, ears, and hearts can dispute. That these evils are on the increase, none who have watched the fluctuations of grade, the sinking price of labor, the growth of pauperism, and the increase of crime, will dispute. Little need be said here to the people of Philadelphia. The researches made by the public spirited among their own citizens, have but too well substantiated the suffering condition of a large mass of their population. In Boston, in New-York, in Baltimore, the voice of distress hath, in like manner, burst the barriers raised, and so long sustained, by the pride of honest industry, unused to ask from charity what it hath been wont to earn by the sweat of the brow. In each and every city necessity has constrained inquiry; and in each and every city inquiry has elicited the same appalling facts: that the hardest labor is often without a reward adequate to the sustenance of the laborer; that when, by over exertion and all the diseases, and often vices, which excess of exertion induces, the laborer, whose patient, sedulous industry supplies the community with all its comforts, and the rich with all their luxuries—when he, I say, is brought to an untimely grave by those exertions which, while sustaining the life of others, cut short his own—when he is mowed down by that labor whose products form the boasted wealth of the state, he leaves a family, to whom the strength of his manhood had barely furnished bread, to lean upon the weakness of a soul-stricken mother, and hurry her to the grave of her father.

Such is the information gleaned from the report of the committee lately appointed by the town meeting of the city and county of Philadelphia, and as verbatim reiterated in every populous city throughout the land. And what are the remedies suggested by our corporation, our newspaper editors, our religions' societies, our tracts, and our sermons? Some have ordained fasts, multiplied prayers, and recommended pious submission to a Providence who should have instituted all this calamity for the purpose of fulfilling the words of a Jewish prophet, "The poor shall never cease from the land." Some, less spiritual-minded, have called for larger jails and more poor houses; some, for increased poor rates and additional benevolent societies; others, for compulsory laws protective of labor, and fixing a *minimum*, below which it shall be penal to reduce it; while others, and those not the least able to appreciate all the difficulties of the question, have sought the last resource of suffering poverty and oppressed industry in the humanity and sense of justice of the wealthier classes of society.

This last is the forlorn hope presented in the touching document signed by Matthew Carey and his fellow laborers.

It were easy to observe, in reply to each and all of the palliatives variously suggested for evils, which none profess to remedy, that to punish crime when committed is not to prevent its commission; to force the work of the poor in poor houses is only farther to glut an already unproductive market; to multiply charities is only to increase pauperism; that to fix by statute the monied price of labor would be impossible in itself, and, if possible, mischievous no less to the laborer than to the employer; and that, under the existing state of things, for human beings to lean upon the compassion and justice of their fellow creatures, is to lean upon a rotten reed.

I believe no individual, possessed of common sense and common feeling, can have studied the report of the committee to which I have referred, or the multitude of similar documents furnished elsewhere, without acknowledging that reform, and that not slight nor partial, but radical and universal, is called for. All must admit that no such reform—that is, that no remedy commensurate with the evil, has been suggested, and would we but reflect, we should perceive that no efficient remedy can be suggested, or if suggested, applied, until the people are generally engaged in its discovery and its application for themselves.

In this nation, any more than in any other nation, the mass has never reflected for the mass; the people, as a body, have never addressed themselves to the study of their own condition, and to the just and fair interpretation of their common interests. And, as it was with their national independence, so shall it be with their national happiness—it shall be found only when the mass shall seek it. No people have ever received liberty *in gift*. Given, it were not appreciated; it were not understood. Won without exertion, it were lost as readily. Let the people of America recall the ten years of war and tribulation by which they purchased their national independence. Let efforts as strenuous be now made, not with the sword of steel, indeed, but with the sword of the spirit, and their farther enfranchisement from poverty, starvation, and dependence, must be equally successful.

Great reforms are not wrought in a day. Evils which are the accumulated results of accumulated errors, are not to be struck down at a blow by the rod of a magician. A free people may boast that all power is in their hands; but no effectual power can be in their hands until knowledge be in their minds.

But how may knowledge be imparted to their minds? Such effective knowledge as shall render apparent to all the interests of all, and demonstrate the simple truths—that a nation to be strong, must be united; to be united, must be equal in condition; to be equal in condition, must be similar in habits and in feeling; to be similar in habits and in feeling, *must be raised in national institutions, as the children of a common family, and citizens of a common country.*

Before entering on the development of the means I have here suggested for paving our way to the reform of those evils which now press upon humanity, and which, carried, perhaps, to their acme in some of the nations of Europe, are gaining ground in these United States with a rapidity alarming to all who know how to read the present, or to calculate the future—I must observe, that I am fully aware of the difficulty of convincing all minds of the urgency of these evils, and of the impossibility of engaging all classes in the application of their remedy.

In the first place, the popular suffering, great as it is, weighs not with a sufficiently equal pressure on all parts of the country; and, in the second, affects not equally all classes of the population, so as to excite to that union of exertion, which once made, the reform is effected and the nation redeemed.

Were it my disposition, which, I think, it is not, to exaggerate evils, or were I even disposed to give a fair picture of those really existing among a large mass of the American population, more especially as crowded into the cities and manufacturing districts, easy it were to harrow the feelings of the least sensitive, and, in the relation, to harrow my own.

I know how difficult it is—reared as we all are in the distinctions of class, to say nothing of sect—to conceive of our interests as associated with those of the whole community. The man possessed of a dollar, feels himself to be, not merely one hundred cents richer, but also one hundred cents *better*, than the man who is penniless; so on through all the gradations of earthly possessions—the estimate of our own moral and political importance swelling always in a ratio exactly proportionate to the growth of our purse. The rich man who can leave a clear independence to his children, is given to estimate them as he estimates himself, and to imagine something in their nature distinct from that of the less privileged heirs of hard labor and harder fare . . .

SELECTION 4:
RADICAL REFORM THROUGH DEMOCRATIC LEGISLATION

The revolution now in preparation for this country may assume one of three possible forms.

First: things may be allowed to follow on in the course they have taken up to this hour, and to move uninterrupted and unimpeded in the accelerated ratio which events, like falling bodies, acquire in progress, and which the circumstances we have enumerated, and many others, combine to urge forward with additional velocity. I say, things may be allowed to move forward as they are moving, with no resistance presented on the part of the people, and every momentum applied by the privileged classes.

Under this supposition, the crisis must be consummated by the destruction of American liberty, and with *American* liberty, that of the world.

The second form which the approaching revolution may wear, even in this land, is more than possible; and nothing, indeed, but timely measures, planned with wisdom, and carried with perseverance, can avert it. This second mode supposes some farther supineness on the part of the people, while existing evils and abuses increase and accumulate, until, the cup of popular calamity being filled, the last drop shall make it flow over. The American population, then, not coerced as in Europe by standing armies, and all the convenient machinery of despotism, shall suddenly take their wrongs into their own hands, and rush, without deliberation, and without knowledge, to their remedy.

Alas for the unsullied robe of American liberty, should this be so. Alas for that unspotted shrine which the hands of sages reared, and which the foot of wisdom should alone approach. Oh, not thus—not thus be the victory won. May the means be pure as the end. May the cause which brings us here this night, be secured without one act to raise a blush, one step to wish retracted, one deed to wish undone!

The third mode of revolution, then, be ours; that mode which is alone worthy of a people who have assumed equal liberty for their motto, and declared their *expressed will* the law of the land. Let the industrious class, and all honest men of all classes, unite for a gradual, but radical reform, in all the objects, and all the measures of government; and let this be done through, and by the means supplied in their constitutional code: namely—*through their legislatures.*

First, then, the people must bear in mind, that to be successful they must be united; to be united they must be of one mind; to be of one mind they must distinguish the first best measure to be carried; and, having distinguished that best measure, must set hand to hand, heart to heart, and vote to vote, for its adoption and execution.

I have already delivered it as my opinion, that this measure will be found in a plan of equal, universal, and republican education, and explained how and why I consider it as alone commensurate with the two great objects we have in view—the relief of the present generation, and the improvement of the next . . .

SELECTION 5:
CORRUPTIONS OF GREED OR COMMUNITY AND EQUALITY

Yet however obvious the evils in our present motives and practice—in our present systems of trade and of law, in the multitude of false employments and in the excessive competition which so frequently threatens with ruin all employments, the honest as the dishonest.—However obvious these evils, and however opposed to the *true* interests of all classes and all individuals, it were idle to expect all classes and individuals to cooperate in their correction. Convince the reason, and habit would run counter still. The gambler, how often soever the game may run against him, will still haunt the board which tempts with one chance of gain against a thousand chances of ruin. The speculator, rather than seek a moderate and unfluctuating profit, will risk bankruptcy and starvation in sight of a bare possibility of seizing upon uncertain wealth. The vain man, blinded by a false education to real honor and dignity, will prefer an uneasy conscience and mean dependence, to honest, but, unhappily, despised labor, and even genius will ambition paltry distinctions, the trappings and profits of office, rather than the high consciousness of advancing the public weal.

How salutary then soever reform may be, many will there be found to oppose it. Corruptions of old growth are dear to those who have grown old with them; and, as all reformers have seen, so see we at the present hour, that the misguided partisans of error will cling to the false, antisocial, and anti-American fabric, raised on the noble foundation laid by the fathers of this people, until it crumble to dust before the magic influence of a more enlightened public opinion, and give place, in a new generation, to an edifice truly American, the pillars of which shall rest on republican education, and its walls shall embrace a nation of freemen, equal in knowledge, in rights, in duties, and in condition.

Such is the change "in the present order of things," the reformers of the present day have dared to anticipate; the people of this city and commonwealth have sworn to effect, and the American nation will be found ready to imitate. No other than a change thus peaceful has been proposed; no other than a change thus gradual could be feasible, and no less than a change thus radical can effect the practical development of American principles.

Upwards of half a century these principles have claimed the love of this people and the admiration of the world. Upwards of half a century has "Liberty and Equality" been the motto of this nation. Upwards of half a century has this motto existed in words, these principles in theory; and now that the people have resolved the practical development of the same, we hear them, at this hour, in this city, denounced as visionary, impeached as iniquitous, and their advocates and vindicators blasphemed as incendiaries and infidels!

Is it come to this? Has treason gone so far in this land, for EQUALITY to be denounced as a dream of enthusiasts, an innovation of foreigners and a doctrine of Marats and Robespierres? Fathers of this nation! well are ye asleep in your graves! By the sword of Washington, by the wisdom of Franklin, by the honest democracy of Jefferson, it is time for Americans to arouse, and to vindicate the words of this charter!

Fellow citizens! the season is arrived when what is here set forth as abstract truth, must be referred to with a view to practice. The equal rights of human beings are here proclaimed self-evident to reason, inherent in the nature of things, and inalienable in justice. Life, liberty, and the pursuit of happiness, stand particularized among the equal, inherent, and inalienable rights held in virtue of our existence.

The truths here set forth as self-evident—for which the blood of patriots has been shed, and to which the honor of the dead and the living has been pledged or is pledged—these truths self-evident involve all that the sage ever pictured, or the philanthropist desired. In the equal rights of all to life, liberty, and happiness, lies the sum of human good. Let us pause, fellow citizens! on the words, and see what is required for their fulfillment.

Life. Respected as it is in this land, compared to all other lands beside, our laws still sanction homicide—enforcing the decree of an ignorant and cruel superstition, "blood for blood."

Liberty. Fresh and ever gathering in strength as she dwells under the shadow of this charter, how trammelled as yet are her young limbs and her glorious mind! Still bigotry challenges her thoughts, and prejudice her actions. Still sex, and sect, and class, and color, furnish pretences, for limiting her range, and violating her purity!

Happiness! Alas! where is it on the face of the earth? Who pursues that whose pursuit is here guaranteed to all? Every one or none. Every one, if we listen to the vague assertions of men; none, if we look to their actions. Happiness enters not even into human calculation. Man has placed his pleasures, and his affections, yea! even his honor and his liberty, at the mercy of gold. From youth to age he sees but money; and, in pursuing it, pursues the shadow of a shade.

Selection 6:
Universal Improvement of Our Human Condition

What is then that object, my friends? What is the purpose of our souls? When we speak of reform, what hope we to produce? *The universal improvement of our human condition*. When we bend our minds and efforts to the great measure of a republican system of education, what do we intend to effect? *The equalization of our human condition*; the annihilation of all arbitrary distinctions; the substitution of the simple character of human beings for that of all others—the honorable title of American citizen, for that of all the silly and mischievous epithets introduced by sectarian superstition and antisocial prejudice, to the confounding of our understandings, the corrupting of our feelings, the depraving of our habits, and the subversion of our noble institutions.

I said that our object was at once the *equalization* and the *universal improvement* of our common condition. It is necessary to bear this two-fold specification in view, as otherwise, it may convey alarm to many, and false impressions to all.

Under the existing arrangements of society—the misapplication of human labor, devoted by more than one half to what is useless or mischievous, and rewarded, not only unequally and arbitrarily, but in a ratio inverse to its utility—the misapplication also of machinery acting, at the time present, not to the relief but to the oppression of the human laborer—the false operation of money, as now in use, laying ever at the mercy of the holder of specie or its paper representative, the real wealth of society—namely, *the productions of human industry.*—Under such and other existing circumstances, to speak of equalizing the general condition excites vague apprehensions on the part of the more favored classes, that benefit is intended to the mass, at expense of injury to individuals.

Frederick Douglass.

CHAPTER 5

FREDERICK DOUGLASS

Frederick Douglass (1817–1895) was born in Talbot County, Maryland, of an unknown white father and an African–American slave named Harriet Bailey—"Douglass" being a name he adopted after gaining his freedom. He escaped from bondage in 1838, finding employment as a wage-worker in New Bedford, Massachusetts. From his early youth as a slave he'd had a voracious appetite for learning. As a free worker in a brass foundry, he continued to study:

> Hard work, night and day, over a furnace hot enough to keep metal running like water was more favorable to action than thought, yet here I often nailed a newspaper to the post near my bellows and read while I was performing the up and down motion of the heavy beam by which the bellows were inflated and discharged.

Becoming active in the movement to abolish slavery in 1841, he himself would soon be writing things that many others would read. His experience of slavery and his escape to freedom were recounted in *The Narrative of the Life of Frederick Douglass* (1845), which became a bestseller in the United States and Britain, with translations into French and German. In 1855, this was expanded into the more substantial work, *My Bondage and My Freedom*, a literary classic that caused one reviewer to comment: "The mere fact that the member of an outcast and enslaved race should accomplish his freedom, educate himself up to an equality of intellectual and moral vigor with the leaders of the race by which he was held in bondage, is in itself so remarkable that the story of the change cannot be otherwise than exciting."

Douglass's writings make clear that the question of slavery involved the subjugation of labor—that the slaves were a specially oppressed sector of the working class, that their struggle for survival, dignity, and freedom was an integral part of the class struggle. His analysis of the power dynamics and psychology involved in slavery therefore provides food for thought on the situation of the larger working class, as do his disturbing insights—drawn from his own bitter experience—into the anti-black prejudice of many white workers. Douglass, as an abolitionist and also in his post-abolitionist period, must be seen as an impressive champion of the struggle to emancipate labor.

More than an orator and writer, Douglass was an activist. In Rochester, New York, he was deeply involved in the work of the Underground Railroad, a highly organized network of escape routes and safe houses that helped thousands of slaves find freedom. He increasingly played a leadership role in the radical wing of the abolitionists, vigorously participating in controversies over the strategy and tactics of the movement. Seeking his own voice (one of the issues leading to his break with abolitionist leader William Lloyd Garrison), he founded a new paper, *The North Star*, and later, *Frederick Douglass's Paper*. He spent time in Britain building support and raising money for the cause. Douglass was a central force in defining the struggle for liberation. C. L. R. James has recounted:

> In the struggle for women's emancipation as in all the causes of the day, Douglass was in the forefront. His paper, *Frederick Douglass's Paper*, was the official organ of the Free Soil Party in New York State. At the second convention of that party he was elected secretary by acclamation . . . From 1841 to his recruiting for the Northern army [during the Civil War], Douglass was the voice of the American Revolution. Stage by stage he embodied its development until in 1860 he gave critical support to the Republican party while defiantly proclaiming he was still a radical abolitionist.

Douglass was active in the campaigns of Abraham Lincoln for president, in efforts to push Lincoln to abolish slavery, and in the organization of the Fifty-fourth Massachusetts regiment—one of the first and most famous bodies of African–American combatants in the Civil War, He also labored tirelessly for the enactment of the thirteenth, fourteenth, and fifteenth amendments to the U.S. Constitution—ending slavery, extending the right to vote, and expanding the power of civil rights.

During the post-war Reconstruction period (1866–1877), as W. E. B. DuBois noted, "the great form of Frederick Douglass, the greatest of American Negro leaders, still led the host" in advancing a program of "self-assertion and self-development" of African–Americans, and "ultimate assimilation [into the enjoyment of equal rights as Americans] *through* self-assertion." But the Republican Party coalition of Northern businessmen, small farmers, white workers, and black laborers that had won the war pulled apart with the reassertion of diverging interests. Eventually, Republican Party leaders, pursuing the economic program of capitalist industrialization, compromised with the old Southern elite—and the results undermined the dignity of African–Americans in a manner eloquently described in the final selection presented here.

Sharply critical of the betrayal of Reconstruction hopes, Douglass never developed a perspective that took him beyond the Republican Party—he accepted a number of positions from Republican administrations (ambassador to Haiti, recorder of deeds for the District of Columbia, and so on)—and was unable to offer the incisive leadership characteristic of earlier years. Yet his insights of the 1880s would be relevant to the struggles of black labor and to the entire working class for many years to come.

Sources for Biographical Sketch

W. E. B. DuBois, *The Souls of Black Folk* (New York: New American Library, 1969).

Philip S. Foner, "Introductions," in *The Life and Writings of Frederick Douglass*, 5 vols. (New York: International Publishers, 1975).

Scott McLemee and Paul Le Blanc, eds., *C. L. R. James and Revolutionary Marxism, Selected Writings 1939–1949* (Atlantic Highlands, NJ: Humanities Press, 1994).

August Meier and Elliott Rudwick, *From Plantation to Ghetto* (New York: Hill and Wang, 1976).

Walter White, "Frederick Douglass," in *Encyclopedia of the Social Sciences*, vol. 5 (New York: Macmillan Co., 1931).

Sources for Selections

Selections 1–7, Frederick Douglass, *My Bondage and My Freedom* (New York: Dover, 1969), pp. 38–39, 89–91, 159, 160–162, 246–247, 251, 263–264, 308–310, 312, 348–350, 354, 355–356, 357, 359–360, 457, 459–460.

Selections 8–11, Philip S. Foner, ed., *The Life and Writings of Frederick Douglass*, 5 vols. (New York: International Publishers. 1975), vol. II, p. 437; vol. III, pp. 387, 402–403; vol. IV, pp. 381–383, 443, 444.

SELECTION 1:
EARLY YEARS AS A SLAVE (1855)

Living here, with my dear grandmother and grandfather, it was a long time before I knew myself to be a slave. Grandmother and grandfather were the greatest people in the world to me; and being with them so snugly in their own little cabin—I supposed it to be their own—knowing no higher authority of grandmamma, for a time there was nothing to disturb me; but, as I grew larger and older, I learned by degrees the sad fact, that the "little hut," and the lot on which it stood, belonged not to my dear old grandparents, but to some person who lived a great distance off, and who was called, by grandmother, "Old Master." I further learned the sadder fact, that not only the house and lot, but that grandmother herself (grandfather was free) and all the little children around her, belonged to this mysterious personage, called by grandmother, with every mark of reverence, "Old Master." Thus early did clouds and shadows begin to fall upon my path. Once on the track—troubles never come singly—I was not long in finding out another fact, still more grievous to my childish heart. I was told that this "old master," whose name seemed ever to be mentioned with fear and shuddering, only allowed the children to live with grandmother for a limited time, and that in fact as soon as they were big enough, they were promptly taken away, to live with the said "old master." These were distressing revelations indeed; and though I was quite too young to comprehend the full import of the intelligence, and mostly spent my childhood days in gleesome sports with the other children, a shade of disquiet rested upon me.

The absolute power of this distant "old master" had touched my young spirit with but the point of its cold, cruel iron, and left me something to brood over after the play and in moments of repose. Grandmammy was, indeed, at that time, all the world to me; and the thought of being separated from her, for any considerable time, was more than an unwelcome intruder. It was intolerable . . .

The heart-rending incidents . . . [which followed] led me, thus early, to inquire into the nature and history of slavery. *Why am I a slave? Why are some people slaves, and others masters? Was there ever a time when this was not so? How did the relation commence?* These were the perplexing questions which began to claim my thoughts, and to exercise the weak powers of my mind, for I was still but a child, and knew less than children of the same age in the free states. As my questions concerning these things were only put to children a little older, and little better informed than myself, I was not rapid in reaching a solid footing. By some means I learned from these inquiries that "God up in the sky" made everybody; and that he made *white* people to be masters and mistresses, and *black* people to be slaves. This did not satisfy me, nor lessen my interest in the subject. I was told, too, that God was good, and that He knew what was best for me, and best for everybody. This was less satisfactory than the first statement, because it came, point blank, against all my notions of goodness. It was not good to let old master cut the flesh off Esther, and make her cry so. Besides, how did people know that God made black people slaves? Did they go up in the sky and learn it? Or did He come down and tell them so? All was dark here. It was some relief to my hard notions of the goodness of God that, although he made white men to be slaveholders, he did not make them to be *bad* slaveholders, and that in due time he would punish the bad slaveholders; that he would, when they died, send them to the bad place, where they would be "burnt up." Nevertheless, I could not reconcile the relation of slavery with my crude notions of goodness.

Then, too, I found that there were puzzling exceptions to this theory of slavery on both sides, and in the middle. I knew of blacks who were *not* slaves; I knew of whites who were *not* slaveholders; and I knew of persons who were *nearly* white, who were slaves. *Color*, therefore, was a very unsatisfactory basis for slavery.

Once, however, engaged in the inquiry, I was not very long in finding out the true solution of the matter. It was not *color*, but *crime*, not *God*, but *man*, that afforded the true explanation of the existence of slavery; nor was I long in finding out another important truth: what man can make, man can unmake. The appalling darkness faded away, and I was master of the subject. There were slaves here, direct from Guinea; and there were many who could say that their fathers and mothers were stolen from Africa—forced from their homes, and compelled to serve as slaves. This, to me, was knowledge; but it was a kind of knowledge which filled me with a burning hatred of slavery, increased my suffering, and left me without the means of breaking away from my bondage. Yet it was knowledge quite worth possessing . . .

[After reading the selections on freedom in the used school book *The Columbian Orator*,] I had now penetrated the secret of all slavery and oppression, and had ascertained their true foundation to be in the pride, the power and the avarice of man. The dialogue and the speeches were all redolent of the principles of liberty, and poured floods of light on the nature and character of slavery. With a book of this kind in my hand, my own human nature, and the facts of my experience, to help me, I was equal to a contest with the religious advocates of slavery, whether among the whites or among the colored people, for blindness in this matter is not confined to the former. I have met many religious colored people, at the south, who are under the delusion that God requires them to submit to slavery, and to wear their chains with meekness and humility. I could entertain no such nonsense as this; and I almost lost my patience when I found any colored man weak enough to believe such stuff. Nevertheless, the increase of knowledge was attended with bitter as well as sweet results. The more I read, the more I was led to abhor and detest slavery, and my enslavers. "Slaveholders," I thought, "are only a band of successful robbers who left their homes and went to Africa for the purpose of stealing and reducing my people to slavery." I loathed them as the meanest and the most wicked of men. As I read, behold! the very discontent so graphically predicted by Master Hugh [who had sought to prevent Douglass from learning how to read], had already come upon me. I was no longer the light-hearted, gleesome boy, full of mirth and play, as when I landed first at Baltimore . . .

I have often wished myself a beast or a bird—anything rather than a slave. I was wretched and gloomy, beyond my ability to describe. I was too thoughtful to be happy . . . Once awakened by the silver trump of knowledge, my spirit was roused to eternal wakefulness. Liberty! the inestimable birthright of every man, had for me, converted every object. It was ever present, to torment me with a sense of my wretched condition. The more beautiful and charming were the smiles of nature, the more horrible and desolate was my condition. I saw nothing without seeing it, and I heard nothing without hearing it. I do not exaggerate when I say that it looked from every star, smiled in every calm, breathed in every wind, and moved in every storm.

I have no doubt that my state of mind had something to do with the change in the treatment adopted by my once kind mistress toward me. I can easily believe that my leaden, downcast, and discontented look was very offensive to her. Poor lady! She did not know my trouble, and I dared not tell her. Could I have freely made her acquainted with the real state of my mind, and given her the reasons therefore, it might have been well for both of us. Her abuse of me fell upon me like the blows of the false prophet upon his ass; she did not know that an *angel* stood in the way; and—such is the relation of master and slave—I could not tell her. Nature made us *friends*; slavery made us *enemies*. My interests were in a direction opposite to hers, and we both had our private thoughts and plans. She aimed to keep me ignorant; and I resolved to know, although knowledge only increased my discontent.

My feelings were not the result of any marked cruelty in the treatment I received; they sprung from the consideration of my being a slave at all. It was *slavery*—not its mere *incidents*—that I hated. I had been cheated. I saw through the attempt to keep me in ignorance; I saw that slaveholders would have gladly made me believe that they were merely acting under the authority of God, in making a slave of me, and in making slaves of others; and I treated them as robbers and deceivers. The feeding and clothing me well could not atone for taking my liberty from me. The smiles of my mistress could not remove the deep sorrow that dwelt in my young bosom. Indeed, these, in time, came only to deepen my sorrow. She had changed; and the reader will see that I had changed, too. We were both victims to the same overshadowing evil—*she*, as a mistress, *I*, as a slave. I will not censure her harshly; she cannot censure me, for she knows I speak but the truth, and have acted in my opposition to slavery, just as she herself would have acted, in a reverse of circumstances.

SELECTION 2:
SUCCESSFULLY PREVENTING A SLAVE-BREAKER FROM WHIPPING HIM

Covey at length (two hours had elapsed) gave up the contest. Letting me go, he said—puffing and blowing at a great rate—"now, you scoundrel, go to

your work; I would not have whipped you half so much had you not resisted."
The fact was, *he had not whipped me at all* . . .

Well, my dear friends, this battle with Mr. Covey . . . was the turning point
in "*my life as a slave.*" . . . He can only understand the effect of this combat
on my spirit who has himself incurred something, hazarded something, in
repelling the unjust and cruel aggressions of a tyrant. Covey was a tyrant, and
a cowardly one, withal. After resisting him, I felt as I had never felt before.
It was a resurrection from the dark and pestiferous tomb of slavery, to the
heaven of comparative freedom. I was no longer a servile coward, trembling
under the frown of a brother worm in the dust, but my long-cowed spirit
was roused to an attitude of manly independence. I had reached the point at
which *I was not afraid to die*. This spirit made me a freeman in *fact*, while I
remained a slave in *form*. When a slave cannot be flogged, he is more than
half free . . .

Slaves, generally, will fight each other, and die at each other's hands; but
there are few who are not held in awe by a white man. Trained from the cradle
up to think and feel that their masters are superior, and invested with a sort
of sacredness, there are few who can outgrow or rise above the control which
that sentiment exercises. I had now got free from it, and the thing was known.
One bad sheep will spoil a whole flock. Among the slaves, I was a bad sheep.
I hated slavery, slaveholders, and all pertaining to them; and I did not fail to
inspire others with the same feeling, wherever and whenever opportunity
was presented. This made me a marked lad among the slaves, and a suspected
one among the slaveholders. A knowledge of my ability to read and write
got pretty widely spread, which was very much against me . . .

SELECTION 3:
A GOOD MASTER AND THE PASSION FOR FREEDOM

Beat and cuff your slave, keep him hungry and spiritless, and he will follow
the chain of his master like a dog; but feed and clothe him well—work him
moderately—surround him with physical comfort—and dreams of freedom
intrude. Give him a *bad* master, and he aspires to a *good* master; give him a
good master, and he wishes to become his *own* master. Such is human nature.
You may hurl a man so low, beneath the level of his kind, that he loses all
just ideas of his natural position; but elevate him a little, and the clear
conception of rights rises to life and power, and leads him onward . . .

SELECTION 4:
WORKING IN THE SHIPYARD—AND THE HOSTILITY OF
WHITE WORKERS

Very soon after I went to Baltimore to live, Master Hugh succeeded in getting
me hired to Mr. William Gardiner, an extensive ship builder on Fell's Point.

I was placed here to learn to calk, a trade of which I already had some knowledge, gained while in Mr. Hugh Auld's shipyard when he was a master builder . . .

After the end of eight months, Master Hugh refused longer to allow me to remain with Mr. Gardiner. The circumstance which led to his taking me away was a brutal outrage committed upon me by the white apprentices of the shipyard. The fight was a desperate one, and I came out of it most shockingly mangled. I was cut and bruised in sundry places, and my left eye was nearly knocked out of its socket. The facts leading to this barbarous outrage upon me illustrate an important element in the overthrow of the slave system, and I may therefore state them with some minuteness. That phase is this: *the conflict of slavery with the interests of the white mechanics and laborers of the south.*

In the country, this conflict is not so apparent; but in cities such as Baltimore, Richmond, New Orleans, Mobile, etc., it is seen pretty clearly. The slaveholders, with a craftiness peculiar to themselves, by encouraging the enmity of the poor, laboring white man against the blacks, succeed in making the said white man almost as much a slave as the black slave himself. The difference between the white slave and the black slave is this: the latter belongs to *one* slaveholder, and the former belongs to *all* the slaveholders collectively. The white slave has taken from him by indirection what the black slave has taken from him directly, and without ceremony. Both are plundered, and by the same plunderers. The slave is robbed by his master of all his earnings, above what is required for his bare physical necessities; and the white man is robbed by the slave system, of the just results of his labor, because he is flung into competition with a class of laborers who work without wages.

The competition, and its injurious consequences, will one day array the non-slaveholding white people of the slave states against the slave system, and make them the most effective workers against the great evil. At present, the slaveholders blind them to this competition by keeping alive their prejudice against the slaves, *as men*—not against them *as slaves*. They appeal to their pride, often denouncing emancipation as tending to place the white working man on an equality with negroes, and by this means they succeed in drawing off the minds of the poor whites from the real fact that, by the rich slave-master, they are already regarded as but a single remove from equality with the slave . . .

SELECTION 5:
A SHIPYARD WORKER IN THE NORTH AFTER ESCAPING
TO FREEDOM

Once assured of my safety in New Bedford [Massachusetts], I put on the habiliments of a common laborer, and went on the wharf in search of work. I had no notion of living on the honest and generous sympathy of my colored brother, Johnson, or that of the abolitionists. My cry was like that of Hood's laborer, "Oh! only give me work." Happily for me, I was not long in searching. I found employment the third day after my arrival in New Bedford, in stowing a sloop with a load of oil for the New York market. It was new, hard, and dirty work, even for a calker, but I went at it with a glad heart and a willing hand. I was now my own master—a tremendous fact—and the rapturous excitement with which I seized the job may not easily be understood, except by some one with an experience something like mine. The thoughts—"I can work! I can work for a living; I am not afraid of work; I have no Master Hugh to rob me of my earnings"—placed me in a state of independence, beyond seeking friendship or support of any man. That day's work I considered the real starting point of something like a new existence.

Having finished this job and got my pay for the same, I went next in pursuit of a job at calking. It so happened that Mr. Rodney French, the late mayor of the city of New Bedford, had a ship fitting out for the sea, and to which there was a large job of calking and coppering to be done. I applied to that noble-hearted man for employment, and he promptly told me to go to work; but on going on the float-stage for the purpose, I was informed that every white man would leave the ship if I struck a blow upon her. "Well, well," thought I, "this is a hardship, but yet not a very serious one for me." The difference between the wages of a caulker and that of a common laborer was a hundred percent in favor of the former; but then I was free, and free to work, though not at my trade. I now prepared myself to do anything which came to hand in the way of turning an honest penny; sawed wood—dug cellars—shoveled coal—swept chimneys with Uncle Lucas Debuty—rolled oil casks on the wharves—helped to load and unload vessels—worked in Ricketson's candle works—in Richmond's brass foundry, and elsewhere; and thus supported myself and family for three years.

SELECTION 6:
BECOMING PART OF THE ABOLITIONIST MOVEMENT

In four or five months after reaching New Bedford, there came a young man to me, with a copy of the *Liberator*, the paper edited by William Lloyd Garrison and published by Isaac Knapp, and asked me to subscribe for it. I told him I had but just escaped from slavery and was of course very poor, and remarked further that I was unable to pay for it then; the agent, however, very willingly took me as a subscriber, and appeared to be much pleased with securing my name to his list. From this time I was brought into contact with the mind of William Lloyd Garrison. His paper took its place with me next to the bible.

The *Liberator* was a paper after my own heart. It detested slavery—exposed hypocrisy and wickedness in high places—made no truce with the traffickers in the bodies and souls of men; it preached human brotherhood, denounced oppression, and, with all the solemnity of God's word, demanded the complete emancipation of my race . . .

I had not long been a reader of the *Liberator*, and a listener to its editor, before I got a clear apprehension of the principles of the anti-slavery movement. I had already the spirit of the movement, and only needed to understand its principles and measures. These I got from the *Liberator*, and from those who believed in that paper. My acquaintance with the movement increased my hope for the ultimate freedom of my race, and I united with it from a sense of delight, as well as duty . . .

In the summer of 1841, a grand anti-slavery convention was held in Nantucket, under the auspices of Mr. Garrison and his friends. Until now I had taken no holiday since my escape from slavery. Having worked very hard that spring and summer, in Richmond's brass foundry—sometimes working all night as well as all day—and needing a day or two of rest, I attended this convention, never supposing that I should take part in its proceedings. Indeed, I was not aware that anyone connected with the convention even so much as knew my name. I was, however, quite mistaken . . .

Here opened upon me a new life—a life for which I had had no preparation. I was a "graduate from the peculiar institution," Mr. Collins used to say when introducing me, "*with my diploma written on my back!*" The three years of my freedom had been spent in the hard school of adversity. My hands had been furnished by nature with something like a solid leather coating, and I had bravely marked out for myself a life of rough labor, suited to the hardness of my hands, as a means of supporting myself and rearing my children . . .

Young, ardent, and hopeful, I entered upon this new life in the full gush of unsuspecting enthusiasm. The cause was good; the men engaged in it were good; the means to attain its triumph, good; Heaven's blessing must attend all, and freedom must soon be given to the pining millions under a ruthless bondage. My whole heart went with the holy cause, and my most fervent prayers to the Almighty Disposer of the hearts of men were continually offered for its early triumph. "Who or what," thought I, "can withstand a cause so good, so holy, so indescribably glorious. The God of Israel is with us. The might of the Eternal is on our side. Now let the truth be spoken, and a nation will start forth at the sound!" In this enthusiastic spirit, I dropped into the ranks of freedom's friends, and went forth into battle.

SELECTION 7:
FINDING MEANING IN THE STRUGGLE FOR HUMAN LIBERATION

A grand movement on the part of mankind, in any direction or for any purpose, moral or political, is an interesting fact, fit and proper to be studied. It is such, not only for those who eagerly participate in it, but also for those who stand aloof from it—even for those by whom it is opposed. I take the anti-slavery movement to be such a one, and a movement as sublime and glorious in its character as it is holy and beneficent in the ends it aims to accomplish . . .

Present organizations may perish, but the cause will go on. That cause has a life, distinct and independent of the organizations patched up from time to time to carry it forward. Looked at apart from the bones and sinews and body, it is a thing immortal. It is the very essence of justice, liberty, and love. The moral life of human society, it cannot die while conscience, honor, and humanity remain. If but one be filled with it, the cause lives . . . The man who has thoroughly embraced the principles of justice, love, and liberty, like the true preacher of Christianity, is less anxious to reproach the world of its sins than to win it to repentance. His great work is to exemplify, and to illustrate, and to engraft those principles upon the living and practical understandings of all men within the reach of his influence. This is his work; long or short his years, many or few his adherents, powerful or weak his instrumentalities, through good report, or through bad report, this is his work.

It is to snatch from the bosom of nature the latent facts of each individual man's experience, and with steady hand to hold them up fresh and glowing, enforcing with all his power their acknowledgement and practical adoption. If there be but *one* such man in the land, no matter what becomes of abolition societies and parties, there will be an anti-slavery cause and an anti-slavery movement.

Selection 8:
A Guide to Successful Struggles for Social Change (1857)

Let me give you a word of the philosophy of reform. The whole history of progress of human liberty shows that all concessions yet made to her august claims have been born of earnest struggle. The conflict has been exciting, agitating, all-absorbing, and for the time being, putting all other tumults to silence. It must do this or it does nothing. If there is no struggle, there is no progress. Those who profess to favor freedom and yet deprecate agitation are men who want crops without plowing up the ground, they want rain without thunder and lightning. They want the ocean without the awful roar of its many waters.

This struggle may be a moral one, or it may be a physical one, and it may be both moral and physical, but it must be a struggle. Power concedes nothing without a demand. It never did and it never will. Find out just what any people will quietly submit to and you have found out the exact measure of injustice and wrong which will be imposed upon them, and these will continue till they are resisted with either words or blows, or with both. The limits of tyrants are prescribed by the endurance of those whom they oppress. In the light of those ideas, Negroes will be hunted at the North, and held and flogged at the South so long as they submit to those devilish outrages, and make no resistance, either moral or physical. Men may not get all they pay for in this world, but they must certainly pay for all they get. If we ever get free from the oppressions and wrongs heaped upon us, we must pay for their removal. We must do this by labor, by suffering, by sacrifice, and if needs be, by our lives and the lives of others.

SELECTION 9:
THE CIVIL WAR—SECURING DEMOCRACY BY FREEING BLACK LABOR (1864)

The saying that revolutions never go backward must be taken with limitations. The revolution of 1848 was one of the grandest that ever dazzled a gazing world. It overturned the French throne, sent Louis Philippe into exile, shook every throne in Europe, and inaugurated a glorious Republic. Looking from a distance, the friends of democratic liberty saw in the convulsion the death of kingcraft in Europe and throughout the world. Great was their disappointment. Almost in the twinkling of an eye, the latent forces of despotism rallied. The Republic disappeared. Her noblest defenders were sent into exile, and the hopes of democratic liberty were blasted in the moment of their bloom. Politics and perfidy proved too strong for the principles of liberty and justice in that contest. I wish I could say that no such liabilities darken the horizon around us. But the same elements are plainly involved here as there. Though the portents are that we shall flourish, it is too much to say that we cannot fail and fall. Our destiny is to be taken out of our own hands. It is cowardly to shuffle our responsibilities upon the shoulders of Providence. I do not intend to argue but to state facts . . .

The hour is one of hope as well as danger. But whatever may come to pass, one thing is clear: The principles involved in the contest, the necessities of both sections of the country, the obvious requirements of the age, and every suggestion of enlightened policy demand the utter extirpation of Slavery from every foot of American soil, and the enfranchisement of the entire colored population of the country. Elsewhere we may find peace, but it will be a hollow and deceitful peace. Elsewhere we may find prosperity, but it will be a transient prosperity. Elsewhere we may find greatness and renown, but if these are based upon anything less substantial than justice they will vanish, for righteousness alone can permanently exalt a nation.

I end where I began—no war but an Abolition war; no peace but an Abolition peace; liberty for all, chains for none; the black man a soldier in war, a laborer in peace; a voter at the South as well as at the North; America his permanent home, and all Americans his fellow-countrymen. Such, fellow-citizens, is my idea of the mission of the war. If accomplished, our glory as a nation will be complete, our peace will flow like a river, and our foundations will be the everlasting rocks.

SELECTION 10:
THE LABOR QUESTION TWENTY YEARS AFTER EMANCIPATION
(1883)

Not the least important among the subjects to which we invite your earnest attention is the condition of the labor class at the South. Their cause is one with the labor classes all over the world. The labor unions of the country should not throw away this colored element of strength. Everywhere there is dissatisfaction with the present relation of labor and capital, and today no subject wears an aspect more threatening to civilization than the respective claims of capital and labor, landlords and tenants. In what we have to say for our laboring class we expect to have and ought to have the sympathy and support of laboring men everywhere and of every color.

It is a great mistake for any class of laborers to isolate itself and thus weaken the bond of brotherhood between those on whom the burden and hardships of labor fall. The fortunate ones of the earth, who are abundant in land and money and know nothing of the anxious care and pinching poverty of the laboring classes, may be indifferent to the appeal for justice at this point, but the laboring classes cannot afford to be indifferent. What labor everywhere wants, what it ought to have, and will some day demand and receive, is an honest day's pay for an honest day's work. As the laborer becomes more intelligent he will develop what capital he already possesses— that is the power to organize and combine for his own protection. Experience demonstrates that there may be a slavery of wages only a little less galling and crushing in its effects than chattel slavery, and that this slavery of wages must go down with the other.

There is nothing more common now than the remark that the physical condition of the freedmen of the South is immeasurably worse than in the time of slavery; that in respect to food, clothing and shelter they are wretched, miserable and destitute; that they are worse masters to themselves than their old masters were to them. To add insult to injury, the reproach of their condition is charged upon themselves. A grandson of John C. Calhoun, an Arkansas landowner, testifying the other day before the Senate Committee of Labor and Education, says the "Negroes are so indolent that they fail to take advantage of the opportunities offered them to procure the necessities of life; that there is danger of a war of races," etc., etc.

His testimony proclaims him the grandson of the man whose name he bears. The blame which belongs to his own class he shifts from their shoulders to the shoulders of labor. It becomes us to test the truth of that assertion by the light of reason and by appeals to indisputable facts. Of course the landowners of the South may be expected to view things differently from the landless. The slaveholders always did look at things a little differently from the slaves, and we therefore insist that, in order that the whole truth shall be brought out, the laborer as well as the capitalist shall be called as witnesses before the Senate Committee of Labor and Education. Experience proves that it takes more than one class of people to tell the whole truth about matters in which they are interested on opposite sides, and we protest against the allowance of only one side of the labor question to be heard by the country in this case. Meanwhile, a little reason and reflection will in some measure bring out truth! The colored people of the South are the laboring people of the South. The labor of a country is the source of its wealth; without the colored laborer today the South would be a howling wilderness, given up to bats, owls, wolves, and bears. He was the source of its wealth before the war. He almost alone is visible in her fields, with implements of toil in his hands, and laboriously using them today.

Let us look candidly at the matter. While we see and hear that the South is more prosperous than it ever was before and rapidly recovering from the waste of war, while we read that it raises more cotton, sugar, rice, tobacco, corn, and other valuable products than it ever produced before, how happens it, we sternly ask, that the houses of its laborers are miserable huts, that their clothes are rags, and their food the coarsest and scantiest? How happens it that the landowner is becoming richer and the laborer poorer?

The implication is irresistible—that where the landlord is prosperous the laborer ought to share his prosperity, and whenever and wherever we find this is not the case there is manifestly wrong somewhere.

This sharp contrast of wealth and poverty, as every thoughtful man knows, can exist only in one way, and from one cause, and that is by one getting more than its proper share of the reward of industry, and the other side getting less, and that in some way labor has been defrauded or otherwise denied its due proportion, and we think the facts, as well as this philosophy, will support this view in the present case, and do so conclusively . . .

SELECTION 11:
THE SO-CALLED "NEGRO PROBLEM" (1886)

To me what you call the *Negro* problem is a misnomer. It were better called a white man's problem. Here as elsewhere, the greater includes the less. The Negro problem is swallowed up in the Caucasian problem and the question is whether the white man can and will yet rise to that height of justice, humanity and Christian civilization as will permit Indians, Chinamen and Negroes an equal chance in the race of life among them? . . .

The great mass of the colored people in this country are now and must continue to be in the south, and there if they are ever to rise in the scale of civilization, their persons must be protected, their rights secured, their minds enlightened, and their honest work receive honest wages. It is something to give the Negro religion. It is more to give him justice. It is something to tell him that there is a place for him in the Christian's heaven, it is more to let him have a place in this Christian country to live upon in peace.

William Sylvis.

Courtesy of the American Catholic History Research
Center and University Archives, Terence Vincent
Powderly Photographic Prints.

CHAPTER 6

WILLIAM SYLVIS

William Sylvis (1828–1869) was born in central Pennsylvania into an impoverished working-class family, the second of a dozen children. He was hired out, at the age of eleven, to the home of a prosperous state legislator, where he did chores for room and board for a period of five years. He had access to modest formal schooling, and to his employer's library, as well as exposure to ideas and information on political issues of the day, before returning home, where his father—a skilled wagon-maker—had finally succeeded in establishing his own shop. Rejecting his father's trade as a wagon-maker, in the industrializing economy of the northern United States, Sylvis decided to become a skilled mechanic in the iron industry. Marrying in 1852, he moved his family to Philadelphia a few years later, where he secured a job in an iron foundry. According to his brother, it was in this period of transition that, "he became a great reader and student of politics, and especially of the elementary principles of political economy."

While a Philadelphia union of iron molders was formed in 1855, it was not until the strike of 1857 that Sylvis joined the union, accepting the position of union secretary. In 1859, he participated in the organization of a national convention of iron molders—out of which came the National Union of Ironmolders, of which Sylvis became treasurer in 1860. With the coming of the Civil War, employers in the iron industry enjoyed considerable leverage in their successful efforts to destroy all attempts by their workers to establish unions—and the iron molders were compelled to witness the destruction of their organization. Sylvis, who had been active in working-class efforts to avert the war, participated briefly in the U.S. army as a Pennsylvania militia man once war came. By the end of 1862, however, he returned to his trade and to trade union efforts.

In 1863, Sylvis and others were successful in reorganizing—establishing the Iron Molders International Union (IMIU), which unanimously elected him as president. In this capacity, he became a tireless organizer for the union. By 1865, the membership rose to over 6,000 (approximately two-thirds of all iron molders in the country), in eighty-eight locals. Two years later, the organization boasted 8,613 members—although a formidable employers' counter-attack would soon push back the workers' gains. This deepened Sylvis's labor radicalism and his determination to build a powerful labor movement to bring about fundamental social change.

In 1866, Sylvis was one of the central organizers and leaders of the NLU, serving as president from its inception until his death. He also became co-editor, with Chicago's Andrew Cameron, of the NLU organ, the *Workingman's Advocate*, which for several years became the nation's most influential labor newspaper.

Increasingly, Sylvis advocated the replacing of capitalism's "wage-slavery" with a national network of worker-owned manufacturing cooperatives, and also the conception of an independent labor party that could compete successfully against the pro-capitalist Republicans and Democrats. He was also drawn to an array of social reforms—including the eight-hour workday, women's right to vote, and far-reaching monetary reforms designed to under-cut the power of finance capital (the so-called "greenback" movement). Initially unsympathetic to the cause of African–American rights, Sylvis began to reach out to black workers—supporting the formation of a National Colored Labor Union, commenting in a tour of the South that, "careful management, and a vigorous campaign, will unite the whole laboring popula-tion of the South, white and black, upon our platform," and that "convincing these people that it is their interest to make common cause with us in these great national questions, we will have a power in this part of the country that will shake Wall Street out of its boots." He also favored NLU affiliation with the London-based IWA (the First International), associated with Karl Marx.

Sylvis's sudden and untimely death, caused by a digestive ailment that may have involved a perforated ulcer, adversely affected labor organizing and reform efforts. This was especially the case with the development of the NLU, which increasingly drifted away from its trade union moorings and finally collapsed in 1874. Even during Sylvis's lifetime, however, it was neither a union nor a federation of unions, but instead was basically a series of annual congresses at which delegates from a variety of trade unions and reform organizations would assemble. Its first congress had delegates from fifty-nine organizations representing about 60,000 workers; this included forty-three local trade unions, eleven local labor assemblies, four eight-hour leagues, plus one national and one international union. Such numbers fluctuated, and, although at its highpoint the NLU claimed to represent 600,000, it had little capacity to do much—aside from gathering prominent labor activists and reformers to discuss the problems facing the working class and what solutions to such problems might be.

Nonetheless, historian David Montgomery notes that, "the National Labor Union congresses were representative of the country's trade union leadership between 1866 and 1870," adding that "for all its frailties, the NLU was a workers' organization—the first enduring, nationwide institution created by the American working class." It certainly helped pave the way for stronger national entities of the future—most immediately the Knights of Labor and the AFL. While his life and efforts were dramatically cut short, it is generally agreed that, in the final six years of his life, Sylvis's impact on the labor movement was profound and far-reaching.

Sources for Biographical Sketch

Philip S. Foner, *History of the Labor Movement in the United States*, vol. 1 (New York: International Publishers, 1947).

Jonathan P. Grossman, *William Sylvis, Pioneer of American Labor* (New York: Columbia University Press, 1945).

David Montgomery, "William H. Sylvis and the Search for Working-Class Citizenship," in Melvyn Dubofsky and Warren Van Tine, eds., *Labor Leaders in America* (Urbana, IL: University of Illinois Press, 1987), pp. 3–29.

James C. Sylvis, ed., *The Life Speeches, Labors and Essays of William H. Sylvis* (New York: Augustus M. Kelley, 1968; originally 1872).

Sources for Selections

All can be found in James C. Sylvis, ed., *The Life Speeches, Labors and Essays of William H. Sylvis* (New York: Augustus M. Kelley, 1968; originally 1872): selection 1 pp. 97–98, 100; selection 2 pp. 106–107, 108, 109–110, 111–112, 114; selection 3 pp. 164–170, 387–390; selection 4 pp. 403–406; selection 5 pp. 446–448.

SELECTION 1:
THE INTERESTS OF LABOR AND CAPITAL ARE NOT THE SAME

The labor question . . . is one that has troubled the minds of men for centuries past. Men in all ages and sections of the civilized world have been found who have endeavored, by laborious and extended writings and researches, to solve the great problem of political and social science, and the origin and distribution of the wealth of nations. Thousands of volumes have been written by as many different men, upon the principles that underlie the present social structure.

Unfortunately, these economists have universally belonged to that class which they are pleased to call the "higher orders," the "cream of society," the "privileged classes," etc. Men whose hands were never soiled by honest labor; men entirely destitute of all practical knowledge of the wants and condition of the masses; consequently, their ideas have ever sympathized with the interests of capital, while the rights of labor, and indeed labor itself, except so far as it may be made an element of wealth in the hands of these "privileged classes," have been entirely ignored. These men have, with but one or two exceptions, taken the ground and founded their arguments upon the assumed facts, that the soil is the source of all wealth. That there is an identity of interests between labor and capital, that labor and capital are co-partners, that the two elements go hand-in-hand, and constitute one vast firm, who carry on and control the vast business of the world; that labor is an article of commerce, and that the price of labor is regulated by the laws of supply and demand.

Nothing, to my mind, can be more absurd than all these propositions. It may be considered presumption in so humble an individual as I to set myself up in opposition to these great authors, but, nevertheless, I claim the right to do so.

Assuming the position that labor is the real source of all wealth, and that its legitimate and proper distribution depends upon a proper and well-regulated political and social system, I shall proceed to discuss the several questions connected with the subject from that stand-point. The condition of the toiling millions forming, as I believe they do, the foundation of all wealth, and the substratum of political and social life, should engage the earnest attention of good men in every station of life; for it must be evident that, unless the condition of the laboring-classes be in strict harmony with the social well-being and commercial wealth of the nation, the people must live in constant dread of a thousand evils that must arise from a neglect of this great principle . . .

This identity of interests amounts to simply this and nothing more. Capitalists employ labor for the amount of profit realized, and workingmen labor for the amount of wages received. This is the only relation existing between them; they are two distinct elements, or rather two distinct classes, with interests as widely separated as the poles. We find capitalists ever watchful of their interests—ever ready to make everything bend to their desires. Then why should not laborers be equally watchful of their interests— equally ready to take advantage of every circumstance to secure good wages and social elevation? Were labor left free to control itself, as it should be and must be instead of there being an identity of interests, a mutual relation between the two classes, there is an antagonism that ever did and ever will exist; a sort of an irrepressible conflict that commenced with the world, and will only end with it.

SELECTION 2:
NECESSITY AND PURPOSE OF TRADE UNIONS

The terrible condition of poverty and degradation to which the working-people of most European countries are reduced, and the awful fact written in dark and portentous characters upon the horizon of the dawning future, that we (the laboring-people of this great continent) must surely, and at no distant day, occupy the same low and miserable condition, has awakened in the mind of every workingman who values his own happiness, and who loves his God, his country, and his family, and who has a proper appreciation of the great blessings of civilization and human progress, from a religious and moral point of view as well as commercial, and wishes to hand down to posterity these inestimable blessings, a strong and earnest desire to adopt some measures whereby to turn back the tide of oppression and human bondage that is threatening to engulf us in mental and moral darkness before it is ever too late. It has long been evident to all that by individual action nothing whatever could be accomplished.

I am fully imbued with that great American idea of individual independence, and much as I admire it as a characteristic of our face, yet I cannot fail to see that, if adhered to in our dealings with capitalists, it must sooner or later bring us to one common ruin ... It became necessary to discover, if possible, some means by which this evil could be avoided. Combination was thought of. Men began to talk about harmony of action, unity of purpose, oneness of interests, which shortly took practical shape in the formation of trades unions; and it is astonishing to see with what rapidity these fraternizing influences drew men together ...

But upon the threshold of our efforts, we are met by the opposition of capitalists. They deny us the right to combine; not that they have any legal objections to offer (for happily there is no law against it yet), but they raise a question of right and wrong ... Capitalists, and the professional robbers of the hard earnings of the toiling millions, political and professional demagogues, and other drones upon society, have long used to molding us to their fashions, and making of us the stepping-stones to their wealth, ease, and elevation, that any effort by us to shake off this power that has been "grinding us to the dust of misery," threatening with mental and moral darkness, misery, and despair not only ourselves but our posterity for all time to come, is looked upon by them as dangerous to the best interests of society. They see in this great reformation the ultimate destruction of their power over the people ... This explains the holy horror and the flow of pious rhetoric with which they of late cajole the "dear people," and cry out against the immoral tendencies of "trades unions."

I believe that all men are "endowed by their Creator with certain inalienable rights," among which is the divine right to labor, the right to an interest in the soil, the right to free homes, the right to limit the hours of toil to suit our physical capacities, the right to place a valuation upon our own labor proportionate to our social and corporeal wants, the right to a voice in the councils of the nation, the right to control and direct legislation for the good of the majority, the right to compel the drones of society to seek useful employment (or become public instead of private paupers), and the right to adopt whatever means we please within the pale of reason and law to secure these rights . . .

They tell us we have no right to combine to protect all that we hold dear in the world; that these combinations are immoral, unnatural, and an interference with the individual rights of each other. In the face of these protestations we find them combining for every conceivable purpose: and these combinations, when formed for good purposes, have been the source of vast benefit to the world; but capitalists combine for evil as well as good purposes. We find combinations almost everywhere for the purpose of speculating in every article of commerce, and monopolizing and controlling every branch of industry and every source of wealth. Against many of these combinations, and especially those for the purpose of speculating in the necessaries of life, and making fortunes from the necessities of the poor, we might raise objections founded upon moral principles. But we will not stop to do so; we will not waste our time in useless controversy with these sanctimonious hypocrites, but pursue the even tenor of our way, and hew out our destiny in our own way . . .

I do not believe the time will ever come when the "lion will lie down with the lamb," when "nations will cease to war against nations," or when the rich man will take the poor man into his parlor and acknowledge him his equal, and treat him as such. All visionary schemes and theoretical abstractions must be discarded. We must know just where we are, what we want, and how to get it.

Is there any reason why we should not occupy a social position equal to other men? Labor is the foundation of the entire political, social, and commercial structure. Labor is the author of all wealth; it is labor that breathes into the nostrils of inert matter its commercial existence. And yet we are told by the aristocracy—by these sticklers for the divine right to rule the world— that we are only fitted to be the "hewers of wood and drawers of water;" and, therefore, should be kept in constant subjection . . .

To secure these blessings, two things are absolutely necessary. We want more time and more money; fewer hours of toil, and more wages for what we do. These wants we will supply, and these evils we will remedy through the instrumentality of our organizations. We must have a thorough combination of all branches of labor. And then by co-operation we must erect our own workshops, and establish our own stores, and till our own farms, and live in our own houses—in short, we must absolutely control within ourselves the two elements of capital—labor and money. Then we will not only secure a fair standard of wages, but all the profits of our labor. We must erect our own halls wherein we can establish our own libraries, reading- and lecture-rooms, under the control and management of our own men; and we must have time to use them. We must do our own thinking, and infuse into the minds of our people a high tone of morals. We must learn to respect ourselves, and be proud of our occupations and positions. We must hold up our heads, and not be ashamed nor afraid to walk upon the fashionable side of the street.

SELECTION 3:
FROM TRADE UNIONISM TO A COOPERATIVE ECONOMY

We will now return to the consideration of what we believe to be the remedies for the present unsatisfactory state of society. Combination, or union among workingmen, may be looked upon as the first step towards competence and independence. Long years ago the few more intelligent among the laboring-classes saw that by individual action no change in their condition could ever come; and they also saw that, without an effort on the part of the masses themselves, their condition must forever remain the same; and they also clearly saw that an effort to be successful must be a united one.

These ideas were not long in taking practical shape in the organization of "trades-unions." Foremost among these, and one that preserved its organization, and went on increasing in magnitude, importance, and influence against the most fearful odds, breaking down every barrier and removing every opposition, and one which now, at the end of *fifty-five years*, can boast of a combination superior to any other in the world, stands the Moulders' Union of England, Ireland, and Wales, with a branch from the same in Scotland. This organization was founded in 1809. Similar organizations have sprung up in all sections of the Old World, where they are not interdicted by law. The same cause, the same "necessity," produced similar results here, and to-day we find almost every branch of labor, skilled and unskilled, with its organization. In the front rank, though not the oldest, but without a rival, stands the "Iron-Moulders' International Union." To enter upon a summing up of the good these unions have accomplished, or of the two specified, would be a herculean task; nor is it necessary that I should do so; it is sufficient to know that the most beneficial and astonishing results have sprung from them.

In this country our unions, as a general thing, contain but the protective feature—that is, to force capital, by the power of numbers, to concede to our demands. Although what is termed the beneficial feature is discarded, they embrace, besides the protective, many other splendid features. The wages of labor here are fully fifty per cent above what it would be had the idea of union never entered the brain of a man in this country, except, perhaps, in a few isolated cases. One of two things is always present when an advance of wages is given—either a demand on the part of the men, or a fear that such a demand will be made. Had no union ever been formed, and employers felt perfectly sure that no demand for increased pay would be made, would they ever have given it?

Workingmen throughout the States are now working for considerable less wages than they received four and five years ago; and how, let me ask, have we got the small advance thus far secured? By fighting for it—by making demands, and backing them up by whatever power we could command. So persistent and bitter has been the opposition to an increase of wages, that what little we have secured, has cost us very nearly as much as the amount received. It is no difficult matter to see what would now be our condition, had we no unions.

The benefits secured by *our* union, aside from an increase of wages, are beyond calculation. A strong desire for mental cultivation has infused itself throughout the entire body. Schools, libraries, reading- and lecture-rooms, and other institutions for the diffusion of useful knowledge, are springing up among us; and were it not for the opposition of the "better classes," the progress in this direction would be much more rapid. One of the most beautiful and beneficial results flowing from our organization is the universal and widespread acquaintance that has sprung up among the members: a feeling of brotherhood everywhere exists; an interest in each other's welfare has broken down, to a vast extent, that old feeling of selfishness that used to exist among us; a feeling of manly independence has taken the place of that cringing and crawling spirit that used to make us the scorn of honest men. Indeed . . . it is impossible for the true man to cast his eyes over the past, and contemplate the present proud position our organization has attained, and the glorious future that lies invitingly before us, without being carried away by those lofty feelings of manly pride and hope which have animated the true reformer—the true friend of right—in all ages of the world.

These are but a few of the benefits and beauties of combination as applied to labor, and but briefly told. But . . . however widely extended may be the principles of combination, with their teachings of unity and brotherhood, and however great may be their influences upon our people; yet I do not agree with those who believe that combination is *the* great idea, and that by its agency alone we can carry forward this great reformation to an entirely successful issue . . . Combination is only the first great step on the road to emancipation and success.

Protective combination has gone forward and marshaled the forces of the great army of labor; has caused a ray of light to penetrate the midnight darkness of the mind; has opened our eyes to a true sense of our condition; has shown us the true reasons why that condition is poor and miserable; has given us a true conception of the principles of justice and common sense, and taught us to reason upon the great issues before us, as man should reason with equal; has shed abroad in the land that great and divine principle of universal brotherhood, without which man can never rise to that lofty elevation which alone can fit him for self-government; has led us on by glittering hopes and promises to the very threshold of the promised land; and as the mind warmed into new life, animated with bright and cheering hope, reaches forward to grasp the great idea, and begins to realize the glorious future which lies just beyond, the soul enlarges, we draw nigher to the great Author of our existence, and we begin to *feel* that we are men.

A new idea has been born to the children of industry. "Co-operation" has dawned upon the world. "Co-operation" is the next great step; this taken, and we will have crossed the boundary which has so long separated man from his true destiny. This is the true remedy for the evils of society; this is the great idea that is destined to break down the present system of centralization, monopoly, and extortion. By co-operation, we will become a nation of employers—the employers of our own labor. The wealth of the land will pass into the hands of those who produce it. The idle drone, who fattens upon the substances of the poor, will be forced to seek an occupation; the rum-seller, who, with an ungodly hand, deals out ruin to mankind, will be forced to honest industry, or left to starve. The devil won a great victory when he introduced whiskey into the world. He knew what he was about. It was his business to fill his region with souls, and he knew that whiskey was the best recruiting officer for the armies of perdition he could employ. Don't touch it; it is a vile practice in which politicians, common people, all the rest of mankind, and even editors and lawyers indulge.

The vile, the vicious, the evil-doers, and the idle of every class will be driven from society. The body politic, which is now a mass of festering sores, will become clean and healthy; honesty and integrity will be rewarded; genius will be developed; the principles and powers of production will be understood and multiplied, and the wealth of the world vastly augmented; the penalties attached to a violation of nature's laws—war, famine, pestilence, and all the vast train of disturbing causes—will disappear; population and production will take care of themselves, and God will take care of the race. Such ... is destined to be the glorious future of the labor movement, wrought out by *our* remedies—brotherhood, combination, and co-operation. But let us not forget that success depends upon our own efforts. "*It is not what is done for people, but what people do for themselves, that acts upon their character and condition.*"

But ... we are told that we cannot succeed; that our plans and theories are chimerical, and therefore impossible of execution; that society, as now existing, is founded upon the experience of all ages, and that so firmly is it established, that to overturn it is impossible, and that none but designing and corrupt men are found advocating the cause of labor. The mind of that man must be dull indeed, who can see in this great movement nothing more than a momentary excitement, produced by the condition of the country, and the influences of ambitious and designing men. And those statesmen and journalists who pretend to ignore this the greatest reformation the world has ever witnessed, are false lights, and are doing more to retard the progress of the age, and fasten upon the masses the chains of slavery, superstition, ignorance, and moral darkness, than any and all other causes.

I do not believe the doctrine taught by many, that man has, at different periods of the world, risen to the highest state of civilization attainable, and then gradually sunk back into a state of comparative barbarism, from which, after long years of darkness, he would advance; and thus rise and fall like the succeeding waves of the ocean. No, sir; I believe that man is a progressive animal, and that, notwithstanding civilization has received many and severe checks, and has been thrown back hundreds of years at different times, the march of the empire of knowledge has been steadily forward, and that we are a long way in advance of any other people of any other age.

Man is a progressive animal, and has been from the beginning; or at least from the first great transgression, making steady progress upwards. Slow sometimes, to be sure; so slow, indeed, as to cause the best men, in all ages, to weep and mourn over the perverseness of the race, and even to doubt the possibility of his rising to that lofty elevation designed by his Creator. But sure, if slow; and that progress is destined to go forward until that point has been reached so devoutly to be wished—when all mankind shall be free, when the whole human family shall become united in one common brotherhood; when the broad banner of political, social, and religious freedom shall wave over every land, under whose ample folds all the nations of the earth can find protection, and when reason, directed by moral principle, shall rule all the nations of the earth.

SELECTION 4:
FOR AN EIGHT-HOUR WORK DAY

No question of greater magnitude than the eight-hour law can be placed before the American people. Theorists and philosophers may prate of social and political economy till doomsday, and rack their brain for chimerical or practical hobbies; but, in our opinion, nothing of more vital importance, or more deeply interesting, could possibly claim public attention. Much that we could hope for in humanity, and still more that is due us on the broad principles of justice, is involved in this struggle. Upon the issue depends the existence of present wrong, or incalculable blessings to a large portion of the human family. We want a precedent in this great work of mercy—a landmark—beyond which avarice or oppression cannot go—a data, a fixed fact, upon which to base the amelioration of workingmen in all coming time.

Although the time is comparatively short since this great reform began to claim public attention, we already find it in the legislative halls of almost every State, as well as in the national Congress. City and town councils are importuned by petitions, immense mass meetings are being held all over the land. The forum, the pulpit, the workshop, and the family circle, are alike invaded by the agitation of this vital question. The surging masses are disciplining their numbers by forming organizations in village, town and hamlet; and a demand has already gone forth for a national congress of workingmen, with the view of concentrating our forces, and creating a parent body, which shall bring together and unite all the fragmentary efforts now in progress. If we are correctly informed, this movement is designed, when completed, to make one *general* and simultaneous effort throughout the country. We need not say that this proposition meets our cordial approbation, and that we shall omit no opportunity to advocate it.

It is somewhat singular to witness the rapidity with which this great idea of shortening the hours of labor has penetrated every avenue of society, even to the remotest corners of our country, if we except our own State of Pennsylvania; for, more singular still, we find that three millions of people in this commonwealth, the interests of a vast majority of whom are directly and intimately connected with this movement, appear to be unconcerned, or wholly indifferent to the result. Centrally located, unsurpassed for its manufacturing, mechanical, and mineral wealth, possessing every facility for sea and inland commerce, rich in its resources, and furnishing a broad field for enterprise and labor; yet, *here*, where the deepest interest should be felt in the eight-hour movement, we find a coldness that almost amounts to opposition.

This is a strange position for the State of Pennsylvania to occupy; and none can regret more than ourselves, that she contrasts so unfavorably with her sister States. Truth, however, compels us to allude to the want of energy, and the spiritless efforts, which lock the wheels of progress in this State. If we are mistaken, we shall be happy to receive some assurance, some *evidence*, to warrant us in changing our estimate of the home *zeal* manifested in this cause.

The motives and desires of men can only be known by their words and actions; and as we deem it impossible that a question of such vital importance can admit of either indifference or neutrality, we hold all those who are not for us to be against us. We believe the workingmen of Ohio, Massachusetts, and elsewhere, to be in favor of shortening the hours of labor, because we find them earnestly at work, using every means to further the cause; but how can we come to the same conclusion, as far as Pennsylvania is concerned, when we see her workingmen silent and inactive amid all the surrounding excitement?

The workingmen of Philadelphia, but very recently, had a splendid opportunity for the display of their zeal, when one of their representatives introduced an eight-hour bill before the Legislature, granting this special privilege to that city. But there was no meeting—no demonstration—no enthusiasm—*no gratitude?* It fell upon the community as a still-born, listless event, powerless to create a ripple on the social surface. Without stopping to question the honesty or sincerity of the member who presented the bill, we should give him credit for no small degree of moral courage, when he fearlessly braved consequences to forward a reform although uncheered and unsupported by that portion of the community which it was designed to benefit. Under such discouragements, legislators will be slow to incur responsibilities which render their best efforts a thankless office on the one hand, while it brings upon them censure and proscription on the other.

And more recently still, an eight-hour bill, which embraces the entire State, passed the lower house by a large majority, without the slightest manifestation of joy. Having yet to pass the ordeal of the Senate, now is the time to recognize the faithful services of those members who were true to our interests, by enthusiastic expressions of approval, and such ovations as will strengthen our friends in the Senate. In the meantime, pour in the petitions. Let them come from foundry and furnace, from forge and loom, from manufactory and workshop. Be earnest, active, and prompt.

SELECTION 5:
THE DIGNITY OF LABOR

A great deal of distinction is made between the different trades, arising from a silly prejudice which concedes more respectability to one trade than another. Labor is labor all the world over, and the only difference consists in the various modes of its application. The shoemaker plies his awl and hammer, the tailor his needle and shears, the carpenter his jack-plane, the molder his rammer, and so on, through the whole catalogue of mechanism. Each and all give brain and muscle to these several occupations; and, for the life of us, we cannot see the claim to superiority of a single one over another. The grubbing-hoe, the hod, or the mud-spud, are equally honorable implements of industry, although coming under the class of unskilled labor; but, should all receive equal compensation, where shall the higher grade of respectability begin? If we accept the difference justly existing between a mechanical trade which takes years of apprenticeship to acquire, and that species of labor which depends more upon physical than mental capacity, we see nothing at variance with a common interest and a common destiny.

We look upon every kind of labor as respectable, because *necessary*; and no man, should he reach the most exalted position in life, could possibly lessen the dignity of himself, or compromise the sphere in which he moved, by resuming the humble occupation from which he sprung, for either pastime or convenience, so long as he faithfully discharged the duties of that position. Would Abraham Lincoln, while President, have degraded himself or his office had he "took a turn" at splitting rails, or grasped the helm of a flat-boat? Could Andrew Johnson have done the same by patching his coat, or sewing up a rip in his pantaloons? On the contrary, the one felt a glow of honest pride when living, as the other does now, while alluding to their past occupations. Then, if proud to boast, as Presidents, of the trades they followed in poverty, why should they not, with equal pride and satisfaction, split a rail or mend a coat, as Presidents?

It is evident that neither of these great men recognized a distinction between the labor of the mechanic or workman, and that of a President. In fact, while free to boast of their performance as laborers, they were by no means vain-glorious while occupying the highest position in the country. It is the wide difference of compensation which creates the distinction, and not the occupation. We have often read sneering criticisms of both, whenever they made allusions to their past history; but while the occupation of either may stink in aristocratic nostrils, one had, and the other has, the moral courage to throw the mantle of respectability around the humblest calling.

TERRENCE VINCENT POWDERLY, GRAND MASTER WORKMAN, KNIGHTS OF LABOR.
PHOTO. BY KUEBLER.—SEE PAGE 116.

Terence V. Powderly.

Courtesy of the Library of Congress, Prints
and Photographs Division, LC-USZ62-83168.

CHAPTER 7

TERENCE V. POWDERLY

Terence Vincent Powderly (1849–1924) was born in northeastern Penn-sylvania of Irish parents, the eleventh of twelve children. At the age of thirteen he became a wage-worker as a railroad switchman, then, at age seventeen, he became an apprenticed machinist. By 1871, he was a member of the Machinists and Blacksmiths Union in Scranton, and, by 1876, was active in the Knights of Labor, which had begun as a secret labor society in 1869. The Knights of Labor was a combination of fraternal organization, trade union, educational society, social club, and reform group. It welcomed all workers—skilled and unskilled, professionals, even small business people who supported labor's cause (with the exception of saloon keepers and lawyers).

Historian Richard Oestreicher has aptly described Powderly's context as "a world of homeowners, workers, and small businessmen who made their livings working with their hands, producing goods or serving those who did, and the social boundaries between classes were indistinct." The way of life in such communities was permeated by a democratic–republican ideology strongly flavored by the revolutionary traditions expressed in the Declara-tion of Independence, plus a pervasive Christianity that saw all people as equal before God, and understood Jesus as an advocate of the poor who taught the egalitarian ethic of the Golden Rule. All of this was coming increasingly into collision with the rapidly growing concentrations of wealth and power associ-ated with an industrializing capitalist order. Such perceptions animated Powderly and many others who would be drawn to the Knights of Labor.

The year 1877 saw the militant nationwide labor upsurge in which rail workers were joined by many others in spontaneous mass strikes, demon-strations, and street battles in July and August. Before the upsurge and after its violent suppression, Powderly became strongly identified with union activity and strikes, and soon found himself unemployed and blacklisted.

He also found himself in the midst of the flourishing of radical electoral action that consequently swept through much of the country. Millions across the country were drawn into the Greenback–Labor Party, combining pro-labor reforms with support for a proposed monetary reform (increasing the supply of paper currency) that presumably would decrease the power of finance capital. In 1878, Powderly ran for mayor of Scranton on the Greenback–Labor ticket. While the local Scranton newspaper warned against the Greenback–Labor upsurge with the banner headline "COMMUNISM," the fact that Powderly won three two-year terms as mayor did little more than introduce "good government" in the city (although while in office he also secretly held membership in the recently formed SLP).

Shortly after becoming Mayor of Scranton, Powderly was elected to the top position of Grand Master Workman, a position he held from 1879 to 1893. The Knights had about 10,000 members at that time—but rose to an estimated 700,000 or more by 1886. Powderly was a strong advocate of African–American equality and women's rights, and, by 1886, 10,000 women and 50,000 blacks are said to have been members of the order. He also worked with the sympathetic Catholic cleric, Bishop James Gibbons, to remove long-standing sanctions against Roman Catholics who joined unions. The Pope was persuaded to make this move when the Knights, in the early 1880s, did away with the secret membership rituals influenced by freemasonry and removed the words "The Holy and Noble Order of" from the name of the Knights of Labor.

Powderly became something of a media "superstar," particularly after a successful Knights of Labor strike in 1885 against the southwestern railroad conglomerate controlled by Jay Gould (the notorious "robber baron," who said: "I can hire one-half of the working class to kill the other half".) Up to this time, the Knights had not always fared so well in strikes, and Powderly, along with others in the leadership of the Knights, sought to steer the organization away from strikes and other forms of class conflict, seeing themselves primarily as educators for broadly based social reforms—especially for consumer and producer cooperatives—that would benefit the working class and the entire nation. This contributed to growing factional conflicts within the Knights with those who favored trade union action, and it also caused growing tensions with the newly formed trade union federation, the AFL.

Labor radicals increasingly became exasperated with what they viewed as Powderly's conservative trajectory and quest for "respectability," especially when he refused to defend members of the Knights (such as Albert Parsons) associated with anarcho-communist currents in Chicago falsely accused of murdering police in the Haymarket "riot" of 1886, and after being out-maneuvered by Jay Gould when he sought to mediate a second rail strike in 1886. Internal conflicts and increasing assaults by employers and the employer-controlled media resulted in the dramatic decline of the Knights and Powderly's removal from leadership. His active involvement in the labor movement ended, and he soon found a position with the U.S. Bureau of Immigration—but he never repudiated his ideals and labor activism of earlier years.

Sources for Biographical Sketch

Philip S. Foner, *History of the Labor Movement in the United States*, vol. 2 (New York: International Publishers, 1955).

Richard Oestreicher, "Terrence V. Powderly, the Knights of Labor, and Artisanal Republicanism," in Melvyn Dubofsky and Warren Van Tine, eds., *Labor Leaders in America* (Urbana, IL: University of Illinois Press, 1987), pp. 30–61.

Terence V. Powderly and Harry J. Carman, *The Path I Trod: The Autobiography of Terence V. Powderly* (New York: Columbia University Press, 1940).

Sources for Selections

First four selections can be found in Terence V. Powderly, *Thirty Years of Labor, 1859–1889* (New York: Augustus Kelley, 1967; originally 1890): selection 1 pp. 31–32; selection 2 pp. 136–138; selection 3 pp. 250–251; selection 4 pp. 349–350, 352.

Last three selections can be found in Terence V. Powderly and Harry J. Carman, *The Path I Trod: The Autobiography of Terence V. Powderly* (New York: Columbia University Press, 1940): selection 5 pp. 38–49; selection 6 pp. 264–266, 267, 276, 283, 362–363, 374–375; selection 7 pp. 383–384, 387, 388.

SELECTION 1:
ENDING TYRANNY OVER LABOR

For several years prior to 1861 the constitutional right of man to "life, liberty and the pursuit of happiness" was being discussed by men of advanced ideas, and a public opinion was being moulded which held that property in man was iniquitous and degrading; that it was entirely inconsistent with the "Bill of Rights," dangerous to morals, and a standing menace to the liberties of the toiling masses in all parts of the United States. The time had gone by when the American people believed that a nation should be regarded as the exclusive property of those who rule its political destinies.

The experience gained since the establishment of the Republic was of a most beneficial character, and it was not thrown away on the reading workingman. He had learned to know that the right of kings to waste the substance of the people in riotous living, under the shadow of divine authority, was a myth, and that the doctrine once held to be sacred was deserving only of the hatred and scorn of all lovers of equity and fair dealing. The rudiments of the science of co-operation in the affairs of government by all the people were being learned.

That a portion of the dwellers on the soil should be bound down in chains, and continue to remain in that condition for any length of time after the doctrine of industrial emancipation had been launched before the people, was inconsistent with every consideration of justice; it was totally at variance with every aspiration of the men who pioneered the movement which had for its ultimate aim the establishment of a system which would make the statement "that all men are created equal" a brilliant, blazing truth instead of a mere empty sound.

"Life, liberty and the pursuit of happiness" are words that were being read and studied by the mechanics of the United States. Every time that these words were read they took on a deeper meaning. Liberty to live meant more than to be a slave to the whim or caprice of any man. The man who held ownership in his fellow-man had the right to so misuse that fellow-man as to deprive him of life, and, while the conditions of servitude were somewhat different between the white toiler of the North and his sable brother of the South, yet the result was the same when the master decided to use his power. Shutting off the supply of food from the black slave while holding him to the plantation was no worse than the discharge of the white mechanic and the sending of the blacklist ahead of him when he left his home to seek for employment elsewhere.

Only a change of color made it possible for the Southern slave-owner to rule, with power most absolute, the destinies of his bondman. The white mechanic felt that only a change of conditions was necessary to place him in the same category with the colored man. No wonder then that the desire to secure freedom for all the inhabitants of the United States began to grow among the members of labor organizations, and gave them renewed zeal in the work of emancipation. The right to live, the right to work and the liberty to work for home and family instead of for a master is inherent in man, but the mechanic could not feel secure in that right while the slave-owner had it in his power to hold one portion of mankind in serfdom the most degrading and brutalizing.

The anti-slavery agitation and the organization of the mechanics of the United States kept pace with each other; both were revolutionary in their character; and though the agitations differed in methods, the ends in view were the same, viz.: the freedom of the man who worked. Though both were revolutionary in character, one agitation reached the climax, burst into flame, was fought out upon the battlefield and resulted in victory for the black slave, whose walk to liberty was tracked in the blood of millions whom he had never known.

SELECTION 2:
DIGNITY OF LABOR

In order to successfully reach all who are engaged in "productive industry," it is necessary that the members of the Order should know who may appropriately come under that head. The belief was prevalent, until a short time ago, among workingmen that only the man who was engaged in manual toil could be called a workingman. The man who labored at the bench or anvil, the man who held the throttle of the engine or delved in the everlasting gloom of the coal mine, did not believe that the man who made the drawings from which he forged, turned or dug could be classed as a worker. The draughtsman, the time-keeper, the clerk, the school-teacher, the civil engineer, the editor, the reporter, or the worst paid, most abused and illy appreciated of all toilers—woman—could not be called a worker. It was essential that the mechanics of America should know who were workers.

A more wide-spread knowledge of the true definition of the word labor must be arrived at, and the true relations existing between all men who labor must be more clearly defined. Narrow prejudice, born of the injustice and oppressions of the past, must be overcome, and all who interest themselves in producing for the world's good must be made to understand that their interests are identical. All the way down the centuries of time, in which the man who worked was held in bondage or servitude, either wholly or partially, he was brought directly in contract with the overseer, the superintendent or the boss. From these he seldom received a word of kindness; indeed, it was the recognized rule to treat all men who toiled as if they were of inferior clay.

The conditions which surrounded the laborer of past ages denied to him the right to dress himself and family in respectable garb. The coarsest material, made in the most untidy fashion, was considered good enough for him. Not only did his employer and overseer believe that his dress, habitation, furniture and living should be of the coarsest, cheapest material or quality, but he also shared in that belief, and took it for granted that it was ordained of heaven; that the stay of the laborer on earth was only as a matter of convenience for his master; and that he must put up with every indignity, every insult and privation, rather than violate the rules of government, which were held up to him as being as sacred as the Ten Commandments. The Holy Scriptures were quoted to show to the toiler that it was said in Holy Writ that he should be content with his slavish lot on earth in order that he might enjoy an eternity of bliss in a future world, through the portals of which those who held him in subjection could not get a glimpse of the happiness beyond. "Servants, obey your masters," was written on every wall in letters of fire for those who could read; and the story was told and retold to those who could not, until the worker believed that to ask for better things on this earth was almost a sacrilege. It would be flying in the face of Divine Providence to even remonstrate against the injustice which the employer practiced upon the poor laborer.

It was necessary to teach the laborer that it was not essential for him to grovel in the dust at the feet of a master in order to win his title deed to everlasting bliss in the hereafter; and it cannot be wondered at that many who strove to better the condition of the toiler lost all respect for religion when they saw that those who affected to be the most devout worshipers at the foot of the heavenly throne were the most tyrannical of task-masters when dealing with the poor and lowly, whose unfortunate lot was cast within the shadow of their heartless supervision. Men who kneeled before the altar of the Most High and asked for heavenly grace, men who prayed for their "daily bread," were to be found among those who denied the meanest privileges to the workman; and not only denied to him the right to worship his God in a decent manner, but actually took from his mouth, from the fingers of his half-fed babes, the crust of bread on which they sought to sustain life itself.

It was no wonder that to many workingmen religion seemed to be but a parody when they contrasted their own condition with that of their employers. When they were told that all were children of the same Father, it could not be wondered at that some of them rebelled against the decree which had rung in their ears for centuries: "Servants, obey your masters." "We are children of the one Father, and that Father has given to one brother all the good things of earth, while to us He has given nothing. Can it be possible that Almighty God has ordained that some of His children are but step-children from birth? Are our souls of as much consequence as those of our employers? Does the Almighty think more of them than of us? Does He give all the good things to them, and place it in their power to take everything that we produce without a proper equivalent; and is it essential to the salvation of our souls that we grovel forever beneath the feet of wealth?"

These questions began to loom up before the children of toil, and then their masters sought to fasten the screws still tighter upon them by bringing to their aid the powers of press and pulpit to convince the laborer that he should not aspire to the good things of earth, but should be content to live in that sphere to which it had pleased his God to call him. Workingmen are very imitative, and they saw that if it was possible for the man of wealth to save his soul while enjoying so much of this world's goods, it was also possible for them to do so, and they determined to take the risk and try to die in sin by acquiring some of the wealth which they had helped to create . . .

SELECTION 3:
HOURS OF LABOR

A great many remedies are recommended for the ills that I speak of. Let me deal with what seems to be the most important—the reduction of the hours of labor to eight a day. Men, women and children are working from ten to eighteen hours a day, and two million men have nothing to do. If four men, following a given occupation, at which they work ten hours a day, would rest from their labors two hours each day, the two hours taken from the labor of each, if added together, would give the tramp who stands looking on an opportunity of stepping into a position at eight hours a day. It is said that a vast majority of those who are idle would not work if they had work to do. That statement is untrue; but let us admit that five hundred thousand of the two million idle men would not work, we still have a million and a half who are anxious and willing to work. If but six million of the seventeen million producers will abstain from working ten, fifteen and eighteen hours a day and work but eight, the one million and a half of idle men who are willing to work can again take their places in the ranks of the world's producers.

Need it be said that a million and a half of new hats will be needed; that a corresponding number of pairs of shoes, suits of clothing and a hundred other things will be required; that the wants of these men and their families will be supplied; that shelves will be emptied of their goods, and that the money expended will again go into circulation? It would entail hardship on some branches of business to require men employed in them to work eight hours a day. Miners and those working by contract could not very well adopt the eight-hour plan without lengthening their hours of labor. Before giving the matter a second thought, many of these men look upon the eight-hour agitation as of no consequence to them. If a mechanic is thrown out of employment and cannot find anything to do at his trade, he turns toward the first place where an opportunity for work is presented. If he is re-enforced by two million idle men, the number that apply at the mouth of the mine, or seek to secure contracts at lower figures, becomes quite large, and the miner and contract man grumble because so many men are crowding in upon them in quest of work. Every new applicant for work in the mine makes it possible for the boss to let his contract to a lower bidder; therefore it is clearly to the interest of the miner to assist in reducing the hours of labor in shop, mill and factory, to the end that the idle millions may be gathered in from the streets to self-sustaining positions.

The eight-hour system, to be of value to the masses, must be put in operation all over the country, for the manufacturers of one State cannot successfully compete with those of other States if they run their establishments but eight hours while others operate theirs ten or twelve hours a day. The movement should be national, and should have the hearty co-operation of all men.

Give men shorter hours in which to labor, and you give them more time to study and learn why bread is so scarce while wheat is so plenty. You give them more time in which to learn that millions of acres of American soil are controlled by alien landlords who have no interest in America but to draw a revenue from it. You give them time to learn that America belongs to Americans, native and naturalized, and that the landlord who drives his tenant from the old world must not be permitted to exact tribute from him when he settles in our country.

SELECTION 4:
EQUALITY OF BLACK AND WHITE LABOR

Much has been said and written concerning the events which have transpired in the city of Richmond during the past ten days. As I am responsible for a great deal of the agitation, it is but proper that I should be permitted to speak to as large an audience as that which listened to those who have criticized, misconstrued and distorted the words and the idea intended to be conveyed by my utterances of October 4, when Francis Ferrell introduced me to the meeting assembled in the armory. I stated to the meeting that it was at my request that Mr. Ferrell, a representative of the colored race, introduced me; it was left to me to make the selection, and I did it after mature deliberation and careful thought. I have not seen or heard an argument since then that would cause me to do differently to-day.

Critics have seen fit to decide what I meant by selecting this man to introduce me, and they have asserted that my action must be regarded in the light of an attack upon the laws of social equality. A part of the press of the South has attacked, in a most unjustifiable manner, a man who, under the flag and Constitution of his country, selected another man, and a citizen of the Republic, to perform a public duty in a public place. In acknowledging his introduction I referred to the prejudice which existed against the colored man. If previous to that day I had any doubts that a prejudice existed, they have been removed by the hasty and inconsiderate action of those who were so quick to see an insult where none was intended.

My sole object in selecting a colored man to introduce me was to encourage and help to uplift his race from a bondage worse than that which held him in chains twenty-five years ago—viz.: mental slavery. I desired to impress upon the minds of white and black that the same result followed action in the field of labor, whether that action was on the part of the Caucasian or the negro. Two years ago, in an address delivered in this city, I said to the people of Richmond: "You stand face to face with a stern, living reality; a responsibility which cannot be avoided or shirked. The negro question is as prominent to-day as it ever was. The first proposition that stares us in the face is this: The negro is free; he is here, and he is here to stay. He is a citizen, and must learn to manage his own affairs. His labor and that of the white man will be thrown upon the market side by side, and no human eye can detect a difference between the article manufactured by the black mechanic and that manufactured by the white mechanic. Both claim an equal share of the protection afforded to American labor, and both mechanics must sink their differences or fall a prey to the slave labor now being imported to this country." . . . In the field of labor and American citizenship we recognize no line of race, creed, politics or color . . .

It is not the negro alone who stands ostracized in the South by the remnant of the Bourbon element, which still exists to protest against the progress of the Southern States. The white man who works is held in no higher esteem than the black man, and his ignorance is taken advantage of when he is patted on the back and told that he "is better than the negro."

SELECTION 5:
MODEL FOR LABOR AGITATORS

During all the years I was General Master Workman of the Knights of Labor I had a picture above my desk representing the world's greatest, most sublime agitator. He whose heart, moved to indignation and pity, condemned the wrongs inflicted on the toiling poor by the rich and powerful. Did they not call Him an agitator when they said: "He stirreth up the people." Did He not pay the penalty for being an agitator when they pressed the thorns into His flesh, and nailed His hands and feet to the cross? Had Christ sanctioned or condoned the practices of the rich and great do you suppose He would have been crucified?

Had He looked on in silence and uttered no protest against wrong do you believe He would have ascended the cross as He did? Christ, if I read Him aright, did not die for the unjust rich man any more than He did for the lazy, poor man. He lived and worked for the industrious poor, for them He agitated, for them He died. He could have lived and been honored by the rich of that day. He elected to die rather than pay such a price for life . . . One day in a pessimistic mood I wrote these two lines and placed them on that picture, at the foot of the cross:

> Work for self and humanity honors you,
> Work for humanity and it crucifies you.

I was an agitator. Perhaps I was not wise or prudent in all my agitating but my purpose was to ameliorate conditions that in some instances seemed intolerable. Bear in mind the laborer of that period was not the well-read, self-reliant, sober, independent man you recognize in the workingman of today. There were but few national trade-unions that could boast of a membership of over fifteen or twenty thousand. For the most part men were not organized at all, and as a consequence agitation was a vital necessity.

When through my agitation abuse came to me from press, pulpit, and those I tried to serve, I could always look on the picture of the crucified Christ and find consolation in the thought that a divine example had illuminated nineteen hundred years of the world's history, that it shone as bright as on its first day, and that duty to fellow men called for agitation in their interests. I agitated and am vain enough to believe I did some good by causing the people to see things they never saw before, and set them to thinking of how the abuses pointed out to them could be corrected. During all the years of this agitation I was never for a moment actuated by hatred of, or opposition to, the employing classes as such. The injustice they practiced, sanctioned, or condoned was what I agitated against.

SELECTION 6:
COOPERATIVE COMMONWEALTH

Preliminary to considering cooperation, let me ask you to take a retrospective view of the commercialism that has grown with the years since Jesus Christ said: "love your neighbor." When asked "Who is my neighbor?" He answered in such a way as to cause all who pay heed to His words to believe He meant: "Mankind of every description."

Not only did Jesus Christ urge us to love our neighbors but our enemies as well. He vigorously opposed many of the practices of the commercialists of His day . . .

When Jesus went into the temple of God and cast out all who were using it as a stock exchange in buying and selling there, when He overturned the tables of the financial ancestors of our modern stock gamblers, He was impelled by a virtuous indignation based on a conviction that they were engaged in a very selfish proceeding . . . He did it because they were profiting through the needs of those who were obliged to use money; He did it because they were profiteers. The usury that was odious in His sight then has not been purified since then. What men should not do to wring undue profit from money in His day should not be done in this day with anything that money may buy.

Christianity, although based on the teachings of Jesus Christ, has recognized the kind of commercialism He condemned. Perhaps I should not say it has recognized it, but it has not frowned on it or opposed its practitioners as I believe He would do were He in our midst today.

Commercialists recognize competition up to a point where they are powerful enough, or securely enough entrenched, to control production; then they change from competitors to monopolists. Once it was an axiom that "competition is the life of trade." Whether it gave life to trade or not, it has caused the ruin or financial death of many a trader.

Christianity has never attempted to abolish the kind of commercialism condemned by its Founder. He taught men to love their enemies. I have not been able to discover what particular kind of enemy He would have us love and am persuaded that, as with neighbors, He must have included enemies of all descriptions. Jesus Christ taught us to love our enemies; commercialism teaches us to hinder, to devour and kill them. Oh! yes it does, for love of enemy, or neighbor, cannot survive in an atmosphere where two enemies or two neighbors for that matter, strive to secure possession of the same dollar. Love of the dollar supplants love for neighbor as well as enemy. Have you not heard it said that "love of money is the root of all evil"?

When I was young I frequently heard those words of Timothy quoted in all seriousness, and for a purpose. I do not hear them spoken or referred to so often, now. Too many ministers today regard their calling as a profession or a trade to make a living by and not as a mission from on high. They dig for the root of all evil as industriously as any member of the United Mine Workers Union. The member of the Union digs for it because his bread and butter depend on it and he makes no pretense of laboring for the dollar for any other purpose. The clergyman lays claim to a less selfish motive, but they [sic] dig for the same root and endeavor to secure as much of it "as the traffic will bear.". . .

During the greater part of nineteen hundred years, men were as neighbors and enemies engaged in commerce and trade. Finally nations as well as individuals began to buy from and sell to each other. International commercialists began to strive for as much of the "root of all evil" as they could honestly get or dishonestly gouge each other out of, and Churchianity, which largely supplanted Christianity and is often mistaken for it, has not stayed the grasping hand of an individual trader, a national commercialist, or an international murderer whose greed prompted him to reach out for the market of neighbor and enemy and gather in all that could be gained . . . Striving for the world's trade, or the international "root of all evil," brought on a war that slaughtered men, violated women, starved children, and spread disease, want, and famine where God had blessed with sufficiency for every need . . .

The great power that came to Christianity through the teachings of Jesus Christ has been largely frittered away through the practice of Churchianity. I am led to say this because I can find little or no evidence to prove that the ordained teacher and preacher of Christianity has attempted to walk directly in the footsteps of the crucified One in driving the waterer of stocks, the gambler in life's necessities, the despoiler of children, the exploiter of labor, or the grabber of profits from the temple wherein the products of industry are exchanged . . .

The wage system, as I see it, has broken down all over the world. It has not made the laborer happy or contented, it has not caused him to feel secure in his trade or calling, it has not given him a reward for his toil commensurate with his dignity, his effort, his risks, or his needs, it has not proved a safeguard against an increased cost of living . . .

Factory life is in itself a cooperative life. Workmen who were widely separated and strangers to each other in the past were brought together, introduced to each other, and began a cooperative, even a communal life if you please, inside factory walls . . .

My belief that cooperation shall one day take the place of the wage system remains unshaken. The fundamentals of cooperation will be taught in our schools yet . . .

The assaults made on me right along by the rabid socialist and anarchist elements kept me fairly well employed in defending the Order from their attacks. Here let me say that I refer to the socialist element that laid its plans for reform over the top of a beer glass, and blew their work away in the froth. The anarchist element I speak of is that which resorted to violence in seeking reforms. For the socialist who would make society better by making better laws than we now have, I have respect. For the anarchist who believes that man should be good enough to live without the restraints of law and does his best to teach his neighbor how to be so good without blowing his head off by dynamite, I have respect. It is not of these men I speak when I refer to socialists and anarchists. I have respect for the belief of every man, no matter what it is, if he is honest in it and does not counsel evil in order to effect good . . .

I am not a prophet but I venture this prediction. A day will come when what is best in socialism will prevail, and when that hour dawns the movers on the world's stage will witness the representatives of the Roman Catholic Church occupying front seats on the band wagon, holding the lines, claiming full credit for inaugurating the new era and for being the real authors of socialism. The church never changes, they say. You who read these lines may not live in the time when what I say shall come to pass, and men who shall live in that day cannot of their own knowledge deny or affirm that the church opposed socialism in the closing years of the nineteenth, or the opening days of the twentieth century . . .

SELECTION 7:
THE RIGHTS OF WOMEN AS LABORERS AND CITIZENS

I had grown up in the belief that the product of the human hand or brain, speaking for the producer, proclaimed that there should be no sex in industry, and that the worker should be awarded full and fair compensation as well as recognition for labor done, regardless of sex.

The economic pressure which forced women into stores, shops and factories was not so well understood by men workers at that time as to cause them to realize that the women were not interlopers intent on taking their jobs from them. When I questioned members of the General Assembly of the Knights of Labor as to their willingness to admit women to membership in the organization, I did not strike a very responsive chord.

One of my first moves in the direction of admitting women to membership was to prepare a resolution having that object in view, but, before it was introduced, Phillip Van Patten, one of the delegates, presented the following: "*Resolved*: That working women may become members of this Order and form Assemblies under the same conditions as men." That resolution was offered at the Chicago General Assembly on September 4, 1879, was voted on the following day, failed of passage for want of a two-thirds majority, and, on reconsideration, was laid on the table until the next session. At the Pittsburgh session the matter came on for discussion. I had personally sounded every representative, and when the vote was taken it was unanimous. That was on September 9, 1880 . . .

Woman is obliged to work the same as man. She contracts debts and pays bills; she owns property and she is swindled out of it; she has to obey laws and she has to break them; she must look on and see rascals elected to office, but has no voice in their selection, although the evil results of their election will fall as heavily on her as anyone else. We ask in our Preamble [of the constitution of the Knights of Labor] for equal pay for equal work, but will never get it until we have manhood enough to place the weapon in the woman's hand with which to punish the offenders against law, decency, order and good government . . . Let us be manly enough to demand for her the same rights that man enjoys.

Albert R. Parsons.

CHAPTER 8

ALBERT R. PARSONS

Albert Richards Parsons (1848–1887) was a leading labor activist in Chicago who was centrally involved in what came to be known as "The Haymarket Affair" of 1886—one of the salient incidents in U.S. labor history. Descended from veterans of the American Revolution, Parsons himself was born in Alabama (one of nine children), where his father had moved to seek his fortune through opening a shoe and leather factory. After his parents died while he was a small child, he was raised by his older stepbrother living in Texas. He became an apprentice in the printing trade, but when he was thirteen years old he was swept up in the excitement prevalent in Texas with the start of the Civil War and became active in the Confederate cavalry.

After the Civil War's end, however, he shocked some of his Confederate comrades by associating himself with the Reconstruction reforms advanced by the victorious U.S. government. He connects this about-face with his love for the elderly African–American woman who had helped raise him when he was a child, "Aunt Ester." He joined the Republican Party, strongly supporting passage of the 13th, 14th, and 15th Amendments to the U.S. Constitution that advanced African–American rights, and became prominent in the cause of advancing an interracial democracy in the South. He also fell in love with, and married, the beautiful Lucy Gonzales, who had Mexican, Indian, and African heritage. But the young couple had to flee Texas in the early 1870s, as Reconstruction collapsed amid the spreading terrorist violence of the Ku Klux Klan.

Settling in Chicago, Parsons found employment as a printer, joining the Typographical Union. He soon became prominent as an organizer and leader in the Chicago Knights of Labor, as well as the Eight Hour League. He was a founding member of the first Marxist-influenced party in North America, formed in 1876—the WPUS. This group split in 1878: one portion focused on trade union organizing, eventually helping to generate the AFL; the other—which included Parsons—became the SLP, throwing its energies into electoral activity. This orientation can already be seen in the militant speech (reproduced below) that Parsons gave amid the mass strikes and working-class protests, sparked by railway strikes, which rocked the nation in 1877. For this speech he was fired and blacklisted. Thanks to Lucy Parsons' dressmaking business, he was able to devote even more time and energy to becoming a labor organizer.

As Parsons explains in one of the excerpts below, he and many others soon became disillusioned in the electoral path, turning to an anarchist-influenced orientation that challenged gradualism and the capitalist state with a more revolutionary orientation. A new organization was created, the IWPA, which became particularly strong in Chicago. As can be seen by the excerpts below, however, Parsons (along with others in Chicago's left-wing labor movement) combined notions of socialism, communism, and anarchism into a heady blend of labor radicalism that by no means rejected the ideas of Marx that he had embraced in the 1870s. Albert and Lucy Parsons, along with a growing number of other comrades, were able to build a sizeable mass movement within industrializing Chicago's multicultural working class— especially among the sizeable German–American population, with August Spies and Michael Schwab becoming particularly prominent, but also among others (including an English-speaking section that had close to a hundred members in the city). A daily IWPA paper, the *Arbeiter-Zeitung*, was edited by Spies, while Parsons edited a vibrant and lively English-language weekly, *The Alarm*.

Parsons and his comrades were a powerful influence in the ranks of organized labor. The trade union movement split into moderate and revolutionary components—but when workers in Chicago were mobilized for nationwide strikes and demonstrations for the eight-hour workday, the more radical union federation was able to draw the largest numbers—with 80,000 triumphantly marching through the city's streets and more than 300,000 downing their tools in support of the demand for a shorter workday with no reduction in pay. This nationwide protest, initiated by the AFL, took place on May 1, 1886—the first May Day.

On May 4, however, an incident of brutal police violence generated an emergency protest rally in Haymarket Square. Parsons, Spies, and others spoke. As the rally was winding down, however, it was attacked by police. Someone threw a bomb, killing eight policemen, and others—at least an equal number of workers—were killed in the shooting that followed. Parsons, Spies, and six other prominent labor activists were arrested for murder. Of those arrested, one committed suicide, and four others—including Parsons— were condemned to death. The sentence was carried out in 1887, despite both national and international protests and appeals for clemency. In 1893,

Governor John Peter Altgeld freed the three remaining Haymarket defendants, declaring that the trial had been unfair, and those condemned had been innocent.

Parsons and the other Haymarket Martyrs were seen as labor heroes throughout much of the United States and the world, and their ideas continued to influence labor radicals for many years to come.

Sources for Biographical Sketch

Philip S. Foner, ed., *The Autobiographies of the Haymarket Martyrs* (New York: Monad/Pathfinder, 1977).

Lucy E. Parsons, ed., *The Life of Albert R. Parsons, with a Brief History of the Labor Movement in America* (New York: Elibron Classics, 2005; originally 1889).

David Roediger and Franklin Rosement, eds., *Haymarket Scrapbook* (Chicago: Charles H. Kerr Co., 1986).

Sources for Selections

Selection 1: "Illinois, The Voice of Labor," *Labor Standard*, August 11, 1877, pp. 1–2.

Selection 2: Lucy E. Parsons, ed., *The Life of Albert R. Parsons, with a Brief History of the Labor Movement in America* (New York: Elibron Classics, 2005; originally 1889), pp. 17–18, 161, 165; Albert R. Parsons, *Anarchism: its Philosophy and Scientific Basis* (Honolulu: University Press of the Pacific, 2003; originally 1887), pp. 93–94.

Selection 3: Philip S. Foner, ed., *The Autobiographies of the Haymarket Martyrs* (New York: Monad/Pathfinder, 1977), pp. 51–55; University of Missouri—Kansas City, School of Law, famous trials project: Parsons' autobiography (available online at www.law.umkc.edu/faculty/projects/ftrials/haymarket/autobiography1.html, accessed October 6, 2010).

SELECTION 1:
SPEECH DURING MASS STRIKES AND PROTESTS OF 1877

We are assembled as the grand army of starvation. [Voices: "that's it, good."] Fellow workers, let us recollect that in this great republic that has been handed down to us by our forefathers from 1776, that while we have the republic we still have hope. A mighty spirit is animating the hearts of the American people today. The American people are bowed down with shame and hunger. ["Hear, hear."] When I say the American people I mean the backbone of the country ["Hear," and applause]—the men who till the soil, who guide the machine, who weave the material and cover the backs of civilized men. We are a portion of that people. [Voices: "We are."]

Our brothers in the state of Pennsylvania, in New Jersey, in the states of Maryland, New York, and Illinois have demanded of those who have possession of the means of production—our brothers have made demand that they may be permitted to live, and that those men do not appropriate the life to themselves and that they not be allowed to turn us upon the earth as vagrants and tramps. While we are sad indeed at our distressed and suffering brothers in the states mentioned, that they had to resort to such extreme measures, fellow workers, we recognize the fact that they were driven to do what they have done. [Voices: "They were, hear, hear," and tremendous cheering.] We are assembled here tonight to consider our condition. We have come together this evening, if possible, to find means by which the great gloom that now hangs over our republic can be lifted, and once more the rays of happiness can be shed on the face of this broad land.

Now I would like to call your attention to one thing. Whenever the workingmen assemble to consider their grievances, it has been a characteristic method of the press of this country to denounce us in language of vilification and abuse—to denounce any labor organization, be it a trades union or not a trades union. If it was a labor organization it was enough for the press to denounce it as a communistic organization. But the time has come for us to utter in thunder tones our condemnation of the American press. [Loud applause.] The American press persistently vilifies the American workingmen. The American press ought to be the great means whereby freedom and justice should be protected in this land, but it is not. It fills its columns with cases of bastardy, horse-racing, and accounts of pools on the Board of Trade. [Applause. "Score that down." "That's right."] The American press never has time—never sees fit—to visit the homes of workingmen; it never has time to go to the factories and workshops and see how the toiling millions give away their lives to the rich bosses of the country. ["Hear, hear."] The American press has prostituted its mission, degraded its calling, and today would keep us in blinded ignorance. The American press deserves only the scorn and contempt of the toiling millions. ["Hear, hear."]

I would like to say to you tonight that the time has come when the workingmen shall no longer be trampled in the dust. ["Hear, hear," and applause.] The time has come in the history of this country when the working classes will no longer be starved and ground to death in the interests of the moneyed power. The Union Pacific [Railroad] today has conceded to the demands of its employees, and also the Northwestern [Railroad], which pays its employees 90 cents a day. ["Oh! Oh!"; groans and hisses.] As I was saying, the great Northwestern pays its employees the pinnacle starvation price of 90 cents a day, and charges 10 cents a day to take them out to work. Fellow-workers, it is upon such wages as these that we are expected to riase our children, that we are expected to conform our lives to the lives of Chinamen. It is expected that we should rear virtuous daughters and honest sons to rule this republic on 90 cents a day. [Voice: "We can't, and we won't do it."]

The Great Union Pacific Railroad is controlled by a man named Jay Gould, of the state of New York.

This man was in the territory of Utah three weeks ago and attended a convention of the iron, coal and copper mining bosses. These bosses made complaint to Jay Gould that they were not making dividends, and requested him to reduce the freight rates upon the Union Pacific Railroad. After hearing their case, he said in reply that their demand was very strange if not foolish. Instead of asking the road to reduce freight [rates], they should reduce the wages of their miners. The mine bosses replied that they were already reduced so low that they could scarcely live, when Jay Gould answered them that if the miners refused to stand any further reduction in their wages, they could get thousands of tramps to take their places, and if the tramps would not work at the price offered they could send to China and get workmen who could live on a rat and a bowl of rice a day. What do you think of such a man? [Cries of "hang him"; groans for Jay Gould.] This man Jay Gould in this morning's paper, this President of the Union Pacific Railway, is reported as having said that the recent demonstrations in Pennsylvania and the East are the first steps toward a great revolution which cannot be resisted till it has accomplished the destruction of this republican form of government. This man Gould has said this. What do you think should be done with him? [Voices—"Down with him, hang him," and wild commotion.) This man— Jay Gould—says this: that this movement will be the destruction of the American republic. [Renewed cries of "hang him."] He said he would gladly give one million dollars to see President Grant in the White House. [Voice: "He never will."] What do you think of this? Those men who have joined together and become wealthy from our substance, now undertake to rob us of our liberty. What do you think should be done with these men? [Voices: "String them up to the telegraph poles, down with them!"]

Here, says this great railway king Tom Scott, is a conflict between labor and capital. [Voice: "He is right!"] Then if that is the case, what is our duty? Our duty is to fight it out. A workingman is a peaceful man, and he is willing to remain peaceful so long as these wolves of capital allow him to live and do not drive him to misery and starvation. Let us recollect that these men are making a war on our property. What is our property? The only property a workingman has is his labor; and a workingman cannot separate his property from his labor. And when the workingman sells his labor, he sells his body for the time being.

Let us be careful here tonight. There is a scheme afoot in this country, by the aristocratic classes of America, to deprive us of our rights. They want a splendid despotism in preference to the present form of government. If this condition of affairs continues, it will be our own fault. I would have you understand that what I say tonight is not as an individual, but as a member of the Workingmen's Party of the United States. [Loud applause.] Why is it that starvation stares us in the face? It is owing to the competition system, and under that system there is no chance for the freedom of the American laborer. Let us recollect that if we seek to better our condition we must begin in an orderly and determined manner.

The machine is at present a curse to the mass of mankind. And why? Because it is the servant of the capitalist and the master of the workingmen. The machine is purchased by the capitalist for the purpose of getting rid of the labor of human hands and rendering their employment unnecessary. It is to the employment of machinery by capitalists that we have so many million idle men. [Loud applause.]

A workingman said yesterday to me, "Suppose we go across the world and take up all the machines and put them in one pile and burn them up? This will settle the question." Well, said I, instead of organizing into a body to destroy all the machines, let us so organize our labor that the machine shall become our servant instead of our master. That will settle the question. [Loud applause.] There never can come good times in this country until the idle man has employment. What are we going to do with the idle men? Are we going to take them up and shoot them? Are we going to let them drop dead? [Voices: "No, no."] Then if we are not, what are we going to do? [Voices: "Fight, fight," and tremendous applause.] No, no, if we are to fight we must let them fire the first guns. [Voices: "Down with the capitalists, hang them on the telegraph poles."]

Fellow workers, there is a way to get over this by peaceful means. Say, for instance, there is work for a hundred men. There are two hundred men to do it. If the one hundred men work for fourteen hours a day, let us reduce the hours to seven, and that will give work to two hundred. Let us reduce the hours of work to one-half and then form a combination, and then demand what wages we want. In order to do this we have to combine in some kind of labor organization. And if we form a combination we can get as much for six hours' work as we formerly got for twelve. We have got to make a law on the subject of hours. Every boss and capitalist and monopolist and railway king, and every man who is interested in labor will be opposed to us in this movement. And also the idle rich who live upon our strength. Let us understand our position. If we reduce our hours of labor, the bosses and capitalists will immediately purchase another machine to replace us. Let us then reduce the hours of labor once more, and in that way we can keep pace with them. [Voice: "We can, every time."] Let us remember that we can make it possible for the wealth-producing classes to enjoy civilization by reducing the hours. It will then become possible for the working classes to learn something of poetry and pictures, but a man who works fourteen hours can never be anything else but a downcast, ignorant man. If we become organized we can carry on the great struggle successfully. Let us remember that we are the working classes of America.

Let us give the politician to understand that we don't want him about. We have no votes to give to the Republican or Democratic Party. [Voice: "Or the greenbackers either."] Let us remember that the Democratic, Republican and Greenback parties are composed of the bosses of the country. [Voices: "you bet" and "hear, hear."] . . . Let us not swerve from the right or left. Let us fight for our wives and children, for with us it is a question of bread and meat. Let the grand army of labor say who shall fill the legislative halls of this country. Now if we do this we can go to work and unite as one people, can go to the ballot box and say that the government shall be the possessor of all the railway lines in the country. If the people go to work and take possession of the railroads and telegraphs, we extract the sting from the mouths of Jay Gould and Tom Scott, and they can no longer sting us to death. [Loud applause.] We take out of their hands the means by which they now enslave us.

Let us not forget the fact that all wealth and civilization comes from labor, and labor alone. Let us not forget that while we work ten hours a day, the capitalist puts the value of of seven hours of it in his pocket. It rests with you to say whether we shall allow the capitalists to go on, or whether we shall organize. Will you organize? [Cries, "We will."] Well, then enroll your names in the grand army of labor, and if the capitalist engages in warfare against our rights, then we shall resist him with all the means that God has given us. [Loud and prolonged applause.]

SELECTION 2:
SOCIALISM, ANARCHISM, AND THE RIGHTS OF LABOR

Dissensions began to rise in the Socialist organization over the question of methods. In the fall and spring elections of 1878–79–80, the politicians began to practice ballot-box stuffing and other outrages against the Workingmen's Party. It was then I began to realize the hopelessness of the task of political reformation. Many workingmen began to lose faith in the potency of the ballot box or the protection of the law for the poor. Some of them said that, "political liberty without economic (industrial) freedom was an empty phrase." Others claimed that poverty had no votes as against wealth; because a man's bread was controlled by another, that other could and, when necessary, would control his vote also. A consideration and discussion of these subjects gradually brought a change of sentiment in the minds of many; the conviction began to spread that the State, the Government and its laws, was merely the agent of the owners of capital to maintain economic subjection of the man of labor to the monopolizer of the means of labor—of life—to capital. These ideas began to develop in the minds of workingmen everywhere (in Europe as well as America), and the conviction grew that law—statute law—all forms of Government (governors, rulers, dictators, whether Emperor, King, President, or capitalist, were each and all the despots and usurpers), was nothing else than an organized conspiracy of the propertied class to deprive the working class of their natural rights. The conviction obtained that money or wealth controlled politics; that money controlled, by hook or crook, labor at the polls as well as in the workshop. The idea began to prevail that the element of coercion, of force, which enabled one person to dominate and exploit the labor of another, was centered or concentrated in the State, the Government, and the statute law, that every law and every Government in the last analysis was force, and that force was despotism, an invasion of man's natural right to liberty . . .

[. . .]

First and foremost it is my opinion, or the opinion of an anarchist, that government is despotism; government is an organization of oppression, and law, statute law, is its agent. Anarchy is anti-government, anti-rulers, anti-dictators, anti-bosses and drivers. Anarchy is the negation of force; the elimination of all authority in social affairs; it is the denial of the right of domination of one man over another. It is the diffusion of rights, of power, of duties, equally and freely among all the people.

But anarchy, like many other words, is defined in Webster's dictionary as having two meanings. In one place it is defined to mean "without rulers or governors." In another place it is defined to mean "disorder and confusion." This latter meaning is what we call "capitalistic anarchy," such as is now being witnessed in all portions of the world and especially in this courtroom; the former, which means without rulers, is what we denominate communistic anarchy, which will be ushered in by the social revolution . . .

[. . .]

What is Socialism, or Anarchism? Briefly stated, it is the right of the toilers to the free and equal use of the tools of production, and the right of the producers to their product. That is Socialism . . .

I am a Socialist. I am one of those, although myself a wage slave, who holds that it is wrong—wrong to myself, wrong to my neighbor, and unjust to my fellowmen—for me to undertake to make my escape from wage slavery by becoming a master and an owner of others' labor. I refuse to do it. Had I chosen another path in life, I might be living in my beautiful home with luxury and ease, and servants to do my bidding. But I chose the other road, and instead I stand here today upon the scaffold, as it were . . .

We desire that all the forces of nature, all the forces of society, of the gigantic strength which has resulted from the combined intellect and labor of the ages of the past shall be turned over to man and made his servant, his obedient slave forever. This is the object of Socialism. It asks no one to give up anything. It seeks no harm to anybody. But when we witness this condition of things— when we see little children huddling around the factory gates, the poor little things whose bones are not yet hard; when we see them clutched from the hearthstone, taken from the family altar, and carried to the Bastilles of labor and their little bones ground up into gold-dust to bedeck the form of some aristocratic Jezebel—then it stirs me and I speak out. We plead for the little ones; we plead for the helpless; we plead for the oppressed; we seek redress for those who are wronged; we seek knowledge and intelligence for the ignorant; we seek liberty for the slave; Socialism secures the welfare of every human being.

SELECTION 3:
THE HAYMARKET TRAGEDY

The rapid growth of the whole labor movement had by May first given the monopolists of the country much cause for alarm. The organized power of labor was beginning to exhibit unexpected strength & boldness. This alarmed King Money-Bags who saw in the Haymarket affair their golden opportunity to make a horrible example of the Anarchists, and by "the deep damnation of their taking off" give the discontented American workingmen a terrible warning.

Their verdict is the suppression of free speech, free press, and the assemblage of the people to discuss their grievances. More than that the verdict is the denial of the right of self-defense, it is a condemnation of the law of self-preservation in America.

The execution of this verdict will demonstrate to the working people of the United States that whoever writes, speaks, or works to help organize the working class to obtain their rights is liable to imprisonment and death, but whoever uses a ten-cent bomb in self-defense and destroys those who would have destroyed them, or uses it in the interests of a monopolist conspiracy to put down the labor movement is in no danger at all, if they go about their business and say nothing to anyone. This fact was clearly set forth in the address of the State's Attorney and his assistants to the jury when they said "These eight men were picked out by the grand jury because they were the leaders. They are no more guilty than the thousands of their associates in Chicago. They are leaders and we ask you to convict them & make examples of them to others." These were the words, almost the precise words, of the prosecution. The bomb-thrower goes free; the judge decides that his identity or our connection with him is immaterial if it can be shown we ever said that workingmen ought to defend themselves against the attacks & assaults of the police and militia.

As to the responsibility for the Haymarket tragedy? You have heard the side of the ruling class. I now speak for the people—the ruled. The Haymarket tragedy was the immediate result of the blood-thirsty officiousness of Police Inspector Bonfield. Mayor Harrison (commander of the Chicago Police) was present at this meeting, and testified before the court that he heard the speeches & left just before its adjournment and went to the police station and advised Bonfield that everything at the meeting was peaceable and orderly. The Mayor left for his home. Soon thereafter, Bonfield thirsting for promotion and the blood-money which he knew that monopolists were eager to bestow, gathered his army and marched them down upon a peaceable, orderly meeting of workingmen where he expected to immortalize himself by deeds of carnage and slaughter that would put to shame a horde of Apache Indians. Had he not done such brutal things before with the striking street-car Knights of Labor, Trades Unionists and other workingmen? Why not repeat it that night also? He had received the plaudits of the capitalist press for such acts done on other occasions. Why not again?

But Police Inspector Bonfield was only a willing agent not the dastardly principal in this outrage. He held plenary power and he obeyed what he knew to be the express desires of his masters—the Money Kings—who want to suppress free speech, free press, and the right of workingmen to assemble and discuss their grievances. Let the responsibility for the Haymarket tragedy rest where it belongs, to-wit: Upon the monopolists, corporations and privileged class who rule and rob the working people, and when they complain about it discharge, lock-out and black-list them or arrest, imprison and execute them.

The Haymarket Tragedy was, undoubtedly the work of a deep-laid monopolistic conspiracy originating in New York City and engineered by the Pinkerton thugs. Its object was to break down the eight-hour movement and Chicago was selected by these conspirators as the best place to do the work because Chicago was the center of the movement in the United States.

Now, what are the facts about this conspiracy against the 8-hour movement which has resulted in breaking it down and consigning us to the executioner?

Just prior to the time set apart to inaugurate the 8-hour workday, (the latter part of April, 1886) the *New York Herald*, in reference to that question said: "Two hours, taken from the hours of labor, throughout the United States by the proposed 8-hour movement would make a difference annually of hundreds of millions in values both to the capital invested in industries and existing stocks."

Now what did this mean? It meant that the issue of the hour with the New York and Chicago Stock Exchanges, Boards of Trade, and Produce Exchanges in every commercial and industrial center, was how to preserve the steadiness of the market and maintain the fictitious values of the four-fold watered stocks, then listed and then rapidly shrinking in value under the paralyzing influence of the impending eight-hour demand of the united army of labor. Hundreds of millions in money was at stake. What to do to save it? Clearly, the thing to do was to stop the 8-hour movement. The *New York Times* came promptly forward with its scheme to save the sinking market values. Accordingly, just 4 days before the grand national strike for 8 hours and only one week before the Haymarket tragedy, the *New York Times,* one of the leading organs of rail road, bank, telegraph and telephone monopoly in America, published in its issue of April 25, 1886 an editorial on the condition of the markets, the causes of existing decline and panicky symptoms, in which it said,

The strike question is, of course, the dominant one, and is disagreeable in a variety of ways. A *short* and *easy* way to settle it is urged in some quarters, which is to *indict* for conspiracy every man who strikes and summarily *lock him up*. This method would undoubtably strike a *wholesome terror* into the hearts of the *working classes*.

Another way suggested is to *pick out* the *labor leaders* and make *such examples* of them as to *scare* the *others into submission*.

This sentiment was echoed at once by the *New York Tribune* which said: "The best policy would be to drive the workingmen into open mutiny against the law."

The organs of monopoly, (including the Chicago press) all over the United States took up the cry and re-echoed the diabolical scheme. Something must be done to trump up charges against the leaders.

The first of May arrives, the great 8-hour strike is inaugurated. Forty thousand men are standing out for it in Chicago. Chicago is the stronghold of the movement, and 40,000 more threaten to join in the demand. An 8-hour mass-meeting is held on the Haymarket, Tuesday May 4. A bomb is thrown, several policemen killed, the leaders are arrested, indicted for conspiracy and murder and 7 of them sentenced to death. What's the result?

It worked as the monopolist press said it would. The labor leaders are "picked out and made such examples of as to scare the others into submission." Strikers were "summarily locked up. This method would undoubtably strike a wholesome terror into the hearts of the working classes," said the *Times*.

The 8-hour strike is broken and the movement fell to pieces all over the country.

Commenting on the business situation on the 8th day of May, 1886, 4 days after the Haymarket tragedy, Bradstreet in his weekly review said, as telegraphed through the Associated Press and published in all its Chicago papers,

Of the 325,000 men who struck for 8 hours about 65,000 have gained it. Chicago was the center of the strike but the movement all over the country has greatly weakened in the past few days.

Stocks were very much depressed the first two days of the week (the 3 and 4 of May the day of the McCormick and Haymarket trouble) but have recovered their strength the last days of the week.

The 8-hour strike is practically ended, since the Haymarket affair in Chicago.

The desired result was attained. Prices of stocks, bonds, etc. were restored. It was accomplished by the fatal Haymarket bomb . . .

Without fear or favor or reward I have given the untiring energies of the past ten years of my life to ameliorate, to emancipate my fellow wage slaves from their hereditary servitude to capital. I do not regret it; rather while I feel the satisfaction of duty performed, I regret my inability to have accomplished no more than I have done.

Mary Harris Jones, "Mother Jones."

CHAPTER 9

MARY HARRIS JONES

Mary Jones (?–1930), popularly known as "Mother" Jones, was born in Ireland, and little is known about her early life, there being controversy even regarding the date of her birth, which various historians set at 1830, 1836, 1838, and 1843 (Jones herself proudly claiming the first date). It is said that her grandfather was hanged in the Irish freedom struggle against British colonialism. Her father emigrated to the United States, obtaining employment as a construction worker on the canals and railroads, and was joined by his wife and children afterward. Working as a teacher and dressmaker as a young woman, Mary Harris married iron molder George Jones and began to raise a family in Memphis, Tennessee, but she was the only one among her loved ones to survive a yellow fever epidemic. She then returned to Chicago and worked as a dressmaker, but soon became involved with the Knights of Labor, whose leader, Terence V. Powderly, was to be a lifelong friend. In the 1870s, she began a career as a labor organizer.

By the 1890s, Mother Jones, most closely associated with the UMW, was traveling widely to help organize workers in a variety of occupations and unions. A woman of strong opinions and great physical courage, she was immensely popular among working-class men and women. "When she started to speak, she could carry an audience of miners with her every time," noted John Brophy, who first heard her speak at his mine in 1899. "Her voice was low and pleasant, with great carrying power. She didn't become shrill when she got excited; instead her voice dropped in pitch and the intensity of it became something you could almost feel physically . . . She had a lively sense of humor—she could tell wonderful stories, usually at the expense of some boss, for she couldn't resist the temptation to agitate, even in a joke—and she exuded a warm friendliness and human sympathy."

J. A. Wayland, publisher of the socialist weekly *Appeal to Reason*, one of her favorite periodicals, commented in the same period: "She is the best socialist agitator working among the labor unions." The tough civil liberties lawyer Clarence Darrow praised her as "a born crusader" who "is one of the most forceful and picturesque figures of the American labor movement," and, after her death, the *United Mine Workers Journal* applauded "her great heart and courage for the disinherited," adding: "Neither courts, nor gunmen, nor prisons, nor militia could stop her. Her name will stand at the head among the great of labor's hall of fame."

It has been noted that she had "fervently traditional views on the role of women, notwithstanding her own traditional lifestyle," yet one can discern strongly feminist elements among the selections offered here. It is worth considering this 1904 account of her impact on a meeting of striking miners' wives and daughters in Pennsylvania:

> In about half an hour a strange audience had assembled. There were old bent women of 70 and young, fresh-faced girls of 10. There were young matrons with babes in their arms, and women faded before their time. The faces that looked up from the rude benches of the strikers' hall were at first only curious or somewhat shy and embarrassed.
>
> Walking to the edge of the platform, Mother Jones stretched out her arms to them, and in her thrillingly sweet voice said, "Sisters!" A perceptible wave of emotion like that of wind sweeping the long grasses of downs and meadows passed over he audience. Still the women waited, wondered, watched.
>
> The faces awoke, the souls back of them kindled. For an hour the speaker walked to and fro telling the deeds of the mothers of the past and sisters and wives. The listeners drew nearer. They leaned their elbows on the platform and lifted their faces to drink in the words. Their bosoms heaved and the tears rolled unheeded down their cheeks, but quickly the smiles flashed out again at the will of the speaker . . .

This culminated in a demonstration of 500 women—in defiance of deputy sheriffs, company guards, and state militia—which won new contingents of mineworkers to the strike.

While Mother Jones has often been seen as a passionate agitator, it is worth noting in these selections a tough-minded analysis underlying much of her fiery rhetoric. Sometimes, contradictions cropped up in what she said or did. At various times she had positive things to say about the Socialist Eugene V. Debs, the Democrat Woodrow Wilson, the Republican Calvin Coolidge, about Bolshevism and Catholicism, and so on. At certain times she changed her mind: at first supporting the IWW, then turning away from it with disappointment;

at first opposing World War I, then supporting the U.S. war effort, later concluding that workers had been fooled into supporting it by treacherous leaders. In her final years, she herself concluded that her thinking had gotten more radical with time. What was unswerving was her devotion to the cause of the working class.

Sources for Biographical Sketch

Philip S. Foner, "Mother Jones: Dynamic Champion of Oppressed Multitudes," in Philip S. Foner, ed., *Mother Jones Speaks: Collected Speeches and Writings* (New York: Monad Press, 1983).

Priscilla Long, "Mother Mary Harris Jones," in Mari Jo Buhle, Paul Buhle, and Dan Georgakas, *Encyclopedia of the American Left* (Urbana: University of Illinois Press, 1992).

Sources for Selections

Selection 1: Mary Harris Jones, *The Autobiography of Mother Jones* (Chicago: Charles H. Kerr Co., 1925), pp. 11–16.

Selections 2–7: Philip S. Foner, ed., *Mother Jones Speaks: Collected Speeches and Writings* (New York: Monad Press, 1983), pp. 96–98, 106, 136–137, 140–141, 142, 146–147, 150, 468–469, 470, 471, 535, 366.

SELECTION 1:
EARLY YEARS

I was born in the city of Cork, Ireland in 1830. My people were poor. For generations they had fought for Ireland's freedom. Many of my folks have died in their struggle. My father, Richard Harris, came to America in 1835, and as soon as he had become an American citizen he sent for his family. His work as a laborer with railway construction crews took him to Toronto, Canada. Here I was brought up but always as the child of an American citizen. Of that citizenship I have ever been proud.

After finishing the common schools, I attended the Normal school with the intention of becoming a teacher. Dress-making too, I learned proficiently. My first position was teaching in a convent in Monroe, Michigan. Later, I came to Chicago and opened a dressmaking establishment. I preferred sewing to bossing little children.

However, I went back to teaching again, this time in Memphis, Tennessee. Here I was married in 1861. My husband was an iron molder and a staunch member of the Iron Molders' Union.

In 1867, a yellow fever epidemic swept Memphis. Its victims were mainly among the poor and the workers. The rich and the well-to-do fled the city.

Schools and churches were closed. People were not permitted to enter the house of a yellow fever victim without permits. The poor could not afford nurses. Across the street from me, ten persons lay dead from the plague. The dead surrounded us. They were buried at night quickly and without ceremony. All about my house I could hear weeping and cries of delirium. One by one, my four little children sickened and died. I washed their little bodies and got them ready for burial. My husband caught the fever and died. I sat alone through nights of grief. No one came to me. No one could. Other homes were as striken as was mine. All day long, all night long, I heard the grating of the wheels of the death cart.

After the union had buried my husband, I got a permit to nurse the sufferers. This I did until the plague was stamped out.

I returned to Chicago and went again into the dressmaking business with a partner. We were located on Washington Street near the lake. We worked for the aristocrats of Chicago, and I had ample opportunity to observe the luxury and extravagance of their lives. Often while sewing for the lords and barons who lived in magnificent houses on the Lake Shore Drive, I would look out of the plate glass windows and see the poor, shivering wretches, jobless and hungry, walking along the frozen lake front. The contrast of their condition with that of the tropical comfort of the people for whom I sewed was painful to me. My employers seemed neither to notice nor to care.

Summers, too, from the windows of the rich, I used to watch the mothers come from the west side slums, lugging babies and little children, hoping for a breath of fresh air from the lake. At night, when the tenements were stifling hot, men, women, and little children slept in the parks. But the rich, having donated to the charity ice fund, had, by the time it was hot in the city, gone to seaside and mountains.

In October, 1871, the great Chicago fire burned up our establishment and everything that we had. The fire made thousands homeless. We stayed all night and the next day without food on the lake front, often going into the lake to keep cool. Old St. Mary's church at Wabash Avenue and Peck Court was thrown open to the refugees and there I camped until I could find a place to go.

Nearby in an old, tumbled down, fire scorched building the Knights of Labor held meetings. The Knights of Labor was the labor organization of those days. I used to spend my evenings at their meetings, listening to splendid speakers. Sundays we went out into the woods and held meetings.

Those were the days of sacrifice for the cause of labor. Those were the days when we had no halls, when there were no high salaried officers, no feasting with the enemies of labor. Those were the days of the martyrs and the saints.

I became acquainted with the labor movement. I learned that in 1865, after the close of the Civil War, a group of men met in Louisville, Kentucky. They came from the North and from the South; they were the "blues" and the "grays" who a year before had been fighting each other over the question of chattel slavery. They decided that the time had come to formulate a program to fight another brutal form of slavery—industrial slavery. Out of this decision had come the Knights of Labor.

From the time of the Chicago fire I became more and more engrossed in the labor struggle and I decided to take an active part in the efforts of the working people to better the conditions under which they worked and lived. I became a member of the Knights of Labor.

One of the first strikes that I remember occurred in the Seventies. The Baltimore and Ohio Railroad employees went on strike and they sent for me to come help them. I went. The mayor of Pittsburgh swore in as deputy sheriffs a lawless, reckless bunch of fellows . . . The governor sent the militia . . . One night a riot occurred. Hundreds of box cars standing on the tracks were soaked with oil and set on fire down the tracks to the roundhouse. The roundhouse caught fire. Over one hundred locomotives, belonging to the Pennsylvania Railroad Company, were destroyed. It was a wild night. The flames lighted the sky and turned to fiery flames the steel bayonets of the soldiers.

The strikers were charged with the crimes of arson and rioting, although it was common knowledge that it was not they who instigated the fire; that it was started by hoodlums backed by the business men of Pittsburgh who for a long time had felt that the Railroad company discriminated against their city in the matter of rates.

I knew the strikers personally. I knew they disciplined their members when they did violence. I knew, as everyone knew, who really perpetrated the crime of burning the railroad's property. Then and there I learned in the early part of my career that labor must bear the cross for others' sins, must be the vicarious sufferer for the wrongs that others do.

These early years saw the beginning of America's industrial life. Hand in hand with the growth of factories and the expansion of railroads, with the accumulation of capital and the rise of banks, came anti-labor legislation. Came strikes. Came violence. Came the belief in the hearts and minds of the workers that legislatures but carry out the will of the industrialists.

SELECTION 2:
LESSONS OF A STRIKE IN WEST VIRGINIA (1903)

Fellow workers, 'tis well for us to be here. Over a hundred years ago men gathered to discuss the vital questions and later fought together for a principle that won for us our civil liberty. Forty years ago men gathered to discuss a growing evil under the old flag and later fought side by side until chattel slavery was abolished. But by the wiping out of this black stain upon our country another great crime—wage slavery—was fastened upon our people. I stand on this platform ashamed of the conditions existing in this country . . .

I shall tell you some things tonight that are awful to contemplate; but, perhaps, it is best that you know of them. They may arouse you from your lethargy, if there is any manhood, womanhood, or love of country left in you. I have just come from a state which has an injunction on every foot of ground. Some months ago the president of the United Mine Workers asked me to take a look into the condition of the men in the mines of West Virginia. I went. I would get a gathering of miners in the darkness of the night up on the mountain side. Here I would listen to their tale of woe; here I would try to encourage them. I did not dare to sleep in one of those miners' houses. If I did the poor man would be called to the office in the morning and would be discharged for sheltering old Mother Jones.

Oppression

I did my best to drive into the downtrodden men a little spirit, but it was a task. They had been driven so long that they were afraid. I used to sit through the night by a stream of water. I could not go to the miners' hovels so in the morning I would call the ferryman and he would take me across the river to a hotel not owned by the mine operators.

The men in the anthracite district finally asked for more wages. They were refused. A strike was called. I stayed in West Virginia; held meetings and one day as I stood talking to some break-boys two injunctions were served upon me. I asked the deputy if he had more. We were arrested but we were freed in the morning. I objected to the food in the jail and to my arrest. When I was called up before the judge I called him a czar and he let me go. The other fellows were afraid and they went to jail. I violated the injunction but I wasn't re-arrested. Why? The courts themselves force you to have no respect for that court.

A few days later that awful wholesale murdering in the quiet little mining camp of Stamford took place. I know those people were law-abiding citizens. I had been there. And their shooting by United States deputy marshals was an atrocious and cold-blooded murder [of six workers]. After the crimes had been committed the marshals—the murderers—were banqueted by the operators in the swellest hotel in Pennsylvania. You have no idea of the awfulness of that wholesale murder. Before daylight broke in the morning in that quiet little mining camp deputies and special officers went into the homes, shot the men down in their beds, and all because the miners wanted to try to induce "black-legs" [that is, scabs, or "replacement workers"] to leave the mines.

How It Started

I'll tell you how the trouble started. The deputies were bringing these strikebreakers to the mines. The men wanted to talk with them and at last stepped on ground loaded down with an injunction. There were thirty-six or seven in the party of miners. They resisted arrest. They went home finally without being arrested. One of the officials of the miners' union telegraphed to the men. "Don't resist. Go to jail. We will bail you out." . . . The miners' officials secured the names of the men and gave their representatives authority to bail them out of jail the next morning. But when the next morning arrived they were murdered in cold blood.

These federal judges, who continue granting injunctions, are appointed by men who have their political standing through the votes of you labor union fellows! . . . If you like those bullets, vote to put them into your own bodies. Don't you think it's about time you begin to shoot ballots instead of voting for capitalistic bullets?

A Challenge

I hate your political parties, you Republicans and Democrats. I want you to deny if you can what I am going to say. You want an office and must necessarily get into the ring. You must do what that ring says and if you don't you won't be elected. There you are. Each time you do that you are voting for a capitalistic bullet and you get it . . . A contented workingman is no good. All progress stops in the contented man. I'm for agitation. It's the greater factor for progress . . .

SELECTION 3:
AN APPEAL FOR WORKING-CLASS SOLIDARITY IN COLORADO (1903)

Brothers, you English speaking miners of the northern fields promised your southern brothers, seventy percent of whom do not speak English, that you would support them to the end. Now you are asked to betray them, to make a separate settlement. You have a common enemy and it is your duty to fight to a finish. Are you brave men? Can you fight as well as you can work? I had rather fall fighting than working. If you go back to work here and your brothers fall in the south, you will be responsible for their defeat.

The enemy seeks to conquer by dividing your ranks, by making distinctions between North and South, between American and foreign. You are all miners, fighting a common cause, a common master. The iron heel feels the same to all flesh. Hunger and suffering and the cause of your children bind more closely than a common tongue. I am accused of helping the Western Federation of Miners, as if that were a crime, by one of the National Board members [of the United Mine Workers]. I plead guilty. I know no East or West, North or South when it comes to my class fighting the battle for justice. If it is my fortune to live to see the industrial chain broken from every workingman's child in America, and if then there is one black child in Africa in bondage, there I shall go.

I don't know what you will do, but I know very well what I would do if I were in one of your places. I would stand or fall with this question of eight hours for every worker in every mine in Colorado. I would say we will all go to glory together or we will die and go down together. We must stand together; if we don't there will be no victory for any of us . . .

SELECTION 4:
SPEAKING IN NEW YORK CITY AMID THE RISING OF THE 20,000
FEMALE WAIST-MAKERS (1909)

This is not a play, this is a fight!

Through all the ages you have built a wonderful monument of civilization, but you don't own it. You make all the fine waists, but you do not wear them. You work hard and are poorly paid, and now you have been forced to strike for better conditions of labor, shorter hours and higher wages.

You ought to parade past the shops where you work and up the avenue where the swells who wear the waists you made live. They won't like to see you, they will be afraid of you!

If I belonged to a union and was on strike, I would insist that we parade past the shops and homes of the masters.

You must strike together to win. The boss looks for cheap workers. When the child can do the work cheaper he displaces the woman. When the woman can do the work cheaper she displaces the man. But when you are organized you have something to say about the conditions of labor and your wages. You must stand shoulder to shoulder. The woman must fight in the labor movement beside the man. Every strike I have ever been in has been won by the women.

Whether you know it or not, this is the last great fight of man against man. We are fighting for the time when there will be no master and no slave. When the fight of the workers to own the tools with which they toil is won, for the first time in human history man will be free.

SELECTION 5:
ADDRESS TO A UNITED MINE WORKERS CONVENTION (1911)

Brothers of this convention, perhaps never in the history of the mine workers was there a more important convention than this . . . The master class is watching your convention with keen interest. And so I say to you, be wise, be prudent in your actions. Think before you act. Don't give the master class any weapon to strike you with and laugh about. Let us have the laugh on them.

Now, my brothers, the last year has been a trying year for organized labor all along the line. It has not been alone the miners, it has not been alone the steel workers. For the first time, perhaps, the women in the industrial field have begun to awaken to their condition of slavery. In New York and Philadelphia the women arrayed themselves in battle, and they gave battle fearlessly. They were clubbed, they were jailed, they were insulted, but they bore it all for a principle they believed in. Never can a complete victory be won until the woman awakens to her condition. We must realize that the woman is the foundation of government; that no government is greater or ever can be greater than the woman. It was once asked of Napoleon how the French nation could become a great nation. He considered for a moment and then said: "Never until you have a great motherhood. When you have that you have a great nation."

So it is with us in this nation. Never as long as the women are unorganized, as long as they devote their time to women's clubs and to the ballot, and to a lot of old meow things that don't concern us at all and have no bearing on the industrial battle, can we succeed, and the men will have to make the battle alone. But the century is here when the woman is going to take a mighty hand in these battles, and then we will fight it out and fight it to the finish. Put that down, Mr. Reporter!

Now, I want to call your attention to some things. The industrial war is on in this country. Why? Because modern machinery plays a greater part in the production of wealth in this nation than it does in any other nation of the world. The class that owns the machine owns the government, it owns the governors, it owns the courts and it owns the public officials all along the line . . .

Now, I want to speak to you on this question of machinery, and I want to draw your attention to the fact that they have reached into China and are developing the industries there. Capitalism is in business for profit, and wherever it is going to realize the most profit out of human blood there it is going. So they have reached into China, where they can hire men for eight cents and ten cents a day. The result is we are feeling it here all along the line . . .

I have been in strikes for a good many years—not alone miners' fights, but garment workers' and textile workers' and street car men's strikes . . . You must stop all conflict [between competing workers and unions] and get down to the fight. Instead of fighting each other, turn all your batteries on the other fellow and lick him; then, if there is any fellow in our ranks who needs a licking, let us give it to him. Let us be true to the organization; let us fight to a finish. That field must be organized, and the Southern Colorado strike must be won. You cannot win that field in the North until you do. You are wasting money. I know that field thoroughly. I was up against the guns there too many months not to understand the situation.

Now, I am talking to you miners. I am not talking to the officers. I am talking to you who put up the money to fight those battles and win them. I knew the men who blazed the way. There was no pay, there was no newspaper eulogy, there were no compliments; they slept by the wayside, but they fought the battle and paved the way for this magnificent organization, and, knowing them as I did, this organization is dear to me. It has been bought with the blood of men who are scarcely known today.

Now, I want to say a few more words. I want to call your attention to that magnificent dope institution that was formed to get labor, that mutual admiration society, the [National] Civic Federation. The biggest, grandest, most diabolical game played on labor was played when that was organized . . . That Civic Federation is strictly a capitalist machine. The men or women who sit down and eat and drink with them and become members of the Belmont-Carnegie cabinet are not true to labor . . . "It is so delightful to have labor and capital coming together in a brotherhood." What do you think of such rot? The robber and the robbed, the fellow who brings the militia out to murder my class and representatives of the workingman! Not on you life! . . .

You are in the mightiest conflict of the age. Put away your prejudice, grow big and great and mighty in this conflict and you will win. There is no such thing as fail. We have got to win. You have brave fighters, both in Colorado and Pennsylvania. You have warriors there, but you must stand by them . . .

SELECTION 6:
WORKING-CLASS SISTERHOOD (1915)

No nation can ever grow greater than its women. None ever has; none ever will. It is the women who decide the fate of a nation, and that has always been so, as history proves.

What tremendous power and responsibility, therefore rest with woman-kind. I wonder if they realize it. In the poorer classes I think they do, or are coming to, but the attitude of the rich is appalling.

I called the other day to see Mrs. J. Borden Harriman at the Colony Club. While I sat in the reception room waiting to be received I watched the fashionable women come and go. Nearly all of them, if you asked them, would tell you proudly that they belonged to society. But if you asked them what society meant they could not answer you without covering themselves with shame.

I will tell you why they could not, or would not, answer. Because the word society, as applied to women of today, stands for idleness, fads, extravagance, and display of wealth.

The women I saw parade before me were "bluffs." They glanced at me languidly, because that in society is the correct way to look at anybody not of their own class . . .

As soon as every woman grasps the idea that every other woman is her sister, then we will begin to better conditions. For instance, I saw a girl in a store the other day ready to drop from weariness. Her fatigue was apparent, and yet I noticed a woman customer loaded down with expensive furs and jewels call on this girl to get down several boxes of goods. Then, after glancing over them, she concluded she didn't want to buy anything. This rich woman wouldn't have asked her own sister to do that, but she didn't view the shop girl in that light. Oh no; she was "only a shop girl."

I spoke to this girl after the woman had left and found that she worked about twelve hours a day, and for one dollar a day. Out of this she had to buy her clothes, her lunch, and supply her carfare. What a life!

It is among the poor that you find that sisterly feeling I have spoken about, because the poor know what suffering is and means, and sympathize with others. You never see a well-dressed woman give up her seat in the subway to an old woman, do you? No never; but I have often had a poor, tired shop girl rise with a smile and proffer me her seat because of my white hair . . .

No human being in this country ever ought to go hungry, and there's something radically wrong somewhere when our jails are continually over-crowded. An immense amount of good can be done with playgrounds and supplying other means to give the poor outdoor exercise. Healthy bodies go forward with healthy minds, and a man or woman, though poor, can smile and do more to overcome their condition if minds and bodies are kept in a normal state.

I have always felt that no true state of civilization can ever be realized as long as we continue to have two classes of society. But there is a tremendous problem and it will take a terrific amount of labor to remedy it. I think myself that we are bound to see a revolution here before these questions are straightened out . . .

SELECTION 7:
COMMENTS SHORTLY BEFORE HER DEATH (1930)

Today modern methods of production have far out-stripped the power of America to consume the product of labor. And now that we're into the machine age, neither the government nor the people are preparing for it. The only thing that can be done now is for the government to take hold and reduce the working hours. A five-day week and a six-hour day would mean work for everybody . . .

I'm more radical than I ever was. I've had a lot of chance to think lately, and the more I think the more radical I get. The capitalists are still a bunch of high-class robbers and burglars, and I'm for anything that will keep them from impoverishing the people. And if the unemployment situation gets much worse men are going to do something about it. If they can't get work and fair wages they will change the system so they can . . .

America was not founded on dollars but on the blood of the men who gave their lives for your benefit. Power lies in the hands of labor to retain American liberty, but labor has not yet learned how to use it. A wonderful power is in the hands of women, too, but they don't know how to use it. Capitalists sidetrack the women into clubs and make ladies of them. Nobody wants a lady, they want women . . .

Eugene V. Debs.

CHAPTER 10

EUGENE V. DEBS

Eugene Victor Debs (1855–1926) was born in Terre Haute, Indiana, of Alsatian immigrant parents steeped in the culture of French and German romanticism; Debs was named after the French novelists Eugène Sue and Victor Hugo. His father and mother provided a living for themselves and their six children through a small grocery store. The second-oldest child (and first of two sons), Eugene left school and got a job in a local railroad shop at the age of fourteen. In 1872, he became a locomotive fireman, and in 1875 he helped found and lead the Terre Haute local of the Brotherhood of Locomotive Firemen, also serving as associate editor of the *Firemen's Magazine* in 1878. By 1880, he was editor-in-chief of the union's magazine, as well as grand secretary and treasurer of the national Brotherhood. The personable Debs was also drawn into Democratic Party politics—elected as Terre Haute city clerk in 1879, then to the Indiana state legislature in 1885 (the same year he married Kate Metzel).

Yet this path offered little for the improvement of railroad workers' lives, and, as Debs commented in later years, "When I rise it will be with the ranks, not from the ranks." He turned away from a conventional political career and then from the limited craft organization of the fragmented railroad brotherhoods—helping to found the ARU in 1893. As president of the ARU, Debs became a leading spokesman and tactician for a new form of industrial unionism that quickly proved its ability to challenge the immense power of the railroad corporations in massive and well-organized strikes. With the Pullman strike of 1894, however, the pro-business government—backed by the news media (also pro-business)—used quickly deputized U.S. marshals, U.S. troops, and the Sherman Anti-Trust Act to smash the ARU and jail its leaders. This posed new questions, and Debs spent much of his fortieth year reading Marx's fiery and incisive *Communist Manifesto*, Edward Bellamy's utopian novel *Looking Backward*, and other probing critiques of capitalism. "While there is a lower class I am in it, while there is a criminal element I am of it, while there is a soul in prison I am not free," he commented after his six-month prison sentence. He emerged with a deeper than ever commitment to create a political, social, and economic "rule by the people." In 1896, he supported the presidential campaign of Populist-Democrat William Jennings Bryan, but soon turned definitively away from the two major parties.

Debs and his co-thinkers went on to form the Social Democratic Party in 1897, and then the broader Socialist Party of America in 1901. In the years from its founding to the 1917 U.S. entry into World War I, the Socialist Party was an increasingly important force in the labor movement, a fact reflected in the vote totals Debs got when he ran for president: 96,000 in 1900; 402,400 in 1904; 420,973 in 1908; 901,062 in 1912 (6 percent of the total vote); and 919,799 in 1920, when he ran from Atlanta penitentiary after being imprisoned for opposing World War I. Many local SP candidates were elected to office in those years; approximately one-third of AFL unions chose open Socialists as leaders; prominent intellectuals and writers (such as Upton Sinclair, Jack London, Carl Sandburg, John Reed, and Sinclair Lewis); women's rights activists (such as Mary White Ovington, Crystal Eastman, and Margaret Sanger); fighters for African–American rights (such as W. E. B. DuBois and A. Philip Randolph); clergymen; young people, and both immigrant and native-born workers in large numbers joined the Socialist movement. The weekly *Appeal to Reason*, published in Girard, Kansas, had a circulation of 761,000, and there were innumerable other Socialist periodicals, books, and pamphlets with broad circulations.

In this context, Debs labored tirelessly, making speeches throughout the country, to bring his message to more and more people. He helped inspire many to devote their energies, sometimes their whole lives, to the cause of labor. Intensely involved in supporting practical trade union struggles, Debs felt strongly that the narrow craft orientation, the exclusionary policies, and the "pure and simple" unionism predominant in much of the AFL were detrimental to the interests of the working class. For this reason, he supported the 1905 formation of the IWW. Pulling back from the organization because he was critical of a tendency toward sectarianism, he remained sympathetic to many IWW goals, activists, and struggles. Although he generally held aloof from internal disputes in the Socialist Party, he identified with its left wing, which rejected reformist compromises. Debs strongly favored worldwide working-class solidarity, opposed the policies of imperialist economic expansionism, and condemned the militarism that culminated in World War I. He was also hopeful that the 1917 Russian Revolution, led by Lenin and Trotsky, would lead to similar working-class insurgencies elsewhere (although he would later express sharp criticisms of the dictatorial trends in Soviet Russia that ultimately culminated in Stalinist tyranny, and he did not agree with the creation of a new Communist Party).

Debs's radical and outspoken anti-war position resulted in his prosecution under the so-called "Espionage Act" in 1918, and, along with many other socialist militants, he was imprisoned—which severely damaged his health, at the same time that government "anti-red" repression severely damaged the socialist and militant labor movements. Pardoned in 1921, Debs no longer had the strength to play the role he once did in the workers' movement. But he did what he could to advance united left-wing and labor efforts in defense of workers' rights and civil liberties, and he struggled to spread socialist ideas in the more conservative atmosphere of the 1920s. Increasingly incapacitated by illness, he died in 1926.

Safely dead, Debs was treated as a saintly man whose lofty notions placed him far above the rest of us—but he would not have accepted such trivialization of his beliefs. "The story of Debs becomes the story of a whole generation of wage earners and dirt farmers," commented his outstanding biographer, Ray Ginger. "While the people learned something from the Socialist leader, he learned even more from them. His awesome strength in time of crisis was made possible by his confidence in his fellows. At such moments his finite self seemed to merge with the agonized wanderings of the nameless multitude."

Sources for Biographical Sketch

James P. Cannon, "Eugene V. Debs and the Socialist Movement of His Time," in *The First Ten Years of American Communism, Report of a Participant* (New York: Lyle Stuart, 1962).

Ray Ginger, *Eugene V. Debs, The Making of an American Radical* (New York: Colliers Books, 1962).

Scott Molloy, "Eugene V. Debs," in Mari Jo Buhle, Paul Buhle, and Dan Georgakas, *Encyclopedia of the American Left* (Urbana: University of Illinois Press, 1992).

Nick Salvatore, "Eugene V. Debs: From Trade Unionist to Socialist," in Melvyn Dubofsky and Warren Van Tine, eds., *Labor Leaders in America* (Urbana: University of Illinois Press, 1987).

Arthur Schlesinger, Jr., "Introduction," in Joseph M. Bernstein, ed., *Writings and Speeches of Eugene V. Debs* (New York: Hermitage Press, 1948).

Sources for Selections

Selections 1, 3 and 5: Joseph M. Bernstein, ed., *Writings and Speeches of Eugene V. Debs* (New York: Hermitage Press, 1948), pp. 43–47, 323, 324–325, 329–330, 425–426, 427–428, 430, 432–433.

Selections 2 and 4: Henry M. Tichenor, ed., *Labor and Freedom, The Voice and Pen of Eugene V. Debs* (St. Louis: Phil Wagner, 1916), pp. 107–110, 119–120, 125–127, 131–132, 169, 171–174, 175.

SELECTION 1:
EARLY YEARS IN THE LABOR MOVEMENT (1902)

On the evening of February 27, 1875, the local lodge of the Brotherhood of Locomotive Firemen was organized at Terre Haute, Indiana, by Joshua A. Leach, then grand master, and I was admitted as a charter member and at once chosen secretary. "Old Josh Leach," as he was affectionately called, a typical locomotive fireman of his day, was the founder of the brotherhood, and I was instantly attracted by his rugged honesty, simple manner and homely speech. How well I remember feeling his large, rough hand on my shoulder, the kindly eye of an elder brother searching my own as he gently said, "My boy, you're a little young, but I believe you're in earnest and will make your mark in the brotherhood." Of course, I assured him that I would do my best. What he really thought at the time flattered my boyish vanity not a little when I heard of it. He was attending a meeting at St. Louis some months later, and in the course of his remarks said: "I put a tow-headed boy in the brotherhood at Terre Haute not long ago, and some day he will be at the head of it." . . .

My first step was thus taken in organized labor and a new influence fired my ambition and changed the whole current of my career. I was filled with enthusiasm and my blood fairly leaped in my veins. Day and night I worked for the brotherhood. To see its watchfires glow and observe the increase of its sturdy members were the sunshine and shower of my life. To attend the "meeting" was my supreme joy, and for ten years I was not once absent when the faithful assembled.

At the convention held in Buffalo in 1878 I was chosen associate editor of the magazine, and in 1880 I became grand secretary and treasurer. With all the fire of youth I entered upon the crusade which seemed to fairly glitter with possibilities. For eighteen hours at a stretch I was glued to my desk reeling off the answers to my many correspondents. Day and night were one. Sleep was time wasted and often, when all oblivious of her presence in the still small hours my mother's hand turned off the light, I went to bed under protest. Oh, what days! And what quenchless zeal and consuming vanity! . . .

My grip was always packed; and I was darting in all directions. To tramp through a railroad yard in the rain, snow or sleet half the night, or till daybreak, to be ordered out of the roundhouse for being an "agitator," or put off a train, sometimes passenger, more often freight, while attempting to deadhead over the division, were all in the program, and served to whet the appetite to conquer . . . I rode on the engines over mountain and plain, slept in the cabooses and bunks, and was fed from their pails by the swarthy stokers who still nestle close to my heart, and will until it is cold and still.

Through all these years I was nourished at Fountain Proletaire. I drank deeply of its waters and every particle of my tissue became saturated with the spirit of the working class. I had fired an engine and been stung by the exposure and hardship of the rail. I was with the boys in their weary watches, at the broken engine's side and often helped to bear their bruised and bleeding bodies back to wife and child again. How could I but feel the burden of their wrongs? How could the seed of agitation fail to take deep root in my heart?

And so I was spurred on in the work of organizing, not the firemen merely, but the brakemen, switchmen, telegraphers, shopmen, track-hands, all of them in fact, and as I had now become known as an organizer, the calls came from all sides and there are but few trades I have not helped to organize and less still in whose strikes I have not at some time had a hand.

In 1894 the American Railway Union was organized and a braver body of men never fought the battle of the working class.

Up to this time I had heard but little of Socialism, knew practically nothing about the movement, and what little I did know was not calculated to impress me in its favor. I was bent on thorough and complete organization of the railroad men and ultimately the whole working class, and all my time and energy were given to that end. My supreme conviction was that if they were only organized in every branch of the service and all acted together in concert they could redress their wrongs and regulate the conditions of their employment. The stockholders of the corporation acted as one, why not the men? It was such a plain proposition—simply to follow the example set before our eyes by their masters—surely they could not fail to see it, act as one, and solve the problem ...

The skirmish lines of the ARU were well advanced. A series of small battles was fought and won without the loss of a man. A number of concessions were made by the corporations rather than risk an encounter. Then came the fight on the Great Northern, short, sharp, and decisive. The victory was complete—the only railroad strike of magnitude ever won by an organization in America.

Next followed the final shock—the Pullman strike—and the American Railway Union again won, clear and complete. The combined corporations were paralyzed and helpless. At this juncture there was delivered, from wholly unexpected quarters, a swift succession of blows that blinded me for an instant and then opened wide my eyes—and in the gleam of every bayonet and the flash of every rifle *the class struggle was revealed*. This was my first practical lesson in Socialism, though [I was] wholly unaware that it was called by that name.

An army of detectives, thugs and murderers was equipped with badge and beer and bludgeon and turned loose; old hulks of cars were fired; the alarm bells tolled; the people were terrified; the most startling rumors were set afloat; the press volleyed and thundered, and over all the wires sped the news that Chicago's white throat was in the clutch of a red mob; injunctions flew thick and fast, arrests followed, and our office and headquarters, the heart of the strike, was sacked, torn out and nailed up by the "lawful" authorities of the federal government; and when in company with my loyal comrades I found myself in Cook Country jail at Chicago with the whole press screaming conspiracy, treason and murder, and by some fateful coincidence I was given the cell occupied just previous to his execution by the assassin of Mayor Carter Harrison, Sr., overlooking the spot, a few feet distant, where the anarchists were hanged a few years before. I had another exceedingly practical and impressive lesson in Socialism.

Acting upon the advice of friends we sought to employ John Harlan, son of the Supreme Justice, to assist in our defense—a defense memorable to me chiefly because of the skill and fidelity of our lawyers, among whom were the brilliant Clarence Darrow and the venerable Judge Lyman Trumbell, author of the thirteenth amendment to the Constitution, abolishing slavery in the United States.

Mr. Harlan . . . gravely informed us that he could not afford to be identified with the case, "for," said he, "you will be tried upon the same theory as were the anarchists, with probably the same result." That day, I remember, the jailer, by way of consolation, I suppose, showed us the blood-stained rope used at the last execution and explained in minutest detail, as he exhibited the gruesome relic, just how the monstrous crime of lawful murder is committed.

But the tempest gradually subsided and with it the blood-thirstiness of the press and "public sentiment." We were not sentenced to the gallows, nor even to the penitentiary—though put on trial for conspiracy—for reasons that will make another story.

The Chicago jail sentences were followed by six months at Woodstock and it was here that Socialism gradually laid hold of me in its own irresistible fashion. Books and pamphlets and letters from Socialists came by every mail and I began to read and think and dissect the anatomy of the system in which workingmen, however organized, could be shattered and battered and splintered at a single stroke. The writings of Bellamy and Blatchford early appealed to me. *The Co-operative Commonwealth* of Gronlund also impressed me, but the writings of Kautsky were so clear and conclusive that I readily grasped, not merely his argument, but also caught the spirit of his Socialist utterance—and I thank him and all who helped me out of darkness into light.

It was at this time, when the first glimmerings of Socialism were beginning to penetrate, that Victor L. Berger—and I have loved him ever since—came to Woodstock, as if a providential instrument, and delivered the first impassioned message of Socialism I had ever heard—the very first to set the "wires humming in my system." As a souvenir of that visit there is in my library a volume of *Capital* by Karl Marx, inscribed with the compliments of Victor L. Berger, which I cherish as a token of priceless value.

The American Railway Union was defeated but not conquered—overwhelmed but not destroyed. It lives and pulsates in the Socialist movement, and its defeat but blazed the way to economic freedom and hastened the dawn of human brotherhood.

SELECTION 2:
UNITY AND VICTORY: ADDRESS TO THE KANSAS STATE AFL (1908)

Mr Chairman, Delegates and Fellow Workers: It is with pleasure, I assure you, that I embrace this opportunity to exchange greetings with you in the councils of labor. I have prepared no formal address, nor is any necessary at this time. You have met here as the representatives of organized labor and if I can do anything to assist you in the work you have been delegated to do I shall render that assistance with great pleasure.

To serve the working class is to me always a duty of love. Thirty-three years ago I first became a member of a trade union. I can remember quite well under what difficulties meetings were held and with what contempt organized labor was treated at that time. There has been a decided change. The small and insignificant trade union has expanded to the proportions of a great national organization. The few hundreds now number millions and organized labor has become a recognized factor in the economics and politics of the nation.

There has been a great evolution during that time and while the power of the organized workers has increased there has been an industrial development which makes that power more necessary than ever before in all the history of the working-class movement.

This is an age of organization. The small employer of a quarter of a century ago has practically disappeared. The workingman of today is confronted by the great corporation which has its iron-clad rules and regulations, and if they don't suit he can quit.

In the presence of this great power, workingmen are compelled to organize or be ground to atoms. They have organized. They have the numbers. They have had some bitter experience. They have suffered beyond the power of language to describe, but they have not yet developed their latent power to a degree that they can cope successfully with the great power that exploits and oppresses them. Upon this question of organization, my brothers, you and I may differ widely, but as we are reasonable men, we can discuss these differences candidly until we find common ground upon which we can stand side by side in the true spirit of solidarity—and work together for the emancipation of our class.

Until quite recently the average trade unionist was opposed to having politics even mentioned in the meeting of his union. The reason is self-evident. Workingmen have not until now keenly felt the necessity for independent working class political action. They have been divided between the two capitalist parties and the very suggestion that the union was to be used in the interest of one or the other was in itself sufficient to sow the seed of disruption. So it isn't strange that the average trade unionist guarded carefully against the introduction of political questions in his union.

But within the past two or three years there have been such changes that workingmen have been compelled to take notice of the fact that the labor question is essentially a political question, and that if they would protect themselves against the greed and rapacity of the capitalist class they must develop their political power as well as their economic power, and use both in their own interest. Workingmen have developed sufficient intelligence to understand the necessity for unity upon the economic field. All now recognize the need for thorough organization. But organization of numbers of itself is not sufficient. You might have all the workers of the country embraced in some vast organization and yet they would be very weak if they were not organized upon correct principles; if they did not understand, and understand clearly, what they were organized for, and what their organizations expected to accomplish.

I am of those who believe that an organization of workingmen, to be efficient, to meet the demands of this hour, must be organized upon a revolutionary basis; must have for its definite object not only the betterment of the condition of workingmen in the wage system, but the absolute over-throw of wage slavery that the workingman may be emancipated and stand forth clothed with the dignity and all other attributes of true manhood . . .

Now, these [capitalist party] candidates are trying to carry water on both shoulders. They declare that they will give both labor and capital a square deal, and I want to say that is impossible. No man can be for labor without being against capital. No man can be for capital without being against labor.

Here is the capitalist; here are the workers. There is so much coal produced. There is a quarrel between them over a division of the product. Each wants all he can get. Here we have the class struggle. Now is it possible to be for the capitalist without being against the worker? Are their interests not diametrically opposite? . . .

We have now no revolutionary organization of the workers along the lines of this class struggle, and that is the demand of this time. The pure and simple trade union will no longer answer. I would not take from it the least credit that belongs to it. I have fought under its banner for thirty years. I have followed it through victory and defeat, generally defeat. I realize today more than ever before in my life the necessity for thorough economic organization. It must be complete. Organization, like everything else, is subject to the laws of evolution. Everything changes, my brothers. The tool you worked with twenty-five years ago will no longer do. It would do then; it will not do now. The capitalists are combined against you. They are reducing wages. They have control of the courts. They are doing everything they can to destroy your power. You have got to follow their example. You have got to unify your forces. You have got to stand together shoulder to shoulder on the economic and political fields and then you will make substantial progress toward emancipation . . .

Let me impress this fact upon your minds: the labor question, which is really the question of all humanity, will never be solved until it is solved by the working class. It will never be solved for you by the capitalists. It will never be solved for you by the politicians. It will remain unsolved until you yourselves solve it. As long as you can stand and are willing to stand for these conditions, these conditions will remain; but when you unite all over the land, when you present a solid class-conscious phalanx, economically and politically, there is no power on this earth that can stand between you and complete emancipation.

As individuals you are helpless, but united you represent an irresistible power.

Is there any doubt in the mind of any thinking workingman that we are in the midst of a class struggle? Is there any doubt that the workingman ought to own the tool you work with under the present system? This whole system is based upon the private ownership by the capitalist of the tools and the wage-slavery of the working class, and as long as the tools are privately owned by the capitalists the great mass of workers will be wage-slaves.

You may, at times, temporarily better your condition within certain limitations, but you will still remain wage-slaves, and why wage-slaves? For just one reason and no other—you have got to work. To work you have got to have tools, and if you have no tools you have to beg for work, and if you have got to beg for work the man who owns the tools you use will determine the conditions under which you shall work. As long as he owns your tools he owns your job, and if he owns your job he is the master of your fate. You are in no sense a free man. You are subject to his interest and to his will. He decides whether you shall work or not. Therefore, he decides whether you shall live or die. And in that humiliating position anyone who tries to persuade you that you are a free man is guilty of insulting your intelligence. You will never be free, you will never stand erect in your own manly self-reliance until you are the master of the tools you work with, and when you are you can freely work without the consent of any master, and when you do work you will get all your labor produces.

As it is now, the lion's share goes to the capitalist for which he does nothing, while you get a small fraction to feed, clothe and shelter yourself, and reproduce yourself in the form of labor power. That is all you get out of it and all you ever will get in the capitalist system . . .

No man can serve both capital and labor at the same time.

You don't admit the capitalists to your union. They organize to fight you. You organize your union to fight them. Their union consists wholly of capitalists; your union consists wholly of workingmen. It is along the same line that you have got to organize politically. You don't unite with capitalists on the economic field. Why should you politically? . . .

SELECTION 3:
INDUSTRIAL UNIONISM (1909, 1910)

The term Industrial Unionism is used to express a modern form of labor organization whose jurisdiction is not confined to any particular trade or craft, but is co-extensive with the industrial development, and embraces the entire working class . . .

The concentration of capital and the highly complex productive mode of the present day, grouping in vast industrial establishments thousands of workers engaged in scores of different trades, forcing them into closer and closer cooperation, based upon the minutest division of labor, have tended to obscure, or perhaps totally obliterate, the lines that once so sharply defined the skilled trades, and in this interweaving of the trades the jurisdictions of the several unions based upon them have overlapped each other, and this has been the prolific source of the increasing friction between many of the larger unions which have approximately reached their maximum of growth and are jealous of maintaining the prestige of an expanding membership regardless of the effect upon a rival union which may lay claim to jurisdiction over the same craft, or division thereof. Following the lines of least resistance the tendency of these unions, so far as external forms are concerned, is toward industrial unionism, and this is undoubtedly the form that will ultimately supersede the trade union of the present and past . . .

I do believe that an industrial union should be organized and it should carry forward a most vigorous and comprehensive propaganda. There are millions of unorganized to whom it can make its appeal, as well as to those who are organized and lean toward industrial unionism. It should be distinctly understood that to smash the existing unions and establish industrial unions by force is not the mission, but that on the contrary, it has come as the most intelligent and effective expression of labor unionism, that its purpose is to build and not to destroy, to help and not to hinder, thus inspiring the confidence of the workers, whether organized or unorganized, and recruiting its ranks from the most intelligent and experienced in every department of industrial activity.

The taunts and sneers of the "pure and simple" [trade union] leaders who have nothing to lose but their jobs, and whose leadership depends upon their keeping the workers segregated in craft unions, may well be ignored, instead of allowing ourselves to be goaded into attacking them, thereby giving warrant to these leaders in charging us, which they are only too eager to do, with seeking to destroy their unions. The effect of this is invariably to fortify these unions more strongly in their reactionary attitude, and their so-called leaders in their corrupt and degrading domination.

It is far wiser, as our experience had demonstrated, to devote our time, means and energy to advocating the principles of industrial unionism, building up our organization and vitalizing our propaganda by an appeal to the intelligence and integrity of the workers, bearing with them patiently and perseveringly, while at the same time aiding and encouraging them in all their struggles for better conditions, than to waste time in denouncing, or seeking to destroy, these reactionary old unions and their leaders.

Industrial unionism, as organized and applied, to find favor with the workers, must give proof of its sympathy with them in all their struggles, rejoice with them when they win, and when they lose cheer them up and point the way to victory.

It matters not what union it is that happens to be engaged in a fight with the master class, or what its attitude may be toward industrial unionism, the invariable policy of the industrial union should be to back up the contestants and help them win their struggle by all the means at its command. This policy will do more, infinitely more to inspire the faith of the workers in industrial unionism and draw them to its standard than any possible amount of denunciation or attempted destruction of the old unions.

Nor do I believe in organizing dual unions in any case where the old union substantially holds the field. Where an old union is disintegrating it is of course different. Here there is need of organization, or rather reorganization, and hence a legitimate field for industrial unionism.

Industrial evolution has made industrial unionism possible and revolutionary education and agitation must now make it inevitable. To this end we should bore from within and without, the industrial unionists within the old unions working together in perfect harmony with the industrial unionists upon the outside engaged in laying the foundation and erecting the superstructure of the new revolutionary economic organization, the embryonic industrial democracy.

The difficulties we have encountered on this side since organizing the Industrial Workers [of the World] have largely been overcome and, I believe the time is near at hand when all industrial unionists will work together to build up the needed organization and when industrial unionism will receive such impetus as will force it to the front irresistibly in response to the crying need of the enslaved and despoiled workers in their struggle for emancipation.

The economic organization of the working class is as essential to the revolutionary movement as the sun is to light and the workers are coming more and more to realize it, and the triumph of industrial unionism over craft unionism is but a question of time, and this can be materially shortened if we but deal wisely and sanely with the situation.

SELECTION 4:
CAPITALISM AND SOCIALISM (1912)

Political parties are responsive to the interests of those who finance them. This is the infallible test of their character and applied to the Republican, Democratic and Progressive parties, these parties stand forth as the several political expressions of the several divisions of the capitalist class. The funds of all these parties are furnished by the capitalist class for the reason, and only for the reason, that they represent the interests of that class ... The Republican, Democratic and Progressive conventions were composed in the main and controlled entirely by professional politicians in the service of the ruling class ...

Since the foundation of the government one or the other of these capitalist parties has been in power and under their administration the working and producing millions have been reduced to poverty and slavery. Professor Scott Nearing has shown in his work on the wages of American workers that half of the adult males of the United States are earning less than $500; that three quarters of them are earning less than $600 a year; that nine-tenths of them are receiving less than $900 a year, while 10 percent only receive more than that figure.

Professor Nearing also shows the starvation wages which women are compelled to work for in the present system. One-fifth of the whole number of women receive less than $200 per year; three-fifths receive less than $325; nine-tenths receive less than $500. Only one-twentieth of the women employed are paid more than $600 per year. These figures bear out the report of the Chicago vice commission to the effect that the low wages of women and girls go hand in hand with prostitution ...

And in the presence of this appalling condition the professional politicians prattle about tariff revision and indulge in silly twaddle about currency reform and regulation of the trusts. The Socialist party is absolutely the only party which faces conditions as they are and declares unhesitatingly that it has a definite and concrete plan and program for dealing with these conditions.

The Socialist party as the party of the exploited workers in the mills and mines, on the railways and on the farms, the workers of both sexes and all races and colors, the working class in a word, constituting a great majority of the people and in fact THE PEOPLE, demands that the nation's industries shall be taken over by the nation and that the nation's workers shall operate them for the benefit of the whole people.

Private ownership and competition have had their day. The Socialist party stands for social ownership and cooperation. The one is capitalism; the other Socialism. The one industrial despotism, the other industrial democracy.

The Republican, Democratic and Progressive parties all stand for private ownership and competition. The Socialist party alone stands for social ownership and cooperation. The Republican, Democratic and Progressive parties believe in regulating the trusts; the Socialist party believes in owning them, so that all the people may get the benefit of them instead of a few being made plutocrats and the masses impoverished. The Republican, Democratic and Progressive parties uphold the wage system; the Socialist party demands its overthrow.

It is under the wage system that the 22,000 operatives in the cotton and woolen mills at Lawrence, Massachusetts have been compelled to work, or slave rather, according to Commissioner Neill, for an average [per day] of $8.76 per family. To earn this average wage, according to the commissioner's official report, requires the combined service of father, mother, and three children. This is slavery with a vengeance. The mill is a sweat-hole; the hovel a breeding-pen. Home there is none. And there never will be under the wage system.

What have the Republican, Democratic and Progressive parties to offer to the wage-slaves of Lawrence, to the wage-slaves of the steel trust, to the wage-slaves of the mines, to the wage-slaves of the lumber and turpentine camps of the South, the wage-slaves of the railroads, the millions of them, male and female, black and white and yellow and brown, who produce all this nation's wealth, support its government and conserve its civilization, and without whom industry would be paralyzed and the nation helpless? What, I ask, has any of these capitalist parties, or all of them combined, [offered] for the working and producing class in this campaign? Nothing. Absolutely nothing . . .

The most promising fact in the world today is the fact that labor is organizing its power; its economic power and its political power. The workers who have made the world and who support the world, are preparing to take possession of the world. This is the meaning of Socialism and is what the Socialist party stands for in this campaign.

We demand the machinery of production in the name of the workers and the control of society in the name of the people. We demand the abolition of capitalism and wage-slavery and the surrender of the capitalist class. We demand the complete enfranchisement of women and the equal rights of all the people, regardless of race, color, creed or nationality. We demand that child labor shall cease once and forever and that all children born into the world shall have equal opportunity to grow up, to be educated, to have healthy bodies and trained minds, and to develop and freely express the best there is in them in mental, moral and physical achievement.

We demand complete control of industry by the workers; we demand all the wealth they produce for their own enjoyment, and we demand the earth for all the people.

SELECTION 5:
OPPOSING WAR, FIGHTING FOR A BETTER WORLD (1918)

Wars throughout history have been waged for conquest and plunder . . . The master class has always declared the wars; the subject class has always fought the battles. The master class has had all to gain and nothing to lose, while the subject class has had nothing to gain and all to lose—especially their lives . . .

And here let me emphasize the fact—and it cannot be repeated too often—that the working class who fight all the battles, the working class who make the supreme sacrifices, the working class who freely shed their blood and furnish the corpses, have never yet had a voice in either declaring war or making peace. It is the ruling class that invariably does both. They alone declare war and they alone make peace.

> Yours not to reason why;
> Yours but to do and die.

That is their motto and we object on the part of the awakening workers of this nation . . .

What a compliment it is to the Socialist movement to be persecuted for the sake of the truth! The truth alone will make the people free. And for this reason alone the truth must not be permitted to reach the people. The truth has always been dangerous to the rule of the rogue, the exploiter, the robber. So the truth must be ruthlessly suppressed. That is why they are trying to destroy the Socialist movement . . .

If you would be respected you have got to begin by respecting yourself . . . There is something splendid, something sustaining and inspiring in the prompting of the heart to be true to yourself and to the best you know, especially in a crucial hour of your life . . .

The lord of the land is indeed a super-patriot. This lord who practically owns the earth tells you that we are fighting this war to make the world safe for democracy—he, who shuts out all humanity from his private domain; he who profiteers at the expense of the people who have been slain and mutilated by multiplied thousands, under the pretense of the great American patriot. It is he, this identical patriot who is the arch-enemy of the people; it is he that you need to wipe from power . . .

When we unite and act together on the industrial field and when we vote together on election day we shall develop the supreme power of the one class that can and will bring permanent peace to the world. We shall then have the intelligence, the courage and the power for our great task. In due time industry will be organized on a cooperative basis. We shall conquer the public power. We shall then transfer the title deeds of the railroads, the telegraph lines, the mines, mills, and great industries to the people in their collective capacity; we shall take possession of all social utilities in the name of the people. We shall be a free nation whose government is of and by and for the people . . .

Do not worry over the charge of treason to your masters, but be concerned about the treason that involves yourselves. Be true to yourself and you cannot be a traitor to any good cause on earth.

Yes, in good time we are going to sweep into power in this nation and throughout the world. We are going to destroy all enslaving and degrading capitalist institutions and recreate them as free and humanizing institutions. The world is daily changing before our eyes. The sun of capitalism is setting; the sun of Socialism is rising. It is our duty to build the new nation and the free republic. We need industrial and social builders. We Socialists are the builders of the beautiful world that is to be. We are all pledged to do our part. We are inviting—aye challenging you in the name of your own manhood and womanhood—to join us and do your part.

In due time the hour will strike and this great cause triumphant—the greatest in history—will proclaim the emancipation of the working class and the brotherhood of all mankind.

Fannia M. Cohn.

CHAPTER 11

FANNIA M. COHN

Fannia M. Cohn (1885–1962) was born in Kletzk, an industrializing city in the Russian empire, one of five children in a relatively well-to-do Jewish family. Able to benefit from a good private education, her idealistic inclinations brought her into collision with the social realities around her, and by the age of fifteen she had joined the revolutionary underground, in the ranks of the Marxist-influenced populist organization that came to be known as the Socialist Revolutionary Party. In 1904, following an anti-Jewish riot (pogrom) in which her brother was almost killed, she and her brother emigrated to the United States.

Initially, she worked on the staff of the American Jewish Women's Committee at Ellis Island to assist immigrants, but the young Marxist quickly concluded that, "it was too much of a charitable nature"—she believed that the working class must organize to emancipate itself, and she looked to the Socialist Party of America and the growing trade union movement. In 1906, she took a job in the garment industry as a sleevemaker and, by 1909, she was a founding organizer of Local 41 in the ILGWU, participating in the momentous "rising of the twenty thousand" through which women garment workers in New York City electrified workers, and others, throughout the nation.

Older (in her early twenties) and better educated than most of the adolescents where she worked, she became a mentor and educator as well as a strike leader. In 1914, she attended a school in Chicago for labor organizers sponsored by the Women's Trade Union League, and in the following year led a major strike of garment workers in a contract shop of Sears and Roebuck workers. In 1916, she returned to New York, where she was elected as a vice president of the ILGWU—the first woman in the United States to hold such high office in the labor movement. She was re-elected four times, serving for ten years on the union's executive board.

Now a policy-maker, in 1917 she launched ILGWU programs in workers' education, going on for the next several decades to play a pioneering role in this field. In addition to fostering a proliferating number of worker education programs in New York and cities throughout the country, Cohn played a key role in the establishment of the famed Brookwood Labor School, a left-wing labor institution and the first residential workers' college in the United States, initially headed by A. J. Muste. She was also a leader and board member of the Workers' Education Bureau, an umbrella organization of labor education projects and institutions, and she became an internationally recognized figure among prominent educators and labor activists.

Latter-day scholars have identified and documented the problem that Thomas Dublin has summarized:

> As a woman in a male-dominated union hierarchy and an idealist among bureaucratic functionaries, her efforts to promote workers' education met stiff opposition. She made enemies in the anti-communist 1920s by tolerating socialists and communists in the workers' education movement. She saw workers' education as a valuable aspect of trade unionism in its own right, while ILGWU officers saw it as a tool to build their own power.

Especially damaging to Cohn's position was the 1920s "civil war" inside the ILGWU between communists and a coalition of socialists, anarchists, and "pure and simple" trade unionists—in which the former were driven out of the organization. "It is awfully difficult now, for one who follows a progressive policy to function in the labor movement," she wrote to a British friend. "Each side wants you to hate for the sake of love, to fight . . . for the sake of unity and solidarity." Many militant rank-and-file members, influenced by Cohn's educational efforts, were drawn into the rebellion and the union's established leadership, and many were expelled, while some abandoned the ILGWU as the union's officers pulled in a more conservative direction. This exodus, plus an economic depression, dramatically eroded Cohn's base in the union. Yet she herself maintained what Annelise Oreleck terms an "unshakeable loyalty to the ILGWU," and she was therefore vulnerable to the pressures of those who remained in the union's leadership.

Increasingly, she was marginalized, although her reputation and her caution helped prevent her elimination from the union's staff. ILGWU president David Dubinsky referred to her as "our cross to bear." Ex-socialist Dubinsky's view was that "trade unionism needs capitalism like a fish needs water." For many leaders in the union movement of the 1930s through the 1960s, this meant close ties with the Democratic Party, a growing sense of collaboration with employers, and an integration of labor in institutions of the "capitalist state"—a far cry from the perspectives of Eugene Debs's Socialist Party to which many from the ILGWU had once adhered.

Adapting in order to survive in this milieu, Cohn's work and writings—while diluted and muted in various ways—nonetheless reflect a continued commitment to some of the earlier ideals which, Cohn more than once emphasized, were essential to the survival and health of the labor movement. Such commitments succeeded in influencing and inspiring many.

Sources for Biographical Sketch

Thomas Dublin, "Fannia Cohn" (Jewish Women's Archive, available at: http://jwa.org/encyclopedia/article/cohn-fannia-m, accessed October 6, 2010).

Alice Kessler-Harris, "Three Jewish Women and Their Union," *Labor History*, vol. 17, no. 1, Winter 1976.

Huey B. Long and Constance Lawry, "Fannia Mary Cohn: An Educational Leader in Labor Workers' Education, Her Life and Times" (College of Education, University of Oklahoma, available at: www-distance.syr.edu/long.html, accessed October 6, 2010).

Annelise Orleck, *Common Sense and a Little Fire: Women and Working-Class Politics in the United States, 1900–1965* (Chapel Hill, NC: University of North Carolina Press, 1995).

Sources for Selections

Selection 1: Fannia M. Cohn, "Winning Workingwomen to Unionism: Not an Impossible Task," *Labor Age*, March 1927, pp. 18–19.

Selection 2: Fannia M. Cohn, "Getting the Message to Women: New Methods in Organizing," *Labor Age*, September 1927, pp. 20–21.

Selection 3: Fannia M. Cohn, "Shaw Speaks to Women: Aims at Men Too," *Labor Age*, October 1927, pp. 22–23.

Selection 4: Fannia M. Cohn, "Workers Education Aims at Power: Encouraging Ideals That Will Win," *Labor Age*, November 1927, p. 9.

Selection 5: Fannia M. Cohn, *Workers' Education in War and Peace* (New York: Workers Education Bureau of America, 1943), pp. 6, 7, 9.

Selection 6: Fannia M. Cohn, "Workers' Education—The Dream and the Reality," reprinted from *Workers Education Bureau News Letter*, July–August 1948.

SELECTION 1:
WORKING WOMEN AND UNIONISM (1927)

Can women be organized? Does not their temporary character as workers make that impossible? Have we developed any technique that promises success? I have been hearing questions like these for too many years. I'm getting tired of them. They lead nowhere. Today, when we recognize the value of experimentation in the social as well as the physical sciences, they seem particularly abstract. If we want to know whether women can be organized, and what technique is most effective to that end, we must attempt organization. Only after we have tried out a number of techniques, will we be able to decide whether the job can be done and how best to do it.

At best organization is a difficult task. The American labor movement has made strenuous efforts in that direction for sixty years and even today has organized only about 4,000,000 of the more than 17,000,000 men and women in industry. Yet we have never been discouraged in our task—never stopped to ask: "Can men be organized?"

From the earliest days, the problem of working women has been regarded as a particularly different one because of "feminine character." Women were *different,* with mystical sex traits which made it impossible to reach them. Their psychology was not like men's; they did not want what men wanted, nor act as men did.

Fortunately, all that is changing. We are coming to see that women are human beings—with the same likes and dislikes, the same capacity for love and hatred as men possess. Their passions and desires, we see respond to stimuli very like those which appeal so strongly to men. With only minor variations, women desire of life what men desire, and they come to resemble each other more closely in their ways of thinking.

Recognizing this, we must look for an explanation of our past difficulties in organizing workingwomen in something other than their femininity. We find it first of all in their character as workers—they are young, in unskilled industries largely, and consequently poorly paid. Everywhere, among both men and women—the semi-skilled, the poorly paid, and the young are not easy to organize.

Nevertheless in those organized industries where the conditions of the workingman depend upon those of the workingwoman—those industries where women are employed in great numbers, such as the garment industries —the unions have succeeded in organizing women as well as men . . .

We have examples of industries organized where women were not only present in large numbers but actually were in the majority. Here workingwomen have stopped work when their union was refused recognition, have carried on protracted and intense strikes, have stood all the suffering connected with such struggles. But more important, after the victory they have succeeded in retaining their union in a fighting condition as a proper instrument for their protection . . .

Our failure to organize women in the past has had two other causes. First, our doubt as to its possibility has decreased the confidence of the women workers in their own abilities, and made it harder for them to solve their problems. This attitude is, fortunately, passing, as more men have the opportunity to see the courage and loyalty of their sisters in strikes, their willingness to fight and suffer in the battle of labor . . .

We in the labor movement have found great difficulty in organizing women, because like other human beings, we have an unfortunate tendency to be too greatly influenced by the past. We are all readier to change our clothes and our way of living than our prejudices and our platitudes. We examine our households from time to time to make changes; we watch our clothes carefully to keep them in style. But we forget the necessity of keeping our minds and ideas abreast of changing conditions . . . In organizing women, the labor movement has been too much influenced by the past, particularly by past failures . . .

Failure in organizing women in the past has been due in large part to historic reasons. When the Industrial Revolution freed women from some of their home duties and made it possible for them to enter industry, few of them became craftsmen. Usually they were unskilled workers, subordinates of the skilled men workers. Working men looked on them with suspicion; they saw in this invading army of working women a danger to their own position in the industries upon which they depended for their livelihood. They defended this position either by trying to shut women out of industry altogether, or by giving them subordinate positions and permitting their exploitation by employers.

In time, however, working men learned that trying to keep working women in subordinate positions in factories, and outside unions, could not keep women out of industry. The exclusion instead of solving the problem made conditions worse by increasing the number of unorganized workers. Had working men realized at the beginning that the problem of all wage-workers is the same, they would have shared their experience with these newcomers and urged them to join the labor movement.

But not alone for these historic reasons have women remained outside the labor movement. Trade unions have not been exempt from the prejudice against the participation of women which exists in every social institution where men dominate. Although consciously we all believe in social and economic justice and equality for both sexes, nevertheless, like people in other organizations, we are subject to the limitations of the human mind—we change more slowly than the institutions are changing . . .

It is essential to the labor movement that women be organized. A better understanding of how to approach women will render it less difficult. Men trade unionists are coming to realize this more and more, are coming to bring it about. They can help personally by using their influence with the women with whom they come in contact, many of whom do not belong to any trade union. They can help as trade unionists by opening their ranks to women and making active efforts to draw them in.

SELECTION 2:
NEW METHODS OF ORGANIZING (1927)

We can lay down no hard and fast regulations for organization . . . But some methods have been shown to be most uniformly successful. Many of these methods appeal to people in general rather than to women alone—such as in literature the use of effective language, plain presentation of facts and careful arrangement . . .

In the preparation of pamphlets [often] the organizer has found the question form with answers given where necessary decidedly the most useful. By giving the reader an opportunity to answer questions out of her own experience and this giving room for thought, the pamphlets stimulate to independent activity . . .

A meeting hall to be used in an organizing campaign among women workers, we know, is preferably centrally located to avoid a long walk from the factories; it is near the transit lines; it has a presentable entrance and a clean, cheerful cozy and attractively decorated meeting room . . . These seemingly little things all work together to create a proper atmosphere, to bring the women into a friendly, receptive mood. And the organizer knows, too, that a speaker can be more convincing, more inspiring in speaking of how organization can help workers to more of the beautiful things of life, if he is undistracted by ugly surroundings.

Another very important consideration of which the experienced organizer is aware is the length of the meeting. After a day's work, everyone is eager to be home in time for dinner and to get ready for an evening's amusement. For a number of fairly obvious reasons, this is even more true of women workers. The organizer thus knows that it is essential that the organization meeting be short . . .

An intelligent organizer knows that the organization campaign should have two phases—the general and the specific. In the preparation of literature, for instance, the problems with which all working women are confronted should be touched on as well as those in the specific industry being invaded. The general appeal tends to overcome time-honored prejudices of women and their families against organization, and to show not only the importance to women of trade unions, but the possibility of building them up. The specific appeal, dealing as it does with conditions in a particular industry, and the possibility of improving them, comes much closer to home.

Every organizer knows that, in addition, local shop problems must be touched on. But unless a plant is very large, an organizer may find it impossible to prepare special literature for it. If he cannot distribute special literature to the shop, he distributes the general literature only. After he has found out all about conditions in the shop, he has well informed committees approach the workers and call them to a shop meeting. Nothing is so impressive to workers as a knowledge of conditions in a shop. Exaggerations defeat their own aims.

It is appreciated nowadays that it is very difficult to plan an effective and successful organizing campaign among workingwomen without the aid of women organizers . . .

The organizer must not speak as if to immature people or try to be funny— I distinguish here between being funny and being humorous. For women, we know, respond most cordially to a serious and earnest appeal. They desire above all to be met on equal grounds, even by organizers who are older and more experienced . . .

Women can be most successfully appealed to through their desire for respect from their menfolk. Many of us women know that though it is difficult, it is not impossible to convince them that by joining trade unions and fighting for their rights and to improve their conditions, they will gain that respect— from father, brother and men friends. Much can be done by impressing upon them the fact that men will welcome them as equals when they, as well as the men in their circle, join the labor movement . . .

SELECTION 3:
INTELLIGENT WOMEN AND SOCIALISM (1928)

In his *Intelligent Woman's Guide to Socialism and Capitalism* Bernard Shaw tells us that the writing of this book was inspired by a woman who asked for a letter on socialism. He thought of referring her to hundreds of books which have been written on the subject, but realized that they were all written in the abstract, academic, dry language . . . [and that] all these books have been addressed to men. "You might read a score of them," says Shaw, "without even discovering that such a creature as woman has ever existed." This probably can be blamed on the prevailing impressions that women are inferior in intellect and, therefore, not interested in the most vital subject, economics. As a consequence, the writer of books on economics addresses himself to men and considers their interests only. Who then, can blame women for not being interested in books on economics as the subject preached by the average author? . . .

It might be that Shaw, in writing this book, meant to give his readers a thorough grasp of modern economics without the assistance of a teacher; again his appeal to women is probably based on the assumption that men, being responsible for the muddle in which our economic system finds itself, are not the ones to correct it; that women, having the advantage of not being directly responsible for our social evils consequently will be more susceptible to criticism of it. It will not hurt their vanity to have the man-made world so brilliantly denounced by Shaw, the most popular and gifted dramatist of our time . . .

Because inequality of income has divided society into social classes which inevitably fight for larger shares in our social production, Shaw thinks that the very existence of these classes poisons every phase of the life of the nation.

It undermines personal happiness, because class differences restrict choice of husbands and wives, and the result is unhappy marriages.

Class difference caused by unequal income means that nine out of every ten children are denied an opportunity to develop their brains and their abilities to serve the community to the fullest extent, and its economic results prevent us from producing more than a fraction of the wealth we could produce because the mass of the people is deprived of the personal power to obtain things that they can collectively produce and that would make their lives more comfortable . . .

In *Intelligent Woman's Guide to Socialism and Capitalism* Shaw has written a textbook on socialism that will be outstanding for some time to come. It is not a cut and dry argument for socialism; but he discusses with his intelligent woman everything that constitutes the life of a civilized nation, politics, religion, medicine, law, education, taxation, Russia, vaccination, birth control, league of nations, prohibition, prostitution, dictators, eugenics, democracy, parents and children, and internationalism.

Science, he tells us, if developed freely will enable people to enjoy life to the fullest extent. Working hours will be reduced to the minimum so as to make the machine our servant rather than our master, as it is now.

Of course, anyone may question whether Shaw does not emphasize too much the importance of the future state and his willingness to clothe it with super-power. Shaw's book is human and simple, in spite of its detached air. He does not refrain from calling things by their real name; he does not attempt to cover them up with such high terms as "theory of rent" or "supply and demand."

Nevertheless, even Shaw cannot escape discussing women's problem from the accepted masculine point of view . . . It seems that Shaw accepts the argument advanced by employers for paying low wages, since women are employed in industry temporarily—until they are married—the employer must compensate himself for the time he wastes teaching them the trade by paying them low wages.

The fact is that women, most of the time, do the simplest work in industry, processes which they can learn in a few days. Therefore, they are easily replaced, as is shown during strikes. The reasons for lower wages are much deeper than that. It is the traditional masculine protest against women in industry, the belief still prevailing that women's place is at home. Therefore, she is not to earn a living but merely some pin-money . . .

SELECTION 4:
WORKERS EDUCATION AIMS AT POWER (1927)

Workers' education, like the labor movement itself, to be most effective must develop naturally. Inevitably its development will be influenced by general economic conditions, since these act upon the lives of the workers engaged in education ... I should like to emphasize that it is decidedly not our idea to standardize a workers' education curriculum—we realize that education must be flexible, experimental, and reflective of the interests of the groups involved. Nevertheless, to have a distinctive character, and to serve the labor movement and progress as a whole, workers' education must have a central ideology, to act as a unifying force bringing together the workers of our whole continent.

Such an ideology would include a number of things—the workers' desire for power to enable them to function as an organized group on the economic, political, social and intellectual field; the workers' desire for a voice in the management of industry, since it affects not only the industrialists, but the workers in industry and the public as a whole. It would include, too, their desire that our vast natural resources be placed at the disposal of our entire population. And it would almost certainly include their feeling that they should have a voice in shaping our international policy, since it affects the lives and happiness of hundreds of millions of men, women, and children. An ideology of this type would naturally not rest on temporary conditions, nor be too much affected by prosperity or depression.

To develop a set of ideals of this character, the labor movement will have to create machinery sufficiently efficient to bring into being such a social program, based, as it is, not on personalities but ideals. This machinery might well include a political labor party, but that labor party will have to be brought into being by a great many independent forces. It cannot be born until the workers as an organized group develop a desire for power—power to enable them to direct their own lives and achieve the ultimate aims that will advance the progress of humanity. So long as the program of the labor movement consists of the temporary everyday needs of the workers alone—though, of course, these must always be its main impulse—so long the workers will feel no need for independent political action ...

SELECTION 5:
WORKERS' EDUCATION IN WAR AND PEACE (1943)

A program of workers' education must of necessity be built around the problems with which labor is confronted. It must be related to the experiences of the workers and provide them with a sound foundation for wise judgments and actions. Nor must it stop there. It must concern itself with everything that stands for progress, everything that contributes to the sum total of our culture ...

Cooperative Character of Workers' Education

... Wherever workers and teachers gather to discuss the domestic and international problems with which they are confronted as workers and citizens, that place becomes their classroom, their school, their college or university.

Workers' education does not segregate itself from other parts of the community. The scholar, the educator, is always invited to contribute to its development. The only requirement is that such educators sympathize with the aims of the workers to make this world a better place for all. Thus the academic world is brought closer to the labor movement as the years go on, and gains a better understanding of labor's role.

Now that the labor education movement has thoroughly established itself, it cooperates with institutions of higher learning interested in labor's objectives. This is indicated by the formation of joint committees for the purpose of conducting summer schools and institutes of the type of the Wisconsin Summer School for Workers ... While workers' education cannot be considered apart from organized labor and is a distinct movement, it is thus being increasingly recognized that it is a sector of the general movement of adult education and has much to contribute to the educational system as a whole ...

Task and Opportunity

... In this country, while we advanced our democratic institutions and processes and our conceptions of freedom, there grew up a mighty power of corporate wealth. The corporations and trusts grew into gigantic economic and political institutions. Their influence was far-flung and of such a character that they became a threat to our democracy and to our conception of liberty. Theodore Roosevelt and Woodrow Wilson unsuccessfully attempted to check that tendency through legislation. Both Presidents realized that the much-talked-of "individual enterprise" had long since been largely superseded by monopolies and semi-monopolies.

Partly as a social defense against the rising tide of big business and employers' organizations, the workers began to form their trade unions. The organized worker began to realize that collective action was essential if poverty and exploitation were to be abolished; if opportunity was to be given to all for adequate development. From bitter experience, the workers began to learn that successful action in the political and economic fields could be accomplished not by individuals but by a united labor movement.

Thence arose the organized labor movement which, by its very character, was destined to become a constructive social force. The two Presidents of "the Big Stick" and of "the New Freedom," in their time, as the "New Deal President" in our time, supported the trade unions as a balance of power in an economy dominated by corporate wealth, trusts and monopolies.

Because the trade union, structurally and functionally, has a framework corresponding to the institutional setup of our country, it has become a training school for democracy in the nation—and by that token throughout the globe.

With the growth of the labor movement, the problem has increasingly become how the growing power of labor can be used most effectively for social progress.

A trade union, like any other democratic institution, depends for its success upon the intelligence and understanding of its members. Unless they are thoroughly informed concerning the social, industrial and political program of the union and the principles and policies underlying that program, the most far-reaching plans of their organization may be brought to naught.

Unions today require an informed, alert and able active membership not only to ensure the efficient and successful conduct of its affairs, but because today they are demanding and receiving increasing representation on various governmental boards and agencies. Workers with ability and promise must be prepared to present the unions intelligently. This is where a purposefully planned workers' education program is essential.

It goes without saying that workers' education must be democratically conducted. Education for democracy must have as its counterpart democracy in education. This is recognized by such labor organizations as the International Ladies Garment Workers Union, where the democratic tradition is followed by inviting active student and teacher participation in planning the educational program . . .

The Three Aims of Workers' Education

Workers' education has at least three important functions to perform. First, it has the function of discovering promising young people with ability to lead and of developing their capacity so that they may be ready, if and when called upon, to serve their union in various capacities. The trade union official must be a well-informed and effective speaker. He must have a knowledge of his industry and of industrial and social trends. He must be a capable negotiator. And he must be able to secure the confidence and active support of the union's membership in his efforts to advance the organization's enlightened program and policies . . .

The second function of workers' education is to assist in democratic processes within the union. If enlightened democracy is to prevail within the union, the membership must be capable of choosing their leadership discriminately, must feel a collective responsibility for their own decisions and must actively and intelligently support the administration in carrying these decisions out. Members must therefore have a knowledge of the economics of the industry and of its interrelation with other industries and its relation to society as a whole. They must have a realization of the importance of the trade union movement as a whole. This knowledge and understanding they can best attain through a meaningful program of education.

Thirdly, workers' education has an ideological function to perform. While the program of workers' education is largely factual when it deals with labor's economic and social problems, its task is not only to give facts but to inspire the workers with confidence in their collective abilities as organized workers and citizens. The development of such a spirit of confidence is a great asset to a union. History teaches that it is those unions with an idealistic social philosophy that have a better chance to weather a storm than have their brother organizations.

Workers' education has faith in the common man. It insists that human nature and human behavior are not static, but are constantly changing. Human beings improve as they are given an opportunity to develop, as their environment becomes a proper and inspiring one. Workers' education is also guided by the belief of modern psychologists that creative imagination and initiative can be developed under improved social conditions. It gives new meaning to the creative effort of workers everywhere. In a word, workers' education emphasizes the importance both of material achievement and of intellectual development . . .

Through labor education the worker gains a full understanding of the important place that labor as an organized movement plays in this country. He is . . . inspired by a feeling of the dignity of labor. And he comes to realize that it is the conditions under which he is working as a member of his union which give him his position in society which makes it possible for him, through his union, to contribute to the common good. This realization of the workers' real role in society is a distinct democratic gain . . .

Post War—Promise or Menace?

. . . The global war found millions of men and women who were eager to work, jobless. For the New Deal, with all its social purposes and progressive tendencies, had failed, after eight years of sincere effort, to solve the all-important problem confronting our nation—the problem of unemployment.

These millions unemployed in the thirties have now been absorbed by the war industries. But the worker is now anxious lest, at the conclusion of the war, the country be faced by another economic depression. He wants to be assured that his government is planning now for the fullest utilization during the post-war period of our technological resources for the welfare of all.

The workers thoroughly believe in the Four Freedoms to which the United Nations are pledged. Freedom of speech and freedom of religious worship are accepted as rights. The worker believes also in freedom from fear of starvation, of insecurity. He wants to know where his next meal is coming from. He likewise desires a state where there shall be freedom from fear of race discrimination and religious prejudice. Our people expect that these fears—as well as the other fears we are fighting—will be banished from the earth. His beliefs are in harmony with the undying pronouncements in the Declaration of Independence that all men have an inalienable right to "life, liberty and the pursuit of happiness."

Workers in the United States, it goes without saying, will not have "the American way" associated with Fascism in any form. Neither do they want "the American way" to be identified again with breadlines or with millions of unemployed living in poverty, with underfed school children looking for work while adults are jobless.

The failure of the democracies to utilize their resources more effectively accounts in large measure for our present plight. In our own land idleness of men and machines and skills has resulted in tremendous social waste and was responsible for such suffering and frustration as well as for a serious dislocation of the economic life of the country.

The problem facing us today is how can we, through the assistance of the government, get effective use of our resources, yet, at the same time, preserve the underlying values of our tradition of liberty and democracy? How can we employ our unemployed, how can we take advantage of the best modern techniques, yet in all this make the individual the source of values and individual fulfillment in society the basic objective? How can we obtain effective organization of resources yet at the same time maximum freedom for the organized workers?

If the democratic way of life is to prevail, it must not be limited to political procedure. It must be extended into the economic, social, and cultural fields, on a real basis of equality.

Few people with imagination, with vision, deny that there is a crying need for real economic and social equality for human values to make our democracy work. Those who possess political or economic power and who dare to oppose such changes will be condemned by history as enemies of our democracy.

The masses will fight for democracy and sacrifice themselves only for a democracy in which they have a stake. In a dynamic period such as ours, it is imperative for us to know what we want. We must plan for present needs with an eye to the future. But the workers ask, "Planning—by whom? For whom?"

The worker does not want his America, the America he loves, the America he is willing to defend with his life, to return to pre-war conditions. To prevent this he is urging planning now for the post-war world; planning for all, through the union of labor with other progressive groups, with a view of shaping the America of tomorrow in a free world . . .

SELECTION 6:
DREAM AND REALITY (1948)

It is axiomatic that the form and content of workers' education must depend upon the needs of organized labor at any given time. When the workers were compelled to struggle on the picket line for recognition against the opposition of powerful economic groups and government by injunction, those subjects were stressed which could serve as tools to keep the union alive. But when the labor movement grew in power and influence, increasing emphasis was placed on interpreting to the worker his role as a responsible member of the union, the community, and the nation.

At a time when the management of labor unions is becoming increasingly complex, technical experts have a very important place in the labor movement. But for the policy-making functions to remain in the hands of the rank and file and its officers, the workers must be well informed. For this, a purposefully, carefully planned workers' education program is most essential —to arouse in the members a great interest in the day-to-day affairs of their union, in addition to stimulating creative thinking . . .

[A] program of workers' education should also include such things as the appreciation of music, art, literature and drama, and should encourage and provide facilities for play . . . Perhaps the next decisive step in the field of workers' education will be purposeful utilization of movies and the radio. Properly conceived and directed, they can become powerful weapons against the deadly enemies of society—confusion and prejudice.

A famous philosopher once observed that "the educator must himself become educated."* The teacher in workers' education cannot be content to heap fact upon fact; he must stress analysis, interpretation and conclusions which can become the basis for intelligent group action . . . Much more skill is required in teaching people who are active participants in the work-a-day world than college youngsters preparing for life. The teacher, therefore, must not only instruct students but must learn from them. A challenging discussion of conflicting opinions between students and teacher helps to clarify views and develop creative thinking . . .

Workers' education has faith in a better future; and the Workers Education Bureau will strive with confidence and resourcefulness to make today's dreams and hopes of humanity become tomorrow's realities. This is the challenge— and our opportunity.

---

* The "philosopher" referred to here is Karl Marx, in his "Theses on Feuerbach."

John L. Lewis.

Courtesy of the Library of Congress, Prints and
Photographs Division, Harris & Ewing Collection,
LC-H22-D-7016.

CHAPTER 12

JOHN L. LEWIS

John Llewellyn Lewis (1880–1969) was born near Lucas, Iowa, of Welsh immigrant parents. The eldest of eight children, he was able to complete all but the final year of high school—which was unusual for children of coal miners in the nineteenth century. Lewis became active in the UMW when he himself became a coal miner. After moving to the newly developed coal-mining region around Panama, Illinois, he became a leader in that town's UMW local. In 1910 he became a full-time organizer for the AFL for a six-year period, all the while maintaining close connections with UMW locals as he traveled around the country, and in 1917 he went on the Mine Workers' staff. Beginning as statistician, moving up as business manager of the union's journal, and then assuming the position of UMW Vice-President, Lewis demonstrated impressive organizational and internal-political skills, and also his abilities in successfully coordinating the 1919 coal strike. This ensured his 1920 election to the presidency of the UMW, which was, at the time, the country's largest union. The UMW also stood out among AFL unions in being organized along inclusive industrial lines, embracing workers of all skills and skill levels in a unified organization.

With left-wing support, Lewis unsuccessfully challenged the aging Samuel Gompers for the AFL presidency in 1921. But, by the end of the 1920s and into the early 1930s, he could be fairly described by labor-radical Len DeCaux as a "big-bellied, oldtime labor leader . . . An autocrat, per capita [dues] counter, egotist, power seeker . . . He was a man who had bowed the knee to capitalism, who had been merciless against the red and the rebellious." He had relentlessly battled and beaten rank-and-file militants and union reformers— led by such tough-minded visionaries as John Brophy and Powers Hapgood, and including socialist and communist currents among mineworkers—who sought to shift the UMW from the relatively conservative policies and undemocratic practices of the Lewis regime. When the Great Depression sent shock waves throughout the labor movement, however, Lewis soon championed in the AFL more militant policies that he had earlier blocked. "I've never really opposed those things," he explained to Powers Hapgood. "I just never felt that the time was ripe and that trying to do those things back in the days when we had our violent arguments would have been suicide for organized labor and would have resulted in complete failure. But now the time is ripe; and now the time to do those things is here." Critics have scoffed that he was an "opportunist" and "careerist"—but there were many of these in the labor movement who never thought of following the course that Lewis now pursued.

In 1935, over the objection of the AFL leadership, Lewis and leaders of seven other unions formed the Committee for Industrial Organization, dedicated to unionizing mass-production workers and promoting relatively advanced social and economic policies within U.S. political life. Embracing one-time opponents such as Brophy and Hapgood, and other left-wingers such as Len DeCaux (hired to edit the CIO News), Lewis drew on the skills, vision, and enthusiasm of diverse forces to move forward the immense organizing work of the CIO. When questioned about his shift away from more conservative unionism, he responded: "I don't give a hang what happened yesterday. I live for today and tomorrow. I will say only this: It takes every man some time to find himself in this world, to decide what he wants to do with his life. It took me longer than most people." By 1936, the CIO was following its own independent course, and by 1938 it became a formal rival of the AFL, adopting the new name "Congress of Industrial Organizations." CIO president, and an uncompromising, often prophetic spokesman for militant industrial unionism, Lewis became a symbol and hero for millions of workers in the 1930s and 1940s.

He was a complex and controversial figure. Forging a firm labor–liberal alliance with Franklin D. Roosevelt's "New Deal" Democrats in 1933, Lewis was troubled by the inconsistent loyalty to labor of this patrician–reformer—for example, when the president proclaimed, "a plague on both your houses" to the steel companies and the steel union, after workers were shot down at the 1937 Memorial Day Massacre. By 1940—convinced that labor must show greater political independence, and that it should also resist an "imperialist" foreign policy that would draw the United States into World War II—Lewis at first sought to generate a new labor-based party, and then reluctantly threw his support to liberal Republican Wendell Willkie. This forced him to relinquish the presidency of the predominantly pro-Roosevelt CIO. In 1942, he led the UMW back to the AFL, after failing to engineer AFL–CIO unity that might facilitate a more aggressive approach toward the government's wartime no-strike policy. He led the UMW out of the AFL in 1947, in a dispute over whether or not an uncompromising struggle should be mounted against the anti-labor Taft–Hartley Act; his warning on what would result from a failure to do so was largely borne out by subsequent developments.

In later years, Lewis and the UMW remained a relatively isolated force in the labor movement, often "a voice crying in the wilderness," and in the face of multiple pressures he compromised his earlier militant unionism without ever repudiating it. It was said that he ran the UMW like a "benevolent dictatorship," and after his 1960 retirement a bureaucratic apparatus under his successor Tony Boyle was shown to have been guilty of corruption and gangster-like violence. Just before his death in 1969, there was indication that Lewis was about to embrace the soon-to-be-martyred UMW reformer Joseph Yablonski.

A disappointed liberal, James Wechsler, who was highly critical of his break with Franklin D. Roosevelt, once wrote: "Lewis's whole career has been a repudiation of democratic doctrine. The 'leader' principle is the keystone of his administration of every movement he has led." The materials reprinted here throw such a judgment into doubt. The more balanced view of biographers Melvyn Dubofsky and Warren Van Tine is that, "his character and behavior combined a peculiar amalgam of individualism, aggressiveness, and possessive materialism balanced against forms of mutualism and social concern."

Sources for Biographical Sketch

Saul D. Alinsky, *John L. Lewis, An Unauthorized Biography* (New York: Vintage Books, 1970).

Melvyn Dubofsky and Warren Van Tine, *John L. Lewis, A Biography* (New York: Quadrangle/New York Times Book Co., 1977).

Melvyn Dubofsky and Warren Van Tine, "John L. Lewis and the Triumph of Mass-Production Unionism," in Melvyn Dubofsky and Warren Van Tine, eds., *Labor Leaders in America* (Urbana: University of Illinois Press, 1987).

Bruce Minton and John Stuart, *Men Who Lead Labor* (New York: Modern Age Books, 1937).

James A. Wechsler, *Labor Baron, A Portrait of John L. Lewis* (New York: William Morrow and Co., 1944).

Sources for Selections

Selection 1: American Federation of Labor, *Report of Proceedings of 1935 Convention*, pp. 534–536, 541–542.

Selection 2: "Towards Industrial Democracy," *Current History*, October 1936.

Selection 3: *Congressional Digest*, May 1937, pp. 157–158.

Selection 4: quoted in Melvyn Dubofsky and Warren Van Tine, *John L. Lewis, A Biography*, p. 327.

Selection 5: Congress of Industrial Organizations, *Report of Proceedings of 1939 Convention*, pp. 25, 48–49.

Selection 6: ibid., p. 173.

Selection 7: Congress of Industrial Organizations, *Report of Proceedings of 1940 Convention*, pp. 91–92.

Selection 8: *New York Times*, April 2, 1940, pp. 1, 4, and July 31, 1940, p. 15.

Selection 9: American Federation of Labor, *Report of Proceedings of 1947 Convention*, pp. 486, 487, 490, 491, 492.

Selection 10: "What Democracy Means to Me," *Scholastic*, May 21, 1938.

Proceedings reports from the AFL and CIO reprinted with permission from the George Meany Memorial Archives.

SELECTION 1:
THE FIGHT FOR INDUSTRIAL UNIONISM IN THE AFL (1935)

I do not speak without some background and some knowledge on this subject acquired in the field of actual experience. I have not gained that knowledge through delving into academic treatises or in sitting in a swivel chair pondering upon the manner in which those upon the firing line should meet their daily problems. I have had perhaps as much experience in organizing workers in the various industries as any member of the Executive Council of the American Federation of Labor or any officer thereof. I served an apprenticeship of five and one-half years as a general organizer for the American Federation of Labor before I became an officer of the United Mine Workers of America. During that period of time I worked in the steel industry, the rubber industry, the glass industry, the lumber industry, the copper industry and other industries in most of the states of this Union.

Then, as now, the American Federation of Labor offered to the workers in these industries a plan of organization into Federal labor unions or local trade unions with the understanding that when organized they would be segregated into the various organizations of their respective crafts. Then, as now, practically every attempt to organize those workers broke upon the same rock that it breaks upon today—the rock of utter futility, the lack of reasonableness in a policy that failed to take into consideration the dreams and requirements of workers themselves, and failed to take into consideration the recognized power of the adversaries of labor to destroy these feeble organizations in the great modern industries set up in the form of Federal labor unions or craft organizations functioning in a limited sphere ... We have claim to a membership of approximately three and a half million out of an organizable number of approximately thirty-nine million ...

There has been a change in industry, a constant daily change in its processes, a constant change in employment conditions, a great concentration of opposition to the extension and the logical expansion of the trade union movement. Great combinations of capital have assembled great industrial plants, and they are strung across the borders of our several states from the north to the south and from the east to the west in such a manner that they have assembled to themselves tremendous power and influence, and they are almost 100 percent effective in opposing organization of the workers under the policies of the American Federation of Labor . . .

There are great influences abroad in the land, and the minds of men in all walks of life are disturbed. We are all disturbed by reason of the changes and the hazards in our economic situation and as regards our own political security. There are forces at work in this country that would wipe out, if they could, the labor movement of America, just as it was wiped out in Germany or just as it was wiped out in Italy.

There are those of us who believe that the best security against that menace and against that trend and against that tendency is a more comprehensive and more powerful labor movement. We believe that the way should be paved so that those millions of workers who are clamoring for admission into our councils might be made welcome upon a basis that they understand and that they believe is suited to their requirements . . .

And so out of my small experience, be it what it may, there is a profound belief on my part that there is a great reservoir of workers here numbering millions and millions of men and women, and back of them stand great numbers of millions of dependents who want the American Federation of Labor to adopt a policy that will be sufficiently flexible and sufficiently modern that it will permit them to join with us in this great fight for the maintenance of the rights of workers and for the upholding of the standards of modern democracy . . .

Is it right, after all, that because some of us are capable of forging great and powerful organizations of skilled craftsmen in this country that we should lock ourselves up in our own domain and say, "I am merely working for those who pay me"? Isn't it right that we should contribute something of our own strength, our own virtues, our own knowledge, our own influence toward those less fortunately situated, in the knowledge that we will be the beneficiary of their changed status and their strength? The strength of a strong man is a prideful thing, but the unfortunate thing in life is that strong men do not remain strong. And that is just as true of unions and labor organizations as it is true of men and individuals.

And whereas today the craft unions of this country may be able to stand upon their own feet and like mighty oaks stand before the gale, defy the lightning, yet the day may come when those organizations will not be able to withstand the lightning and the gale. Now, prepare yourselves by making a contribution to your less fortunate brethren, heed this cry from Macedonia that comes from the hearts of men. Organize the unorganized and in so doing you make the American Federation of Labor the greatest instrumentality that has ever been forged in the history of modern civilization to befriend the cause of humanity and champion human rights.

SELECTION 2:
AIMS OF THE COMMITTEE FOR INDUSTRIAL ORGANIZATION
(MAY 1936)

The primary objective sought is the improvement of the working and living standards of mass-production employees by the development of industrial unions coterminous with industry in extent of organization and coequal in economic power with management. Through such unions genuine collective bargaining with representatives of mass-production industries may be established, due consideration and emphasis, as a matter of course, being given to joint cooperative effort and increased industrial accomplishment.

The other fundamental objective sought is the development of effective political organization and strength by the labor groups, whether hand or brain workers, to the end that it may be used in cooperation with other unselfish groups of our people in establishing sound measures of industrial democracy, and in bringing about other social, economic, and humanitarian reforms which are traditionally and indissolubly associated with the ideals and aspirations of our self-governing republic.

The conviction that these objectives should be attained has come to many labor union executives as the result of their observations and experiences during the period since the World War. It has been apparent to them that American industrial management—engineers, chemists, and other technicians, as well as executives—established such a remarkable record of industrial organization and accomplishment during the ten years immediately following the War as to make America the marvel of other industrial and commercial nations. On the other hand, it has been equally clear to many labor leaders, and profoundly deplorable to them, that operating management has not been able . . . to have industry function in an enlightened way both for itself and for the common good. The reason is that our basic industries have been, and still are, controlled and their policies determined by a small, inner group of New York bankers and financiers . . .

Organized labor has suffered from the selfish and short-sighted policies of this financial dictatorship. It produced the breakdown of 1929 by refusing to allow the wage and salary workers sufficient purchasing power to keep the wheels of industry going. It was responsible in 1930 for the inauguration of the disastrous policy of wage deflation. Finally, in 1934, after stability had been assured through the National Recovery Administration, it refused to permit its representatives on the Code Authorities to approve a policy of shorter hours, higher rates of pay, and minimum profits so that genuine economic recovery might be assured . . .

It is for these reasons that organized labor has determined that this sinister financial and industrial dictatorship must be destroyed. Through the formation of industrial unions it seeks to acquire political organization and strength to contribute toward this end in an orderly American way. Labor's aim is to have a free America for the future, both politically and industrially.

SELECTION 3:
LABOR BATTLES THE BIG CORPORATIONS (DECEMBER 1936)

The Committee for Industrial Organization is carrying its plans forward. Extensive unions have been promoted and expanded in steel, automotive, glass, shipbuilding, electrical manufacturing, oil and by-product coke industries. Unabashed by employer opposition, they are joining the unions in their industries, literally by the thousands ... Labor demands collective bargaining and greater participation by the individual worker, whether by hand or brain, in the bountiful resources of the nation, and in the fruits of the genius of its inventors and technicians.

Employers talk about possible labor trouble interfering with continued expansion and progress of industry. They ignore the fact that unless people have money with which to buy, the wheels of industry slow down, and profits and likewise capital disappear. It would be more fitting and accurate to talk about "employer trouble"—that is something from which wage earners are suffering. I refer you to the refusal of some of the largest and most powerful corporations in this country to follow modern labor practice, or to obey the law of the land. They deny the entirely reasonable and just demands of their employees for legitimate collective bargaining, decent incomes, shorter hours, and for protection against a destructive speed-up system.

It is the refusal of employers to grant such reasonable conditions, and to deal with their employees through collective bargaining, that leads to widespread labor unrest. The strikes which have broken out in the last few weeks, especially in the automotive industry, are due to such "employer trouble." Modern collective bargaining, involving negotiations between organized workers and organized employers on an industry basis, would regularize and stabilize industry relations, and reduce the economic losses occasioned by management stupidity. The sit-down strike is the fruit of mismanagement and bad policy towards labor. Employers who tyrannize over employees, with the aid of labor spies, company guards, and the threat of discharge, need not be surprised if their production lines are suddenly halted.

Huge corporations, such as United States Steel and General Motors, have a moral and public responsibility. They have neither the moral nor the legal right to rule as autocrats over the hundreds of thousands of employees. They have no right to transgress the law which gives to the worker the right of self-organization and collective bargaining. They have no right in a political democracy to withhold the rights of a free people.

The workers in the steel industry are organizing; the workers in the automotive industry are organizing; the workers in other industries are organizing; any sane concept of industrial relations would indicate that the labor problems of these industries should be settled across the council table.

The unlicensed and unrestrained arming of corporations against the workers has no place in any political or industrial democracy. Recent revelations before the LaFollette Subcommittee of the Senate have revealed in part the plans of industry to club, gas and cripple workers with the lethal weapons of warfare. Huge stocks of such weapons have been purchased at enormous expense ... and the expenditure necessary for the purchase of these war supplies is charged to the cost of production.

This real alternative to industrial democracy has been slightly exposed by the LaFollette Committee. This alternative is what industrialists want left undisturbed under this sudden "era of good feeling." They do not want the Senate and workers to discover how the anti-labor policies of great industrialists have filled the land with a fat business of spying and armed strike-breaking and civic corruption ...

Labor now demands the right to organize, and the right to bargain. Labor demands a new deal in America's great industries. Labor holds in contempt those who for mercenary reasons would restrict human privileges. Labor demands legislative enactments making realistic the principles of industrial democracy. It demands that Congress exercise its constitutional powers and brush aside the negative autocracy of the Federal judiciary, exemplified by a Supreme Court which exalts property above human values ...

Time has passed in America when the workers can be either clubbed, gassed, or shot down with impunity. I solemnly warn the leaders of industry that labor will not tolerate such policies or tactics ...

SELECTION 4:
DISAPPOINTMENT WITH A "FRIEND OF LABOR" (1937)

Labor, like Israel, has many sorrows. Its women weep for their fallen, and they lament for the future of the children of the race. It ill behooves one who has supped at labor's table and who has been sheltered in labor's house to curse with equal fervor and fine impartiality both labor and its adversaries when they become locked in deadly embrace.

SELECTION 5:
DEEP-ROOTED ECONOMIC PROBLEMS AND LABOR'S NEEDS (1939)

In the background of any discussion of temporary measures to help the unemployed stands a grim reminder that the only way to solve unemployment is to give everyone a job. Expediencies are valuable only as they may give time to work out permanent means to provide jobs.

The nation's number one problem is work for its population. The displacement and economic exile of 25 percent of our adult population constitute a threat to the stability of the nation. This appalling drift cannot go on forever. Privation is taking a toll from the population that cannot be much longer endured. Our people, unemployed, sweated and exploited, have been patient. But their patience is not inexhaustible. Beyond patience lies despair; and from despair springs action, drastic and unpredictable.

Labor believes that this nation acting within its democratic tradition can solve the problem of unemployment. Labor believes that every worker in this country can have a job, a job paying enough to give him and his family a happy and secure life. Labor believes that the machinery of our nation can be so operated that no wheel need be stopped nor any man idle. That is labor's faith.

The history of the government's attack on unemployment has been one of hesitant half steps towards solution, hastily withdrawn before they could become effective. If we are to justify the effectiveness of our democracy, of our vaunted leadership in the economic field, then we must prove that we can solve this problem of unemployment . . .

We believe that our present tax structure is antiquated and unable to meet modern conditions. The fact of the matter is that with the recent payroll and wage taxes for social security and the numerous sales taxes levied by states, the proportion of governmental revenue derived by direct taxes upon wage earners has increased tremendously. In other words, it is not business but rather labor and consumer groups who are bearing the brunt of our increased expenditures for social welfare. At the same time the old forms of real property taxes are bearing down heavily upon farmers.

While the whole tax problem requires further study before definitive solutions can be provided, certain facts already appear. Government securities, both Federal and State, are now exempt from taxation thus creating a vast reservoir of excess wealth, which goes untouched by taxes. While nothing can be done about existing issues of public securities, in future investments in these securities, which represent vast accumulations of surplus income and wealth, should be taxed. Recent disclosures of the Temporary National Economic Committee show that many large corporations are accumulating tremendous reserves, which are not idle. The increased industrial activity of the past few months, if continued, will mean larger profits for industry and should be used as a basis for obtaining increased income for Government through taxes.

The second vital aspect of our present economic problems is represented by monopoly controls of the big financial and business interests. The Temporary National Economic Committee has demonstrated that the basic mass production industries of this country are dominated by a few large corporations that are tied up with Wall Street. This is true of automobiles, glass, rubber, steel, cement and aluminum. It is also true of the meat packing and many other parts of the food processing industry.

Connected with this monopoly is the control over our monetary policies exercised by Wall Street and a few bankers scattered all over the country. We are now faced with a situation where the banks are swollen with reserves that they are unable to place in productive channels and the interest rates and capital remain beyond the reach of the average small business man and consumer groups . . .

Organized labor and farmers and lower income groups are the victims of the irresponsible power and control in the hands of a few selfish individuals. Through their control they have been able to practice the vicious policy of restricting production whenever their profits are in danger and maintain high price levels irrespective of consumer demands. A further consequence of this monopoly power is represented in technological unemployment. Big industry is able to control technological changes and to place the cost of introducing labor-saving machinery upon the workers directly, by discharging those who no longer become necessary with the introduction of new machinery . . .

Quite often people whose knowledge of economics is superficial or unsound believe that they are taking a very virtuous position when they say that they are quite willing for the wages of the workers of this country to advance in proportion to the increase in the cost of living. That position presupposes that the economic status of the workers of this country is ideal in relation to cost of production, national income and the other varied factors of consideration.

The contrary is true. The relationship of labor, both to the cost of production, to the total value of our commodities produced, to the total national income and the increasing production efficiency of our producing machine is totally inadequate. For labor to accept that philosophy would mean that as increased efficiencies in production came into use, new formulas are devised in chemistry, in engineering and otherwise, that the consequent displacement of labor and the lowering of the cost of production through the utilization of engineering and semi-automatic machines would constantly tend to debase labor, to give labor an increasingly smaller proportion of the total value of its production and a constantly lessening participation in the whole of the national income in proportion of the relationship of labor to the national population.

It is economically unsound, socially unjust and politically unwise. Labor must unceasingly be on guard against the acceptance of this philosophy, because I proclaim that the position of labor in our economy is not ideal or just, or satisfactory. Labor wants a continuously increasing participation in the increased productivity of modern industry, and a larger share in the bounties of our national wealth.

On no other premise can employment be maintained; under no other arrangement can national purchasing power be maintained; upon no other arrangement can we care for the element of our population constantly being dispossessed by participation in our internal economy and our productive establishment by the utilization of energy, the application of new formulas, by the use of automatic and semi-automatic machines.

Labor wants a larger participation and labor must have an increasing participation in the fruits of our men of genius, of our technicians, of our chemists of high and low degree. The chemists of America meet and they inform the country that the wonders and the potentialities of industrial chemistry have scarcely scratched the surface of possibilities. And tomorrow, out of the mind of one man may come an idea that will revolutionize industry; that will make possible for that industry to operate with 50 percent less manpower and twice or ten times its present production. These industries of ours cannot be kept in operation as they constantly increase their producing power, except by constantly increasing the buying power of the American population. Labor cannot be a consumer of the products of men and factories unless labor is given a constantly increasing participation in the increasing efficiency of production and in the natural wealth of the nation . . .

I think it is well that our people should be constantly on guard and, without apology, at all times decline to accept that status that is given labor by those who say, virtuously and sanctimoniously, like Pharisees in the market places, "Oh, yes! I am perfectly willing that if the price of milk goes up in a community, wages shall be increased so that the worker can still get exactly the same amount of milk for his children."

SELECTION 6:
ACHIEVEMENTS OF THE CONGRESS OF INDUSTRIAL ORGANIZATIONS (1939)

You know, one of the things that makes this Convention most remarkable . . . is that the machinery of this Convention and this movement of ours operates to crystallize and translate into expression and action the things that you think and the things that you believe, because, in turn, they are the things that the millions of workers back in their homes throughout this country believe, those things which you have in your heart. So when the committees of this Convention come upon the floor with their resolutions and with their recommendations, they are in truth and in fact recommending that which they believe you want done. Therein lies the power of the leadership of the CIO! Therein lie the factor and the influence which make my voice, when I speak for labor, a voice of some importance, of some influence and of some power! But only because of those things I have said in our Convention before, and I repeat now, because it is an elemental truth that if the day ever comes in the councils of labor that I cease to represent what is truly in the hearts and the minds of our people and to give voice to their yearnings and desires, their needs and their ambitions, then just that day my voice loses its power, my tongue loses its cunning, and the people of the United States will pay no more attention to me than they will the street-sweeper on Market Street outside this door.

There are those in this country who marvel at the so-called influence or power of the leaders of labor, and they cannot understand why millions of men and women support them in their publicly-taken position. It is because they have, perhaps, given their lives and their talents to the accumulation of money or the piling-up of wealth, and, just to that degree, have ignored or forgotten the human equations that exist in the bosoms of men, which, after all, are the real and desirable things in life.

After all, there is no particular credit due to the President of your organization or his associate officers as far as the accomplishments of the Congress of Industrial Organizations are concerned. All that they do is act as moderators for the organization. They are the central vocal chords in the machinery of our great movement. They merely function because of the power, the energy, the force and the determination of each man and woman among the millions of our membership, that force being crystallized into a gigantic influence that is translated and vocalized by the leaders of our movement . . .

For the first time in the history of industrial America these great accumulations of capital, described as modern corporations, which have flaunted and abused and exploited labor in America for half a century, have been compelled by the sheer influence and crystallized power of millions of workers to engage in collective bargaining and to recognize the economic, social and political rights of the workers in America. Some accomplishment! And the end is not yet. The work is appreciated by millions and millions of men and women who are not yet members of labor organizations, who have had their wages increased or their wage structure preserved, or their hours of labor decreased and their working conditions improved, their health and safety conditions made better.

Is there anybody so foolish as to think that they do not know why? Is there anyone so foolish as to think that they believe that the craft form of organization in America accomplished that work and secured for them those blessings? Is there anyone who believes that they do not know that this great, mighty force in America that has enlarged their opportunities and broadened their horizons of thought and stirred within them the slumbering thoughts of ambition to go forward, ever forward in that improvement, is the Congress of Industrial Organizations as exemplified by the leadership in this Convention, as exemplified by the sound and logical American policies which we have uttered in this Convention?

Men and women are not fools merely because they work in factories, mines or shops. There are those in this country who believe that men and women who work for a living are incapable of logical thought, that they possess an inferior intelligence. I give the lie to that assertion on the part of employers, on the part of bankers, on the part of manufacturers' associations and on the part of stubborn statesmen in our legislative halls! I hurl that lie back into their teeth, and I revel and enjoy doing it! [Laughter and applause.]

I make no apology to any interests in the United States for the position of labor upon any questions. From the standpoint of the economic soundness of their policy; from the standpoint of their justifiable human and social rights; from the standpoint of political virtue and soundness I proclaim, I assert that labor's policies are victorious, that its position is sound and that labor intends to go forward under its policy enunciated in its own councils and premised upon a platform that any American can endorse! [Loud applause.]. . .

So we are to be congratulated in this convention upon the record of our organization, and we can rest assured and we can give that word to our membership that tomorrow and the future will reveal greater and greater accomplishments for our membership, and greater and greater pride for every member and every officer in this instrumentality that he and she have created here in defense of the rights of humanity, the liberties of her citizens, and the living standards of our people!

SELECTION 7:
LABOR AND CONTROL OF THE ECONOMY (1940)

We must recognize that in the coming years the basic problems, having a necessary impact upon future legislation, will center about the protection of democratic institutions and civil rights and economic security for young and old.

It is clear that we cannot simply maintain the status quo, but that we must go forward to reach a solution to the fundamental problems that have confronted us for the past ten years. The impact of the European War on the hemisphere has in no way altered the nature of the problems confronting us. It may perhaps have given them new forms, but it has also made them more urgent than ever before.

Every one of our past problems still faces us—the economic insecurity for millions, the necessity for collective bargaining and federal labor standards, the extension of social security, the reshaping of our tax structures according to ability to pay, and above all, the necessity for putting our economy upon a full time expanding basis . . .

By concretely realizing our objectives, we can take hold of the rapid and dynamic flow of events and see to it that the interests of the American people govern the course of our future policies. First, we must see to it that our capacity to produce is utilized to the fullest not for the sole purpose of producing armaments, but also to produce the commodities of our basic industries that go into American standards of living and provide jobs for the presently unemployed workers.

Secondly, we must recognize that adequate wage and hour standards have to be maintained, and collective bargaining securely established so that there will be an adequate distribution of wages to provide mass purchasing power. The right of the people to exercise freedom of speech, of press, of assembly, of worship, and to organize into free unions must not be abridged but ever more securely protected.

Thirdly, the national defense program has made it clear that prices have to be kept under control. The government, in an informal and unofficial way, through the use of its bargaining power, the antitrust laws and public opinion, is now purporting to exercise pressure upon industry to keep the prices of our basic commodities down and prevent price rises that would eat up purchasing power. But more effective measures are essential. At the same time we must insist that our financial system respond quickly and flexibly to meet the demands of industry for credits to purchase materials, pay wages, and keep inventories.

In short, the policies of American industry, which have hitherto been under exclusive control of a few owners and their bankers, must be made subject to the necessities of the public interest and the welfare of the American people. It is along the lines of these potential developments that labor must exert its pressure both so that existing standards can be maintained, and that, more important, we can move forward to the solution of our fundamental economic problems.

Out of the abundance of materials, man power and equipment with which this country is endowed, we can create and maintain a standard of living under democratic institutions that will be a beacon to a troubled world.

SELECTION 8:
TOWARD A PARTY OF LABOR (1940)

Early April

John L. Lewis threatened today to organize labor, youth, old age, Negro and farmers' groups into a third party unless the Democratic party adopts a platform and selects a candidate "acceptable to labor and the common people." He would call a convention of these groups "to meet in some central city," he declared, "to formulate a program that each and every American can support."

The head of the Congress of Industrial Organizations named specifically among the various organizations the American Youth Congress, the National Association for the Advancement of Colored People, the American Negro Congress, "liberal agricultural" organizations, and the Townsend old-age pension group.

He did not mention a third party but said that unless the conditions he laid down were met he would call the convention presumably before the Fall elections. "And we'll see whether mere machine politics in this country are going to be more important than the voice of the people of this land," he shouted . . .

"Some few weeks ago, as chairman of Labor's Non-Partisan League, I addressed the American Youth Congress in Washington, DC," said Mr. Lewis, adding: "I invited them to become affiliated with Labor's Non-Partisan League. They received the invitation with enthusiasm, and since that time a complete and satisfactory working alliance has been worked out and ratified between the American Youth Congress and Labor's Non-Partisan League."

Mr. Lewis said he expected to address the American Negro Congress and the National Association for the Advancement of Colored People conventions before July 4, and asserted he would tell them: "It is an outrage and a shame that 8,000,000 Negroes in America are prevented from voting in eight Southern states because they do not have enough money to pay their poll tax." There are millions of white Americans who are "disfranchised in the same manner," he declared, so that they cannot express themselves at the polls.

Mr. Lewis said he would speak before the Townsend old age organization at a meeting in St. Louis. The CIO, he noted, has already advocated pensions . . . for those over 60. The CIO chieftain said that "after the Republican and Democratic conventions" he would "propose and urge upon these various organizations the assembling of a great delegates' convention" unless the Democrats met his requirements . . .

"Far from settling the unemployment question, the existing Administration is curtailing the meager relief extended to men and women out of work." Speaking scornfully of "national police institutes conducted by the FBI to train men for espionage," he continued: "What a sad commentary it is that we are putting men and women off relief, careless of whether they live or die, when the Congress is asked to appropriate more money to employ more Federal detectives."

"I am serving notice, " he continued, "upon the political parties in this country—and I don't expect anything from the Republicans—that America cannot be permitted to drift, drift, while politicians merely hope, hope. And I am also serving notice that the answer to these problems is not the answer of having America participate in the European war . . . and that this will be an answer to the economic and political questions that beset this nation . . ."

Late July

John L. Lewis, addressing the convention of the United Automobile Workers of America, attacked today the pending conscription bill . . . warned that if such a law were enacted in peacetime it would "mark a turning point in the policies of this republic and constitute a departure from the ideals of this nation such as has never before been contemplated in the life of the republic." . . .

"Build up if you please," he continued, "a gigantic military instrumentality of that character and quarter it upon the people of this nation under a Roosevelt or under any other President; call it a defensive mechanism, if you please, but sooner or later will come a Chief Executive of the United States, a man on horseback, who will believe this instrumentality is not a defensive instrument at all but an offensive instrumentality that will carry out his imperialistic dreams and conceptions."

Inadequate national income and unemployment were still the nation's major problems, he declared, and inquired what the major political parties were doing to solve those problems. "Some day the people of the United States are going to lose confidence in the political parties and form their own party," he told the delegates who applauded enthusiastically. But he added: "Be that as it may, that is for the future to develop." Thus he apparently sounded the death knell to the hopes of those who had been under the impression that he would issue a rallying cry for the formation of a third party.

SELECTION 9:
CONFRONTING THE TAFT–HARTLEY ASSAULT ON WORKERS' POWER: A CALL FOR THE AFL'S NON-COOPERATION WITH AN UNJUST LAW (1947)

The Taft–Hartley statute is the first ugly, savage thrust of fascism in America. It came into being through an alliance between industrialists and the Republican majority in Congress, aided and abetted by those Democratic legislators who still believe in the institution of human slavery. It was bought and paid for by campaign contributions from the industrial and business interests of this country, and the Republican party and the Democratic minority made good by forging these legislative shackles for you and the men and women who pay you to intelligently represent them.

It creates an inferior class of citizens, an inferior category and a debased position politically to the men and women who toil by hand or brain for their daily subsistence and to safeguard the future of their loved ones . . .

The signing of the [non-Communist] affidavit isn't the only thing that an organization has to do to conform to this Act. This Act is a trap, a pitfall for the organizations of labor, and I am surprised that those who have been attempting to analyze it haven't looked down the road just a few months or a year to find out some of the things that are inherent in this Act. This Act was passed to oppress labor, to make difficult its current enterprises for collective bargaining, to make more difficult the securing of new members for this labor movement, without which our movement will become so possessed of inertia that there is no action and no growth, and in a labor movement where there is no growth there is no security for its existence, because deterioration sets in and unions, like men, retrograde . . .

I wonder what built up the labor movement in this country? Was it protecting laws and statutes that protected the organizers of our movement when they went out to meetings? Oh, no! The founders of our Federation had no such protection. They had to fight for the right to be heard. They had to fight for the right to hold a meeting, and men had to sacrifice and sometimes die for the right to join a union. Those were the conditions under which this movement of ours was created. It is a monument to the unselfish sacrifice of millions of men through decades of time and to the unswerving devotion to principles of the great leaders of our movement who have preceded us.

Well, what are we going to do? Are we going to abandon that policy and that course of action that created us, that made strong and courageous men out of our members and great leaders out of their representatives? . . . If there ever was a time in the history of the organized labor movement, in the history of our country when unity of purpose, unity of policy and objections were needed in the interest of every man, woman and child under our flag, then that time is now in this year of our Lord, 1947. Yet we quibble over details, we swallow a camel—the Taft–Hartley Act—and we strain at gnats . . . If you resist the power of the state, the central government will be used against you, and if you don't resist it will be used against you that much more quickly, because they won't lose any sleep at night worrying about what to do with a labor movement that is fleeing before the storm . . .

I am trying to look at the future of our labor movement. I am here to say that if we have the courage to stand together, we are strong enough and powerful enough to protect our membership, our unions and our country from the detrimental effects of this most despicable act. If we don't stand together—well, divided we fall.

Selection 10:
What Democracy Means to Me (1938)

Democracy is the basis of our national development and the guarantor of our liberties. It is our security against the economic, social and political vicissitudes of this constantly changing world. We are living in one of the most interesting and significant ages in all recorded history. We are confronted daily with problems whose solution may affect materially the future of all peoples.

The United States has been an independent nation for 160 years. Our war of independence was followed closely by a period of expansion, we were subjected to the industrial revolution. We were torn by a civil warfare. As a nation, we are not yet completely integrated. Our institutions and our culture are in a fluid state. Their future will depend on whether we maintain democratic principles supreme in the conduct of our government.

Many of us do not realize how deeply the concepts of democracy influence our lives. We cannot conceive of a life in which we are not entitled to the greatest degree of personal liberty, consistent with the orderly government of our nation and the economic and social security of our people. The free-born and high-spirited citizens of the United States would never yield to the harrowing tyranny of a Fascist state.

Democracy does not comprise a perfect system of government. That would be inconsistent with the qualities of human nature. However, it is the closest approach to a perfect system of government which has yet been evolved by man. It is our duty to see that any change is based upon the principles of democracy and not of tyranny. We must guard our most precious heritage of liberty and equality of economic privilege.

So long as corruption may flourish in the police forces of our cities and states, so long as corporate employers may deny the law of this land, our democracy has a stain of dishonor. We cannot say we have real democracy when men and women starve for lack of work and when children are born to a heritage of hopeless misery. It is our responsibility to correct these things. If we fail to safeguard our democratic liberties, we have done less than our duty to ourselves and to posterity.

A. Philip Randolph.

Courtesy of the Library of Congress, Prints and
Photographs Division, LC-USZ62-119495.

CHAPTER 13

A. Philip Randolph

Asa Philip Randolph (1889–1979) was born in Florida of working-class parents—his father a tailor, as well as an ordained minister in the African Methodist Episcopal (AME) Church, his mother a seamstress. A voracious reader, Randolph was profoundly influenced by W. E. B. Du Bois, whose *The Souls of Black Folk* propelled him toward the struggle for black equality.

Moving to New York City in 1911, he soon was drawn into the Socialist Party of America. His excited discovery of the works of Karl Marx, he later commented, was "like finally running into an idea which gives you your outlook on life." He found kindred spirits in a young intellectual named Chandler Owen and a socialist-minded widow and businesswomen, Lucille Green (whom he soon married), and together they produced, beginning in 1917, *The Messenger*, which has been hailed as a vital element within the "Harlem Renaissance" among black intellectuals, artists, and activists, giving "many of them a renewed spirit and feeling of power" in the wake of World War I. "In spite of its turbulent history," notes scholar Sondra Kathryn Wilson, "*The Messenger* proffered an essential radical dimension to African–American social and political thought." In 1921, he also ran on the Socialist Party ticket for New York secretary of state.

On the strength of his well-known and powerful working-class orientation, highlighted by his ringing socialist oratory and the role he played through *The Messenger*, and his reputation for incorruptibility, Randolph attracted a group of Pullman porters who asked him to help lead and organize their new organization, the BSCP. The Pullman porters were an all-black service staff for the Pullman sleeping cars, dining cars, and so on. The fact that Randolph was not a Pullman employee meant that he could not be fired or bought off by the company. Throwing himself into this effort, Randolph transformed *The Messenger* into an organ of the BSCP, and after an arduous ten-year effort, in 1935, the workers under his leadership were finally able to make the union the exclusive bargaining agent of the Pullman porters. Randolph also led a successful fight to affiliate the BSCP with a somewhat reluctant AFL and, for years thereafter, was a powerful voice for the unity of black and white workers and against racist policies and practices predominant in all too many unions.

From that time onward, Randolph became one of the central leaders in the struggle for black rights, always linking the struggles for economic justice and for racial justice, reaching for common cause between workers of all races. From 1935 to 1940 he was president of an influential coalition, the National Negro Congress, leaving it over differences he had with influential elements in the group associated with the Communist Party. Soon after, he began to organize an increasingly powerful March on Washington Movement to protest against racist discrimination in defense industries, government employment, and the military. The march was called off when President Franklin Roosevelt issued an Executive Order making important concessions. After World War II, Randolph led another successful campaign to de-segregate the U.S. military.

In 1955, Randolph became a Vice-President of the AFL–CIO upon the merger of the AFL and the CIO. In the new formation, he continued to play the role of speaking out against racist policies and practices, sometimes coming into conflict with AFL–CIO President George Meany (who once snapped: "Who appointed you the Voice of the Negro People?"). He was also a founder and leader of the Negro American Labor Council, serving as its president from 1960 to 1966.

Randolph's example and ideas had a powerful impact on the rise of the civil rights movement in the 1950s and 1960s. He was a key initiator and organizer of the massive 1963 "March on Washington for Jobs and Freedom," at which Martin Luther King, Jr. gave his famed "I Have a Dream" speech. In later years, critics argued that he had compromised some of his principles— although his opposition to black nationalism and to the seemingly separatist "black power" militancy of the 1960s was actually rooted in long-standing principles. At the same time, some shifts were undeniable. Like Socialist Party leader Norman Thomas, Randolph moved away from opposition to voting for the pro-capitalist Democrats in 1964, to oppose conservative Republican Barry Goldwater (but, unlike Thomas, he muted his own opposition to the U.S. war in Vietnam so as not to antagonize the Democrats and the AFL–CIO leadership).

Beginning in 1966, Randolph worked with others to campaign for a detailed "Freedom Budget for All Americans"—a ten-year plan that would abolish poverty, guarantee full employment, ensure adequate minimum wages, guarantee incomes for all unable to work, ensure a decent home for every family, provide modern health services for all, provide full educational opportunity for all, update social security and welfare programs, and more. Developed by capable economists, with broad support in labor, civil rights, religious, intellectual, and activist circles, it was far too radical for both Democrats and Republicans. Randolph later commented: "This system is a market economy in which investment and production are determined more by the anticipation of profits than by the desire to achieve social justice."

Sources for Biographical Sketch

Jervis Anderson, *A. Philip Randolph, A Biological Portrait* (Berkeley, CA: University of California Press, 1986).

William H. Harris, "A. Philip Randolph, Black Workers, and the Labor Movement," in Melvyn Dubofsky and Warren Van Tine, eds., *Labor Leaders in America* (Urbana: University of Illinois Press, 1987).

Manning Marable, "A. Philip Randolph and the Foundations of Black Socialism," in John Hinshaw and Paul Le Blanc, eds., *U.S. Labor in the Twentieth Century: Studies in Working-Class Struggles and Insurgency* (Amherst, NY: Humanity Books, 2000).

Paula F. Pfeffer, *A. Philip Randolph, Pioneer of the Civil Rights Movement* (Baton Rouge, LA: Louisiana State University Press, 1990).

Sondra Kathryn Wilson, ed., *The Messenger Reader* (New York: The Modern Library/Random House, 2000).

Sources for Selections

Selection 1: A. Philip Randolph, "The Negro in Politics," *The Messenger*, vol. II, no. 7, July 1919, pp. 16–17, 20–21.

Selection 2: A. Philip Randolph, "The Trade Union Movement and the Negro," *The Journal of Negro Education*, vol. 5, no. 1 (January 1936), pp. 54–58.

Selection 3: A. Philip Randolph and Norman Thomas, *Victory's Victims? The Negro's Future*, pamphlet (New York: Socialist Party, 1943), pp. 4–11.

Selection 4: "What They Say," *AFL–CIO American Federationist*, October 1959, p. 32.

Selection 5: A. Philip Randolph Institute, *A "Freedom Budget" For All Americans* (New York: A. Philip Randolph Institute, 1966), pp. iii–v.

SELECTION 1:
BLACK WORKERS AND SOCIALIST POLITICS (1919)

The old Negro leaders have had the intent to serve the interests of the Negroes, but they have lacked the knowledge as to how they could best serve them. And it is recognized today that the possession of an intent to do good without the knowledge is more fatal than the possession of knowledge without the intent ... Even Protestant historians accord to those who maintained the Spanish Inquisition honest intentions while they murdered, massacred and outraged the heretics of their day. The suppression of free speech, the freedom of the press, and the lynching of Negroes and IWW are based upon intent to serve the country's interests ...

Thus it is obvious that the hope of the Negro lies, first, in the development of Negro leaders with the knowledge of the science of government and economics, scientific history and sociology; and second, in the relegation to the political scrap heap of those Negro leaders whose only qualifications are the desire to lead and the intent to do good.

The old Negro leaders have been factors in producing and perpetuating a patent contradiction in American politics: the alliance of a race of poverty, the Negro, with a party of wealth, the Republican Party.

The Republican Party has been the instrumentality in American politics of abolishing agricultural feudalism of the South for the establishment of industrial capitalism of the North. Industrial slavery has been substituted for human slavery.

But how is the Negro to know which party to support? Before answering this question may I observe that a party is a body of individuals who agree upon a political program and who strive to gain control of the government in order to secure its adoption. Its campaigns are made possible by those persons who desire the adoption of its program. It is natural and plain, then, that those who supply the funds will control and direct the party.

Now, it is a fact of common knowledge that the Republican and Democratic parties receive their campaign funds from Rockefeller, Morgan, Schwab, Shonts, Ryan, Armour and other capitalists. It is also a fact of common knowledge that the chief interests of these capitalists are to make large profits by employing cheap labor and selling their goods at high prices to the public.

Thus, since the chief interests of the workers are more wages, less work, cheaper food, clothing and shelter, it is apparent that their chief interests are opposed to those of their employers—the capitalists, which are represented by the Republican and Democratic parties.

Now, since almost all Negroes are workers, live on wages and suffer from the high cost of food, clothing and shelter, it is obvious that the Republican and Democratic parties are opposed to their interests.

But since neither the Republican and Democratic parties represent the Negroes' interests, the question logically arises as to which party in American politics does?

I maintain that since the Socialist Party is supported financially by working men and working women, and since its platform is a demand for the abolition of this class struggle between the employer and the worker, by taking over and democratically managing the sources and machinery of wealth production and exchange, to be operated for social service and not for private profits;

and further, since the Socialist Party has always, both in the United States and Europe, opposed all forms of race prejudice, that the Negro should no longer look upon voting the Republican ticket, as accepting the lesser of the two evils, but that it is politically, economically, historically and socially logical and sound for him to reject both evils, the Republican and Democratic parties, and select a positive good—Socialism.

SELECTION 2:
ORGANIZED LABOR AND THE NEGRO (1936)

The record of the relation of the trade union movement to Negro workers has been and is an unhappy one. This relation constitutes the problem which falls into two main outlines: the first concerns discrimination practiced by labor unions against Negro workers, and second, the displacement of union workers, while on strike, by Negro strike-breakers.

Trade Union Discrimination

The first aspect of the problem, namely, discrimination by trade unions against Negro workers, takes many varied and variegated forms. Twenty-two international and national unions, for instance, flatly and frankly exclude Negro workers by constitutional provision. Other trade unions limit Negro workers to certain types of work, certain shops in which to work, and to certain locals ... There are unions ... that admit Negro members but definitely bar them from representing themselves in conventions or holding office. Negro workers are not excluded by constitutional provision from the [International Brotherhood of] Electrical Workers, Plumbers' and Steam-fitters' or Flint Glass Workers' Union, but they are simply not taken in as members, or rather, they discourage Negro members from joining them ... Separate locals are generally provided for Negro workers by [certain unions] ... The only unions that require Negro workers to join mixed locals are the United Mine Workers' and the Garment Workers' organizations.

These existent forms of discrimination against Negro workers are not denied, but sometimes excused by trade union officials on the tenuous grounds that Negroes are only happy when they are to themselves, or that Negro and white people don't get along so well together.

But the American Federation assumes that it has made adequate and proper provision against the discrimination practiced by trade unions upon Negro workers by permitting them to affiliate with it through federal unions. While inclusion of Negro workers in the trade union movement through the federal unions may be better than leaving them out entirely, the federal union as a mechanism for organizing Negro workers is far from satisfactory, since Negro workers, in an industry which is covered by an agreement on wages and rules governing working conditions negotiated by an international union which excludes Negroes, are impotent to change it, if perchance the agreement has provisions inimical to their interests . . .

Discrimination against Negro workers by the trade union movement is doubtless the greatest challenge to its profession of democracy and its claim of representing a progressive force in American society. Of course, it must be admitted and recognized that the AF of L in its conventions has always expressed a policy for the organization of Negro workers, and has condemned the practice of unions discriminating against workers on account of race, creed, color or nationality. No representative of the AF of L, however, could well deny that these resolutions, which are adopted in conventions, in favor of the organization of Negro workers, are poor and well-nigh meaningless gestures. They have not altered the policy of a single union which elects to discriminate against Negro workers. Something much more drastic is necessary . . .

Negro Strike-Breakers

Relative to the other angle of the problem or role of the Negro worker as a strike-breaker, it is a commonplace that Negro workers as strike-breakers have dealt the labor movement serious blows. In the great stockyards strike, Negro workers were used in large numbers and practically broke it. The steel strike, too, was largely lost because of the importation of Negro workers as strike-breakers in the steel mills. In 1922, the shopmen's railroad strike met with serious handicaps because of Negro strike-breakers. Teamsters and hotel workers and many other crafts and callings have found their lot materially worsened, when on strike, by the invasion of Negro workers. But it is important to recognize in this connection that Negroes are not the only other chief strike-breakers in America. White workers, too, have figured in every strike as strike-breakers, though they cannot claim in extenuation of their action, exclusion from the union conducting the strike. This is different from Negro workers. While strike-breaking is unjustifiable on the part of one worker against another, whether they be of the same or different race, creed or nationality, it is equally unjustifiable for one worker to discriminate against another by preventing him from joining a union because of difference in race or color, creed or nationality.

Besides serving to widen the breach between the two groups of workers and rendering organization in a common labor movement more difficult, strike-breaking on the part of Negro workers has not measurably improved their employment status, while definitely injuring their earning power, since they are invariably accepted at lower wages. Strike-breakers don't only lower the wage for themselves, but tend to weaken and destroy the entire wage structure of a given industry in particular and the country in general.

Remedial Measures

This brings me to the consideration of the solution of the aforementioned problem. While it may seem rather trite and simple, it is nevertheless true that the only remedy for the problem, which has grown out of the relationship of Negro workers to the trade union movement, is the organization of the Negro workers into the trade unions that will accept them and into independent unions of Negro workers to fight for admission into unions that exclude them, as well as to develop economic strength to bargain collectively with the employers for whom they work.

Some organizing device should be planned to develop and promote this program, such as the Italian Chamber of Labor and the United Hebrew Trades . . .

Misleadership

The cause of the organization of Negro workers into the trade union movement has suffered greatly and been incalculably hindered by Negro leadership. The old guard conservative group are simply opposed to organized labor for the same reason that Mellon or Morgan is opposed to it . . . As a matter of fact they would oppose a group of Negro workers organizing to fight for more wages and better working conditions, just as they oppose white workers fighting for more wages and better working conditions.

The Negro intellectual, too, has rendered doubtful service to the cause of the organization of Negro workers, since they have been content merely to proclaim their opposition to the AF of L because of the existence of prejudice in various unions afflicted with it which, of course, nobody denies or condones . . . Discrimination, segregation and Jim Crowism should be systematically exposed and fought wherever found, whether in the church, government, school system, trade union, or what not. Destruction generally precedes construction . . .

Organization of Negro Workers by Negroes

But along with a policy of destruction with respect to discrimination, segregation and Jim Crowism in the trade unions, [there] should also be developed a program of construction. Obviously, the only sound constructive program in dealing with the problem of Negro workers is organization. This is the task of the Negroes themselves. Nobody else will organize Negro workers but Negro workers of hand and brain.

Even if the AF of L and the national and international unions believed thoroughly in the organization of Negro workers, they could not be depended upon to do the job themselves. Jewish workers have organized Jewish workers. Italian and Irish workers have organized Italian and Irish workers. Of course the AF of L has assisted. But the spade [work] and Jimmie Higgins work* is done by the workers that are seeking organization. Not only must the Negro workers organize themselves, but what is as important, they must pay the price in suffering, sacrifice, and struggle. Even if the AF of L could and would organize the Negro workers without the Negro workers going through the ordeal and fire of suffering, struggle and sacrifice, it would be more and more of a bane than a benefit, for Negroes would lack the experience, the class perception, courage and vision that are only born in a struggle for power . . .

The paramount and big question before Negroes today of all strata is the development of a long-range program for the organization of Negro workers in the trade unions, either in or out of the AF of L, for the purpose of developing economic power to improve their lot in terms of wages and hours of work and for the larger objective of industrial and political democracy.

SELECTION 3:
RACISM, HUMAN RIGHTS, AND LABOR RIGHTS IN
WORLD WAR II (1943)

Norman Thomas: Today I am happy to share this period [of radio programming] with another brilliant representative of our common country and his race. My guest A. Philip Randolph is not only an outstanding figure in the whole American labor movement. I know that he is an uncompromising foe of Nazism and fascism everywhere. That gives peculiar weight to his words. He has consented to let me ask him some very direct questions on the race situation in America and its bearing on war and peace. Mr. Randolph, is it true that racial resentment and bitterness are rising in America?

A. Philip Randolph: Yes, Mr. Thomas, it is well-nigh a matter of common knowledge that racial resentment and bitterness are rising in America and what is more disturbing, they are rising with amazing rapidity . . . The story of Jim-Crow in uniform has been aptly styled by Dwight MacDonald, a noted writer, as the "war's great scandal." Negroes occupy the rather strange position of being required to fight for the right to fight and die for their own country. The armed forces are reeking with race discrimination. Negro and white soldiers are segregated in the army, Negro and white women are segregated in the WAACs, and although Dorrie Miller, Negro messman, displayed remarkable heroism in the naval battle at Pearl Harbor, Negroes are not yet permitted to become commissioned officers in the Navy. Negro doctors can

---

* "Jimmie Higgins" is a term utilized by Socialist Party figure Ben Hanford, and later made a character of an Upton Sinclair novel, referring to a dedicated rank-and-file worker who carries out numerous and often mundane practical tasks needed to build and sustain an organization, whether a Socialist Party local or a trade union.

only treat Negro soldiers; in the air corps, Negroes are segregated iin the Jim-Crow school at Tuskegee, Alabama, and up to today, there is not a single Negro air pilot in combat service anywhere.

In the South, Negro soldiers have been denied the right to eat in the diners on railroads while traveling to their camps. At various southern camps, Negro soldiers are being called "niggers" by white officers and shamelessly abused and nothing is done about it. The WAVES and SPARS reject Negro women and the Red Cross Jim-Crows Negro blood although science states there is no difference in the blood plasma based upon race.

Let me cite several instances of the way Negroes are treated in Uncle Sam's uniform in the South:

- At Fort Benning, Georgia, May 2, 1941: The body of a Negro private, Felix Hall, was found hanging from a tee, arms and legs bound. Negro groups charge Private Hall was lynched. The BULLETIN of the NAACP states that at Fort Benning "concentration camp tactics are allegedly being used against Negro soldiers, and torture and killings are taking place at the pleasure of the military police."
- Fayettesville, North Carolina, August 6, 1941: Sergeant E. L. Hargreaves, white military policeman, and Private Ned Thurman, Negro engineer, are killed and four other soldiers are wounded in a gun battle between white and Negro soldiers on a crowded bus. Cause: brutality by white M.P.'s.
- Judge William H. Hastie, former Civilian Aide to War Secretary Mr. Henry L. Stimson, resigned because he found himself helpless in attempting to stop the spread of Jim-Crowism and secure just treatment for Negroes in the armed forces.

These things have happened in an army supposed to be fighting for democracy. They could be multiplied a hundred fold. It is mere accident that this undeclared war against a part of our armed forces has not broken out into devastating riots, bloodshed and lynching on a large scale.

I think it important, too, to state, Mr. Thomas, that in spite of the insult and humiliation visited upon Negroes in the army, navy, air corps, U.S. Marines and WAACs, 16.1 percent of all volunteers in the armed forces in 1941–42 were Negroes, although only 9.8 percent of the population are colored according to the Office of War Information.

Meanwhile lynchings continue, discrimination against Negro boys and girls in the public and private schools nullify our democratic professions—600,000 Negroes in a time of man-power shortage are denied the right to employ their skills because of the Nazi theories of racialism in America.

Thomas: Speaking of discrimination in war industry, Mr. Randolph, you were, I know, a leader in the March on Washington movement which played so large a part in winning the Presidential order against discrimination against Negroes in defense industries. I understand that that movement continues. Would you say a word about its plans?

Randolph: I am glad to say a word about the March on Washington Movement which came into existence in protest against the run-around Negroes were getting when they applied for jobs in defense industries and various government departments. As a result of its mobilization of Negro masses and a threatened march on Washington, July 1st, 1941, Executive Order 8802 was granted under which the President's Committee on Fair Employment Practice was established. The Committee has done splendid work in breaking down barriers against Negro workers in war plants and government departments. Unfortunately, the Committee was almost destroyed when FEPC was put in the War manpower Commission and the railroad hearings were postponed by Mr. Paul V. McNutt. Only recently a new chairman, Father Haas, was appointed by the President. Negroes are now demanding that the railroad hearings be rescheduled immediately and that FEPC be independent, responsible only to the President, with an adequate budget and personnel, and that it adhere to the principle of pubic hearings, and also that the present members of the committee be retained.

The March on Washington Movement plans to hold a national conference in Chicago June 30 to July 4 to map out a program of attack upon Jim-Crow.

Thomas: Of course, Mr. Randolph, I am interested . . . in your own great role in labor. You are the president of a strong union, the Brotherhood of Sleeping Car Employees, AF of L. What is your advice to the labor movement about the Negro and to the Negro about the labor movement?

Randolph: My advice to the American labor movement, Mr. Thomas, is that it wipe out racial discrimination and segregation, for a labor movement divided upon a basis of race, religion or national origin will become easy prey to the rising forces of Fascism and reaction in America. I also urge the Negro workers to join trade unions, both AFL and CIO, according to the one which controls the industries in which Negroes are employed . . .

Thomas: . . . I'd like to know what you think about the present situation here in American in its bearing upon the war and on the peace . . .

Randolph: The question of color and race, Mr. Thomas, in my opinion has become the central historical issue of these times, the reason being that the peoples of color, constituting two-thirds of the population of the world, have reached a higher measure of intellectual, moral and spiritual maturity than obtained in the last war and unless the darker races are brought within the orbit of the democratic tradition and both the imperialisms of the Anglo-American Empire Systems and the totalitarian states are wiped out, this will not be the last war, and democracy and peace will be insecure.

There are some definite things our friends can do.

1. Support the Fair Employment Practices Committee and demand strengthening and enforcement of Executive Order 8802, setting up the committee.
2. Demand that no filibuster in the Senate defeat the Anti-Poll Tax bill.
3. Demand a mixed army and an end to discrimination and segregation in the armed services.
4. Demand an end to a segregated school system which impoverishes Negro education. Insist upon equality in education, elimination of racial barriers against admission to schools and colleges, an end to overcrowding and poor conditions which local governments permit in schools in Negro neighborhoods.
5. Demand passage of a strong anti-lynching bill.
6. Demand low-cost public housing for Negroes and whites, conforming to healthful standards of living.
7. Demand provision of extensive facilities for the training of Negroes in skilled jobs.
8. Demand the abandonment of racial discrimination by such unions as have not yet followed the example of more progressive unions, where workers unite without regard to color, race or creed.
9. Demand abolition of racial segregation of human blood by the Red Cross.
10. Demand abandonment of the Nazi theory of white supremacy, and support cooperation of Negroes and whites for the conquered peoples in Europe, Asia and Africa in their struggle for liberation from imperialist control.

SELECTION 4:
RACE, CLASS, AND A STRONG LABOR MOVEMENT (1959)

Only a strong labor organization is the answer to labor exploitation. A labor organization can be strong only if it brings within its fold all workers in the trade of craft, class or industry. Racially segregated local unions are as morally unjustifiable and organizationally indefensible as racially segregated public schools, housing, recreation or transportation.

Employers who exploit white workers and black workers in the South have effectively played upon the division of labor upon the basis of race. These employers have profited from racial wage differentials.

While Negro workers' wages, as a rule, are lower than the wages of white workers performing the same work, the wages of white workers, too, are lower than the wages of workers performing the same work in other areas under trade union organization. Thus, white workers in the South suffer from substandard wages because of a lack of strong trade union collective baragaining power resulting from the division of labor upon a basis of race.

Organized labor must project a massive revolution within its house to effect a transition of the Negro workers from the status of second-class to first-class economic citizenship.

SELECTION 5:
INTRODUCTION TO *A FREEDOM BUDGET FOR ALL AMERICANS* (1966)

The "Freedom Budget" spells out a specific and factual course of action, step by step, to start in early 1967 toward the practical liquidation of poverty in the United States by 1975. The programs urged in the "Freedom Budget" attack *all* of the major causes of poverty—unemployment and underemployment; substandard pay; inadequate social insurance and welfare payments to those who cannot or should not be employed; bad housing; deficiencies in health services, education, and training; and fiscal and monetary policies which tend to redistribute income regressively rather than progressively. The "Freedom Budget" leaves no room for discrimination in any form, because its programs are addressed to *all* who need more opportunity and improved incomes and living standards—not just to some of them.

The "Freedom Budget" differs from previous worthy efforts to set forth similar goals because it fuses general aspirations with quantitative content, and imposes time schedules. It deals not only with where we must go, but also with how fast and in what proportions. It measures costs against resources, and thus determines feasible priorities. It is not only a *call* to action, but also a *schedule* for action.

The "Freedom Budget" is thus an imperative call to *national action— now*.

Why do we call this a "Freedom Budget"?

The language evokes the struggle of the civil rights movement, its vision of social justice and equality, its militant determination that these goals be rapidly and forthrightly achieved. This is the vision and determination that underlies the "Freedom Budget" and must propel any genuine war on poverty. The moral issues in this war are no less compelling than those of the battle against racism.

We call this a "Freedom Budget" in recognition that poverty and deprivation, as surely as denial of the right to vote, are erosive of human freedom and of democracy. In our affluent nation, even more than in the rest of the world, economic misery breeds the most galling discontent, mocking and undermining faith in political and civil rights. Here in these United States, where there can be no economic nor technological excuse for it, poverty is not only a private tragedy but in a sense a public crime. It is above all a challenge to our morality.

We call this a "Freedom Budget" because it embodies programs which are essential to the Negro and other minority groups striving for dignity and economic security in our society. But their legitimate aspirations cannot be fulfilled in isolation. The abolition of poverty (almost three-quarters of whose U.S. victims are white) can be accomplished only through action which embraces the totality of the victims of poverty, neglect, and injustice. Nor can the goals be won by segmental *ad hoc* programs alone; there is need for welding such *programs* into a unified and consistent *program*.

The main beneficiaries will be the poor themselves. But in the process everyone will benefit, for poverty is not an isolated circumstance affecting only those entrapped by it. It reflects—and affects—the performance of our national economy, our rate of economic growth, our ability to produce and consume, the condition of our cities, the levels of our social services and needs, the very quality of our lives. Materially as well as spiritually, a society afflicted by poverty deprives all of its citizens of security and well-being . . .

In the economic and social realm, no less than in the political, justice too long delayed is justice denied. *We propose and insist the poverty in America can and therefore must be abolished within ten years.*

The means toward this end are spelled out in the following pages, prepared in cooperation with some of the nation's outstanding experts. There may be minor disagreements with regard to statistical data, analysis, and policy proposals, even among those endorsing the "Freedom Budget" in this publication . . . But this limitation is not intended to imply lukewarmness in terms of urgency, nor to question that in its *major* aspects the "Freedom Budget" is essentially sound and imperative.

The "Freedom Budget" contends that this nation has the resources to abolish poverty, for the first time in human history, and to do so within a decade. Indeed, the very process of abolishing poverty will add enormously to our resources, raising the living standards of Americans at all income levels. By serving our unmet social needs—in slum clearance and housing, education and training, health, agriculture, natural resources and regional development, social insurance and welfare programs—we can achieve and sustain a full employment economy (itself the greatest single force against poverty) and a higher rate of economic growth, while simultaneously tearing down the environment of poverty. All these problems interact, whether viewed as causes or results, and they are in truth both . . .

Those drafting this "Freedom Budget" have sought to outline, objectively and fully, the steps required for the abolition of poverty in America. It may be argued that the "Freedom Budget" is too ambitious to be "politically feasible." We contend that the proper question is whether poverty is any longer feasible . . . Who, only a few short years ago, would have acknowledged the "political feasibility" of the tremendous legislative victories of the civil rights movement in our own day?

These breakthroughs were not won by those who thought narrowly of what was "politically feasible," but by those who placed the moral issues squarely before the American people. Having stated the issues clearly, they forged a mighty coalition among the civil rights and labor movements, liberals and religious forces, students and intellectuals—the coalition expressed in the historic March on Washington for Jobs and Freedom . . . To the full goals of the 1963 March the "Freedom Budget" is dedicated. Within this coalition of conscience the strength must be mobilized for the implementation of this "Freedom Budget" for all Americans.

Mrs. Genora Johnson (later Genora Dollinger).

CHAPTER 14

GENORA JOHNSON DOLLINGER

Genora Dollinger, originally Genora Albro (1913–1996), was born in Michigan, one of four children, in a family that blended wage earners and small store-owners (as well as Greenback–Labor, Populist, and Socialist traditions—but also, to her chagrin, a touch of Ku Klux Klan influence in the 1920s). Growing up in the city of Flint, at the age of 17, in 1931, she became a founding member of the city's Socialist Party.

Marrying Kermit Johnson, another member of the Socialist Party, she helped to build a strong branch of the organization, where she came to know other Socialist Party comrades—including the Reuther brothers (Walter, Victor, and Roy). As indicated in the selections below, she became centrally involved in the efforts to organize the UAW in the Flint sit-down strike of 1936–1937, in which her husband played a leading role—during which she helped organize the famed Women's Emergency Brigade.

After the strike, Genora Johnson became active in the National Association for the Advancement of Colored People (NAACP) and she also helped organize, and served as secretary to, the first unemployed union affiliated with the UAW, in 1938–1939. She and some of her comrades were drawn to the revolutionary socialist current influenced by Russian revolutionary and anti-Stalinist leader Leon Trotsky, and in 1938 she became a founding member of the Socialist Workers Party. After the end of her marriage with Johnson, she married Sol Dollinger in 1944. Nine years later, the Dollingers shifted their political affiliations to the short-lived American Socialist Union.

During World War II, Genora Dollinger moved to Detroit, taking a job at Briggs manufacturing, where she was also active in the UAW, serving as chief steward of her union local. After World War II, she sought to expose the ties between the Briggs company and members of organized crime who were behind brutal assaults on two co-workers in her UAW local. In October 1945, she was brutally assaulted in her home by members of the notorious Perrone Gang, who beat her in the face with a lead pipe. In 1948, Walter and Victor Reuther were each wounded in assassination attempts. Ties between Briggs and the Perrone gang were exposed in U.S. Senate hearings in 1951. Dollinger commented:

> Are union leaders so naive as to think labor peace has been established in America? Do they think the beatings and shootings were an aberration of a local industrialist suffering from an overdose of anti-union rabies? If they have these illusions they better get rid of them . . . Not all union militants have gone through the experience of the veterans of the sit-down strikes. If these workers were shot at and tear-gassed as I was in Flint, they would know General Motors doesn't like unions. If they were violently driven out of Saginaw by GM-inspired vigilantes in the same year for trying to organize workers into a union, they would never forget it. If they had lived through the bitterness and violence of the Ford organizing drive in Detroit this conviction would be part of their flesh and bones.

Dollinger became a union dissident, challenging the far-reaching compromises, the undemocratic practices, and "tuxedo unionism" that she associated with Walter Reuther's regime in the UAW. Nor was her activism restricted to trade union activity. She ran for governor in Michigan on the Socialist Workers Party ticket in 1948, served as development director of the Michigan Civil Liberties Union from 1960 to 1966, and was a leader of Women for Peace during the protests against the U.S. war in Vietnam.

In 1977, she helped to organize a protest against the exclusion of women (resulting in her being invited to address the gathering), and she was involved in the making of two documentaries—the British Broadcasting Corporation's *The Great Sit-Down Strike*, and Academy Award-nominated *With Babies and Banners: The Story of the Women's Emergency Brigade*. In her final years, after moving to California, she was active in Labor Party Advocates. When she was inducted into the Hall of Fame of the Michigan Women's Historical Center in 1994, Victor and Sophie Reuther wrote: "Genora is of the great tradition of Mother Jones who in an earlier generation was to the mineworkers what Genora became to the auto workers. A living legend in her own time!"

Sources for Biographical Sketch

Genora Dollinger, "I Warned Reuther," *American Socialist*, February 1954 (available online in the American Socialist Archive at www.marxists.org/history/etol/newspape/amersocialist/gdollinger02.htm, accessed October 6, 2010).

Sol Dollinger, "The Unrelenting Genora Dollinger," *Against the Current*, no. 60, January–February 1996.

Sol Dollinger and Genora Dollinger, *Not Automatic: Women and the Left in the Forging of the Auto Workers' Union* (New York: Monthly Review Press, 2000).

Carlton Jackson, *Child of the Sit-Downs: The Revolutionary Life of Genora Dollinger* (Kent, OH: Kent State University Press, 2008).

Striking Flint: Genora (Johnson) Dollinger Remembers the 1936–37 General Motors Sit-Down Strike, as told to Susan Rosenthal (Chicago, IL: Bookmarks, 1996).

Also see Kathleen O'Nan, "The Role of Women, and of Radicals, in the First Sit-Down Strikes, An Interview with Genora Johnson Dollinger," in John Hinshaw and Paul Le Blanc, eds., *U.S. Labor in the 20th Century: Studies in Working-Class Struggles and Insurgency* (Amherst, NY: Humanity Books, 2000).

Sources for Selections

All can be found in *Striking Flint: Genora (Johnson) Dollinger Remembers the 1936–37 General Motors Sit-Down Strike,* as told to Susan Rosenthal (Author, 1996): selection 1 pp. 8–9, 11–13, 14–17; selection 2 pp. 28–31; selection 3 pp. 24, 25, 27–28; selection 4 pp. 40–41; reproduced in Sol Dollinger and Genora Dollinger, *Not Automatic: Women and the Left in the Forging of the Auto Workers' Union* (New York: Monthly Review Press, 2000).

SELECTION 1:
SIT-DOWN STRIKE AND WOMEN'S EMERGENCY BRIGADE

A considerable amount of preparatory work was done before the strike. That preparatory work was done by radical parties. We had several very active organizations in Flint and Detroit: the Communist Party, the Proletarian Party, the Socialist Labor Party, the Socialist Party and the Industrial Workers of the World (IWW). And, with the exception of the Communist Party, we all had our headquarters in the Pengelly Building, a very old building that became the major strike headquarters of the whole United Automobile Workers Union of Flint. Even as the strike was going on, we still had our rooms on the second floor, while the main activities in the auditorium were on the third floor . . .

Many revolutionaries, so-called, talk about "spontaneous combustion of the workers." I can't see that at all, because it took time for the organizers in various plants of this whole General Motors empire to talk to the workers and to bring them to classes—to make some contact—create a bond. You had to trust your fellow worker if you were going to be an active union member because we had an awful lot of spies in there, a lot of people who would get special favor for squealing on somebody else . . .

The first sit-down was on December 30 in the small Fisher Body Plant 2 over a particularly big grievance that had occurred. The workers were at the point where they had just had enough, and under a militant leadership, they sat down. When the UAW leaders in the big Fisher Body Plant 1 heard about the sit-down in Fisher 2, they sat down, also. That took real guts, and it took political leadership. The leaders of the political parties knew what they had to do because they'd studied labor history and the ruthlessness of the corporations.

Picket lines were established and also a big kitchen in the south end of Flint, across from the large Fisher 1 plant. Every day, gallons and gallons of food were prepared, and anybody who was on the picket lines would get a ticket with notification that they had served on the line so they'd be able to get a good hot meal.

The strike kitchen was primarily organized by the Communist Party women. They brought a restaurant man from Detroit to help organize this huge kitchen. They were the ones who made all of those good meals.

We also had what we called scavengers, groups of people who would go to the local farmers and ask for donations of food for the strikers. Many people in these small towns surrounding Flint were factory workers who would also raise potatoes, cabbages, tomatoes, corn or whatever. So great quantities of food were sent down to be made into dishes for the strikers. People were very generous.

John L. Lewis and the United Mine Workers helped us financially so that if there was somebody in serious difficulty we could help them out a little bit. Later on, the garment workers sent money. But with thousands of workers, you couldn't help everybody, so many families were taken care of by committees forming in plants, whether they were on strike or not. Committees in Buick, Chevrolet, and Fisher Body took care of some of the urgent cases so nobody starved or got into really major medical difficulties.

After the first sit-down started, I went down to see what I could do to help. I was either on the picket lines or up at the Pengelly Building all the time, but some of the strike leaders didn't know who I was and didn't know that I had been teaching classes in unionism and so on. So they said, "Go to the kitchen. We need a lot of help out there." They didn't know what else to tell a woman to do. I said, "You've got a lot of little, skinny men around here who can't stand to be out on the cold picket lines for very long. They can peel potatoes as well as women can." I turned down the idea of kitchen duty.

Instead, I organized a children's picket line. I got Bristol board and paints, and I was painting signs for this children's picket line. One of my socialist comrades came up and said, "Hey, Genora, what are you doing here?" I said, "I'm doing your job." Since he was a professional sign painter, I turned the sign-painting project over to him and that was the beginning of the sign-painting department.

We could only do the children's picket line once because it was too dangerous, but we got an awful lot of favorable publicity from it, much of it international. The picture of my two-year-old son, Jarvis, holding a picket sign saying, "My daddy strikes for us little tykes," went all over the nation, and people sent me articles from French newspapers and from Germany and from other European countries. I thought it was remarkable that the news traveled so far . . .

I should tell you how the Women's Auxiliary was formed. The last days of December 1936 were when the sit-downs began. Following that came New Year's Eve. Among working class families, everybody celebrates New Year's Eve. I was amazed at the number of wives that came down to the picket line and threatened their husbands, "If you don't cut out this foolishness and get out of that plant right now, you'll be a divorced man!" They threatened divorce loudly and openly, yelling and shouting at their husbands. I knew I couldn't go and grab each one of them to talk to them privately. So I could only watch as some of the men climbed out of the plant window up on the second floor, down the ladder to go home with their wives. These were good union members, but they were hooted and hollered at by their comrades in the plant who were holding the fort in the sit-down. This was a very dangerous turn of events because I knew how few men were inside holding that plant, and it worried many of us.

The next day, we decided to organize the women. We thought that if women can be that effective in breaking a strike, they could be just as effective in helping to win it. So we organized the Women's Auxiliary and we laid out what we were going to do.

Now remember, the UAW was still in the process of getting organized. It didn't have elected officers or by-laws or any of the rest of it. So we were free to organize our Women's Auxiliary, to elect our president, vice-president, recording secretary and heads of committees, all on our own.

We couldn't have women sitting down in the plants because the news-papers were antagonizing the wives at home by saying that women were sleeping over in the plant. In fact, GM sent anonymous messages to the wives of some of the strikers alleging that there were prostitutes in those embattled plants. But we knew we could get women on the picket lines.

We organized a child-care center at the union headquarters, so children would have some place to go when their mothers marched on the picket line. Wilma McCartney, who had nine children and was going to have her tenth, took charge of that. At first, the women were scared to death to come down to the union, and some may have been against the union for taking away their paycheck so they couldn't feed their children who were hungry or crying for milk. Then this wonderful woman, this mother of nine children who was pregnant with another, would talk to them about how it would benefit them for their husbands to participate actively. And if they won the strike, it would make all the difference in the world in their living conditions. We recruited a lot of women just through the child-care center.

We also set up a first aid station with a registered nurse in a white uniform and red union arm-band. She was a member of the Women's Auxiliary. The women in the Auxiliary also made house calls to make sure every family had enough to eat, and they gave advice on how to deal with creditors.

But that wasn't enough as far as I was concerned. Women had more to offer than just these services. So we set up public speaking classes for women. Most of the women had never even been to a union meeting. In those days, many of the men would go to union meetings and say to the women, "It's none of your damn business. Don't you mix into our affairs." So the women didn't express any of their ideas about what could be done to better their conditions . . .

Some of the men were very opposed to having their wives at the union headquarters and a few of them never gave up their sexist attitudes. But most of the men encouraged their wives. They thought we were doing a wonderful job, making things better for them at home because their wives under-stood why their husbands had to be on the picket line all day long and do a lot of extra things for the union. They could talk and work together as companions. And the children were learning from their parents' discussions about the strike . . .

The company decided they had to break the strike. On January 11, they attacked the smaller Fisher Body Plant 2. I happened to be on the picket line that day, and I was amazed to see what was happening. The plant guards prevented the men from getting any food for about 24 hours. It was very cold, and they turned off the heat in the building. The men inside were very angry.

Then the company police and the city police started shooting. At first they were shooting tear gas inside the plant, but that was too difficult, so they decided to tear-gas and shoot this huge mass of picketers that had formed in front of the plant. The police were using rifles, buckshot, fire-bombs, and tear-gas canisters. It was a shock to a lot of people. We had thought that General Motors would try to freeze us out or do something in the plants, but never open fire on us right in the middle of the city.

The union picketers took their own cars and barricaded off a section so that the police couldn't get us from both ends. Then, over the radio came the equivalent of saying that there was a revolution starting in Flint. With all the propaganda saying, "The communists are coming into the city to take over the union," people gathered in vast numbers on both sides of this battle. When the police misfired, tear gas and bullets went over our heads into the crowds which had came out to watch. It was very frightening. People would run away and dart into restaurants up the street.

The battle continued for quite some time. Workers overturned police cars to make barricades. They ran to pick up the fire bombs thrown at them and hurl them back at the police. It was very, very cold. The men in the plant were using fire hoses against the police, and when the water ran down, it would quickly ice over.

I saw one of our Socialist Party members, Fred Stevens, jump over a gutter where there was icy water flowing down. A little stream of blood spurted down his leg into the water. I couldn't get my wits together for a moment.

The men wanted to get me out of the way. You know that old "protect the women and children" business. If there are any women or children around, usher them right out, protect them. I told them, "Get away from me. I've got as many weapons as you have." I was the only woman who stayed.

The battle went on for hours. Throughout the whole time, the sound car was giving instructions and trying to bolster the courage of the men inside the plant as well as the picketers on the outside. Victor Reuther spoke for a while and then other men substituted for him, giving him relief. But there were only the voices of men. At one point, Victor came over and told us that the batteries in the sound car were running down.

Lights went on in my head. I thought, "I've never used a loudspeaker to address a large crowd of people, but I've got to tell them that there are women down here." So I asked him, "Victor, can I take the loudspeaker?" He said, "We've got nothing to lose."

The first thing I did was attack the police. I called to them, "Cowards! Cowards! Shooting into the bellies of unarmed men and firing at the mothers of children." Then everything became quiet. There was silence on both sides of the line. I thought, "The women can break this up." So I appealed to the women in the crowd, "Break through those police lines and come down here and stand beside your husbands and your brothers and your uncles and your sweethearts."

In the dusk, I could barely see one woman struggling to come forward. A cop had grabbed her by the back of her coat. She just pulled out of that coat and started walking down to the battle zone. As soon as that happened there were other women and men who followed. The police wouldn't shoot people in the back as they were coming down, so that was the end of the battle. When those spectators came into the center of the battle and the police retreated, there was a big roar of victory. That battle became known as the Battle of Bulls Run because we made the cops run.

By this time, General Motors was going crazy and got Governor Frank Murphy involved. The next day, the National Guard was sent in because it was a very explosive situation. At first, eleven hundred troops were sent, followed by more than two thousand later. By the end of the strike, almost four thousand National Guardsmen were stationed in Flint.

I decided that women could do more than just the duties of the Women's Auxiliary. We could form an Emergency Brigade, and every time there was a threatened battle, we could mobilize. We might make a difference . . .

When we held our big Auxiliary meeting, I got up and asked who would like to join the Women's Emergency Brigade. I said, "It can't be somebody who's weak of heart. You can't go hysterical if your sister beside you drops down in a pool of blood." Oh, I made it a bloody sounding thing! After all, sixteen workers and eleven police had been injured in that battle. Anyone who wanted to join had to stand up, announce publicly that they wanted to join, walk over and sign their names in front of everybody. It wasn't a secret organization and we didn't pressure anyone to join. We made it very difficult.

One old woman in her early seventies stood up. I said, "This is going to be too difficult for you." She said, "You can't keep me out. My sons work in that factory. My husband worked in that factory before he died and I have grandsons in there." She went on and gave a speech. She got applause, then she walked over and signed her name. Then a young girl, I think she was sixteen or seventeen, stood up and said, "My father works in that factory. My brothers work in that factory. I've got a right to join, too." She walked over and signed, and all the women applauded. We recruited about 400 women for the Brigade out of about 1,000 women in the Women's Auxiliary.

I organized the Emergency Brigade on a military basis. I knew a captain gave orders, so I was the captain. Then I picked five lieutenants. We organized groups under each lieutenant. We'd give out an assignment and that lieutenant would find a car, round up her people, and off they'd go to wherever they were needed. Three of my five lieutenants were factory girls. One of them was an A.C. worker who was nineteen years old.

Ruth Pitts was from Fisher Body, and "Teeter" Walker was from Redmans, a supplier plant for GM cars. Those two lieutenants wore jodhpurs, pants that come out on the side like a military or riding habit. They wore big boots that laced up to the knees, short Eisenhower-type jackets, red berets and arm bands. The workers in Fisher Body 1 made blackjacks for them. They laced them up with car leather on the outside and wristlets to go around the arm. They looked pretty jaunty and they meant business. Those two were always on the front lines.

We decided that we would use red berets as our insignia. They were very cheap at the time, something like fifty cents for a good felt beret. The Women's Auxiliary sewed red arm bands with a white E.B. on them for Emergency Brigade. I have one still. We carried heavy wooden clubs with handles carved to fit a woman's grip. Whenever you saw one of those women, you knew that she was ready for action at any time, morning, night, or anytime.

News about the Women's Emergency Brigade made the front page of the New York Times and other papers across the nation. In France when they heard about women organizing and doing it seriously, not just carrying mops and brooms as the newspapers liked to put it, but carrying clubs, they called me the "Joan of Arc" of organized labor—of women warriors. They thought it was very dramatic . . .

SELECTION 2:
UNITY OF EMPLOYED AND UNEMPLOYED WORKERS

After the strike, the unemployed workers were also having great difficulties. We petitioned the International Union to give us the right to organize a WPA and Unemployed Local 12, UAW–CIO, under the International's name and their protection. They didn't give us any money. I guess they didn't know what we were going to do and if they couldn't control it all the way down, they didn't want to fund it. We did organize a very militant union.

Many WPA projects were street repairs. They used to call it "digging holes" and ridicule the workers. These projects kept men and their families barely eating, just barely eating, because the wages were so little.

I was the secretary of Local 12 because at that time a woman wasn't supposed to be president, even though she may have all the ideas. We used the big name and the big, bright lights of the UAW–CIO, and because of the success of the strike, we got an awful lot of WPA workers to join our union. The main organizers were the men who were digging in the streets and the women who worked on the canning projects. We had regular meetings and we had all kinds of projects. We had library projects.

There wasn't office space in the main building for the library project I was working on at the time, so we were put in the building that housed the water department facilities of the city . . .

Local 12 brought in the unemployed people that had almost lost hope. The politicians were taking away milk from the children, instead of giving them more milk which they should have been doing. And they wouldn't give any surplus food to the hungry people. Homes were being repossessed and they were taking the women and children and putting them into one big shelter with the men in another. They were actually splitting up families. They would set furniture out in the street, but we had crews that would set the furniture back in and try to protect it. That became a lot of hard labor without any results so we started organizing big demonstrations. We would burn an effigy of the relief manager, the head of the welfare department, and we'd give out statements.

We finally decided to let the whole city of Flint know what was happening. We had a demonstration and announced that we would hold a "Death Watch." If they were going to do these things to the poor people in Flint, then let everybody see it.

Across from the welfare building there was a big park with a lot of beautiful trees. This park also happened to be across from one end of Buick Motor Car Company, which was rehiring workers to go into automobile production after the 1937 recession.

We put big signs up on each corner of the park inviting the public to come out to see poor people with hungry, starving children—to watch people die. We had whole families down there in great big army tents that we had procured. And we tapped into the street wires so that they had electricity at night in their tents.

Mothers were down there washing out diapers in tubs and hanging them up on ropes we strung between the trees. They built fires in large oil drums to keep warm and to heat water. They would cook their meals out there and heat their water to wash clothes and bathe their babies. They were really living out in public.

People came down to see what was happening. Great big signs on each corner of the park said, "This is the Death Watch" and "If you want to see people in the city of Flint die, here they are." That shook up a lot of people. You'd see cars driving around slowly to view what was happening. This was very bad publicity for the city. It hit the state capital and finally it hit Washington. Washington opened up surplus food to the people in Flint who were on the relief rolls. And they stopped separating families when they repossessed their homes . . .

Unemployed people were inspired by factory workers who had won a union, and they came down to the union meetings which became quite exciting, quite dramatic. They would get up and speak for the first time. Unemployed people found their voice and their strength. It was a wonderful experience, not only for the people that helped, but for the people who were doing it—for everybody.

It is the hardest thing in the world to organize the unemployed. They need strong backing. The strongest backing comes from the established unions, especially those who've had success in a strike. They feel that they have power. Once you see that in a worker or a number of workers, it's something you don't forget. They've been changed from people who have been kept down constantly to people who feel they have strength. They have knowledge and the ability to make changes. Before that, they'd only see the overpowering bureaucracy of the union and the overpowering bureaucracy of the government over their heads constantly with police and badges all around them. But when they have a great victory in a labor struggle, then they begin to feel that they are just as powerful and strong as their opponents.

That's the way that socialism will come in this country—when workers realize that they do have the numbers and the strength and the talents and the abilities. All of the creative things that workers come up with in a strike are usually original, because it pertains to the situation you are in right at that moment. You'll have people offering one suggestion after another, and they will discuss it together. The organizing process is very inspirational.

SELECTION 3:
UNITY OF BLACK AND WHITE WORKERS

Black workers did not generally participate in organizing the union. They used to say at our Socialist Party headquarters, "It's bad enough being Black without being Red, too." You had to understand that they had nobody, not even any White union people, that would fight for them if they were fired. Racial prejudice was so pervasive. Many workers had come up recently from the deep south thinking that Blacks should get off the sidewalk when they passed by. We couldn't eat in the same restaurants. Blacks just wouldn't be served in any restaurant in Flint.

Out of 12,000 workers employed by Chevrolet, only 400 were Black. Fisher 1, Fisher 2, Chevrolet, all ten plants of Chevrolet, hired only White men on production. Black men were allowed to work only in the foundry of Buick and as sanitation workers, cleaning up the men's toilets in the other plants. Black men had no hope of ever getting a raise or getting a job promotion . . .

Conditions for Black workers improved greatly after the strike. Oh, yes! They were now in the union, of course, and they could begin to afford to own their own homes, buying them at so much a month. They took great pride in what had been accomplished by the strikers. Their sympathies were with us all of the time.

For White workers from the recent south, racism was something that was very strong. They had nasty attitudes like, "You wouldn't want to get too close to them. Your daughter might marry one." You heard it all the time. We socialists kept on educating and writing articles in the union paper and doing everything that we could to argue against racism. Certainly, all the socialist auto workers had the right understanding. The success of the union eased things for Blacks but racism was still there. That was the hardest struggle of all.

The only viable anti-racist organization in Flint at the time was the NAACP, and that was not a militant organization nationally—ever. But we formed a NAACP chapter in Flint that became very militant.

We threw out the president, the one they called "the downtown man" because he would go and report everything downtown. We threw him out and elected Edgar Holt, a Black Buick worker who was a graduate of Wilberforce University, to be president. He was a good orator with a wonderful personality—a very inspiring man.

When the city council voted down the Fair Employment Practices Commission, we organized a mock funeral with a casket in a hearse. A black minister in his robe marched with casket bearers wearing white gloves. This funeral procession wound through the city of Flint to stop at the bridge of the Flint River. We took the casket out, proclaimed "The burial of FEPC," and tossed the casket over the bridge into the river. Then the minister gave a long sermon using a loudspeaker . . .

I became very active as a leader of the NAACP following the strike. We always dramatized the actions we organized so we'd get a lot of publicity. Otherwise, it was the policy of a company town like Flint to keep everything quiet. There was no news coverage of working class people's lives, of what they were doing or thinking, and so you had to be dramatic to get attention.

SELECTION 4:
UNDERSTANDING OUR HISTORY PREPARES US FOR THE FUTURE

I think our duty today is to educate all of those who do not understand that they got their present benefits and their present standard of living from organized labor. We have to tell the story of people who suffered and died for the cause of labor. We have to teach people the history of the labor movement, and we have to tell the story that women played, so that women can be encouraged to play more of a role today.

We have won some wonderful economic advantages for working people in this country. But they are slowly being legislated away from us. Now, we've got to fight on the political level. We have to organize politically with the same intensity that we had when we began to organize the unions.

Today, most unions have a bureaucratic leadership that does little for working people and keeps them in a state of apathy. As soon as Walter Reuther found the back door to the White House so he could go in and talk to the President, he was more concerned about what the big politicals and the corporation owners said than his own members—his own members!

Right after the strike, they did away with the stewards collecting union dues on the job. Walter Reuther wanted to have money coming in regularly through an automatic dues check-off system. It was supposed to be more efficient and guarantee that in case of a strike the International Union had the funds available to help in any part of the country. But as soon as they got the regular dues coming in, you know what the bureaucrats did? They were secure, so they made all the decisions and that made the union less democratic.

We fought against this change because we thought it was better to keep the union leadership accountable to the members. Under the old system workers had some power over their leaders. They could say, "I want this done and I want that done and here's my dues." So the leadership had to deliver if they wanted the dues to come in regularly.

At the beginning of the strike, Walter Reuther said no labor leader should get paid more than the highest paid worker in the industry. But he soon forgot those words. He started living a very comfortable life, and he spent a lot of the union's money without talking to the members about it. He built a very beautiful camp at Black Lake with some of that money.

That camp is supposed to be an educational facility, but they don't want radicals in there giving workers the real solution to the problems of people in general and working class people especially. That is socialism, social ownership of the means of production. That is the way to stop the ruling class from dominating humanity, and for working people to achieve their liberation.

Cesar Chavez.

CHAPTER 15

CESAR CHAVEZ

Cesar Chavez (1927–1993) was born in Yuma, Arizona, the second of five children in a close-knit, Mexican–American family. His parents owned a small farm which—due to unpaid bills in the Great Depression—was lost when Chavez was twelve years old. Compelled to become migrant farm workers, the family faced conditions in many ways similar to those movingly documented in John Steinbeck's novel *The Grapes of Wrath*, but in important ways the conditions were different—especially owing to the deeply rooted racism facing Mexican–Americans (Chicanos), Filipinos, and other people of color working in the Western and West Coast fields, vineyards, and orchards. As one biographer notes, however, an awareness of class developed as "Chavez quickly learned that Chicano labor contractors and Japanese growers exploited migrants as readily as did Anglo employers."

In 1943, Chavez's parents decided to make a permanent home in Delano, California, but desperate "to get away from farm labor," he joined the Navy for two years ("the worst of my life"). He returned to Delano in 1946, found work as a farm worker, and married in 1948. In 1952, he got a more secure job in a San Jose lumberyard. At this point, he met activist priest Father Donald McDonnell and veteran community organizer Frank Ross of the Community Service Organization, a self-help group operated under the sponsorship of Saul Alinsky's Chicago-based Industrial Areas Foundation, a semi-radical institute dedicated to community organizing.

Drawn into CSO activities, Chavez's talents were quickly recognized, and he was offered a staff position. Employed by the organization for ten years, he rose to the national position of general director. But he came to feel, according to one sympathetic writer, that, "the CSO was veering too far from its radical origins, that it was attracting too many middle-class professional people— doctors, lawyers, politicians, more interested in the prestige of the organization than mobilizing the poor." When his long-incubating proposal to begin organizing a farm workers' union was turned down at a 1962 convention, he left the CSO to create the National Farm Workers Association (NFWA).

The NFWA was sustained by a core group that included Chavez family members, CSO veterans, Protestant clergy associated with the California Migrant Ministry, Catholic activists, independent secular radicals, and some of the bolder spirits among the farm workers themselves. Chavez was insistent that the NFWA must, at least initially, remain independent of the mainstream of the labor movement, which he felt was too routinist and bureaucratic to offer effective leadership in the new work of organizing agricultural workers. A strong flavor of 1960s radicalism, inspiration from the civil rights movement led by Martin Luther King, Jr., Catholic social doctrine, Mexican culture, and the teachings of Mahatma Gandhi blended together in what was characterized by many as "more of a social cause than a union."

After winning strikes in the mid 1960s, followed by an effective national grape boycott that finally forced the growers to the bargaining table, the NFWA joined with the predominantly Filipino Agricultural Workers Organizing Committee to form the AFL–CIO-affiliated United Farm Workers Organizing Committee, which in 1972 became the United Farm Workers of America, AFL–CIO.

Yet powerful and arrogant agricultural corporations were determined to maintain immense profits through the most brutal exploitation, and they were helped by courts and police and unfair laws (as agricultural workers had been systematically excluded from protections extended to most other workers under the Wagner Act and other labor legislation). The corrupted leadership of the Teamsters Union made an alliance with the growers to secure "sweet-heart" contracts at the expense of Chavez's "radical outfit." The growers also had good friends in President Nixon and Governor Reagan. Red-baiting, intimidation, dirty tricks, and violence were all part of the well-orchestrated anti-UFW program, which succeeded in pushing back vital gains of Chavez and his followers.

Mass demonstrations and rallies, civil disobedience, religious mobilizations, widespread educational and publicity efforts, nationwide boycotts of lettuce and (once again) grapes, assisted by hundreds of support committees in cities throughout the nation (sustained by a broad alliance of student activists, church people, liberal and radical groups, and labor activists) all supplemented the more traditional union activities: steady organizing efforts among farm workers, work stoppages, picket lines—and powerful solidarity from other unions. Under the impact of all this pressure, a number of important things were finally accomplished: legislation was passed in California that extended union protections to farm workers; the Teamsters leadership pulled back from the anti-UFW campaign; and growers showed a greater inclination to seek compromise. "*La Causa*" not only won important improvements that changed the lives of farm workers, but it also suggested new directions for the union movement, consistent with the social idealism that had predominated in earlier periods of U.S. labor history.

As with every major labor figure and organization, Cesar Chavez and the UFW were by no means free from imperfections, contradictions, and limitations. Critics have commented on an over-reliance on Democratic Party politicians, also emphasizing the failure of the UFWA to secure a substantial base outside of California. Some have criticized Chavez for promoting a "personality cult," which prevented the development of democratic structures and drove away loyal dissidents, and which contributed to the union's dramatic decline after Chavez's premature death in 1993.

Yet no one can deny the immense accomplishment of Chavez and those around him in doing what had never been done before, building, for a time, a durable union among super-exploited agricultural workers where many had concluded, after many bitter experiences, that it would be impossible to build one. The reflections on experiences, far-reaching insights, and enduring vision, provided in the selections that follow, constitute a rich legacy, not only for future farm workers' struggles, but also for the revitalization of the labor movement.

Sources for Biographical Sketch

Cletus E. Daniel, "Cesar Chavez and the Unionization of California Farm Workers," in Melvyn Dubofsky and Warren Van Tine, eds., *Labor Leaders in America* (Urbana: University of Illinois Press, 1987).

John Gregory Dunne, *Delano* (New York: Farrar, Strauss & Giroux, 1971).

Miriam Pawel, *The Union of Their Dreams: Power, Hope, and Struggle in Cesar Chavez's Farm Worker Movement* (New York: Bloomsbury Press, 2009).

Sources for Selections

All can be found in Jacques Levy, *Cesar Chavez, Autobiography of La Causa* (New York: W. W. Norton and Co., 1975): selection 1 pp. 4–5; selection 2 pp. 109–111; selection 3 pp. 150, 153, 154–155; selection 4 p. 160; selection 5 pp. 269–270, 271; selection 6 pp. 520–521; selection 7 pp. 536–539.

Reprinted with permission from University of Minnesta Press.

SELECTION 1:
COMMITMENT, COMMUNITY, AND UNION-BUILDING

I saw the trap most people get themselves into—tying themselves to a job for security. It was easier for us and our family to try to escape poverty than to change the conditions that keep so many workers poor. But we inherited the poverty from our fathers and our fathers from our grandfathers and our grandfathers from their grandfathers. We had to stop someplace! . . .

So I resigned my job and set out to found a union. At first I was frightened, very frightened. But by the time I missed the fourth paycheck and found things were still going, that the moon was still there and the sky and the flowers, I began to laugh. I really began to feel free. It was one of my biggest triumphs in terms of finding myself and of being able to discipline myself.

After all, if you're outraged at conditions, then you can't possibly be free or happy until you devote all your time to changing them and do nothing but that. The affluence in this country is our biggest trap, because we can't change anything if we want to hold on to a good job, a good way of life, and avoid sacrifice.

We began to do away with a lot of little things we thought we just had to have, things we really did not need. We began to get that commitment, that gut commitment—"all right, then, this sacrifice won't be for nothing. I made it for six months, nothing will stop me now." Then we began to build a community, we began to build what would become the Union.

Today I don't think our members are going to stop just at building a farm workers' union. In the course of that accomplishment other things are beginning to be revealed to them, not through me, but through the experience of living. I've heard them say, "We're not going to get paychecks. We're willing to put ourselves with our families on the line! Let's go!" You can't stop people like that. They can change the world.

SELECTION 2:
ORGANIZING TECHNIQUES AND BUILDING THE NUCLEUS OF A UNION

I soon realized that you can't do anything by talking, that you can't do anything if you haven't got the power. I realized that the first time I went to a public office to do battle . . .

I always have had, and I guess I always will have, a firm belief that if you muster enough power, you can move things, but it's all on the basis of power. Now I seldom like to go see my opponent unless I have some power over him. I'll wait if it takes all my life. And the only way you can generate power is by doing a lot of work.

It's unfortunate that power is needed to get justice. That suggests a lot about the nature of man. And we also must guard against too much power, because power corrupts, but that was not one of our problems then . . .

We wanted to build power within the community in order to solve some of its problems . . .

Since I had the inclination and the training, helping people came naturally. I wasn't thinking in terms of organizing members, but just a duty I had to do . . .

Well, one night it just hit me. Once you helped people, most became very loyal. The people who helped us back when we wanted volunteers were the people we had helped. So I began to get a group of people around me.

Once I realized helping people was an organizing technique, I increased that work. I was willing to work night and day and night and go to hell and back for people—provided they also did something for [the Union] in return. I never felt bad asking people for that ... because I wasn't asking for something for myself.

For a long time we didn't know how to put that work together into an organization. But we learned after a while—we learned how to help people by making them responsible ... We don't get everybody, but we get enough to get that nucleus. I think solving problems for people is the only way to build solid groups.

SELECTION 3:
LEARNING FROM THE HISTORY OF WORKING-CLASS STRUGGLE

In the past 125 years or more, the farm workers' struggles to organize have been smashed repeatedly by the power of agribusiness. It is a story that should be told—how hundreds of strikes were broken, and everyone destroyed up until now. It's been nothing but a record of defeat after defeat.

The power of the growers was backed by the power of the police, the courts, state and federal laws, and the financial power of the big corporations, the banks, and the utilities.

The first strikes by American Indians more than 120 years ago were called uprisings and put down by the army; not too long ago Governor Reagan referred to one of our strikes as an uprising and threatened to call out the national guard.

Since the start of this century, many unions were involved—the Industrial Workers of the World, or Wobblies, as their members were called; the United Cannery, Agricultural, Packing and Allied Workers of America; the United Packinghouse Workers of America; the Food, Tobacco and Agricultural Workers Union; the AFL; the CIO; and the Teamsters, to name a few. But the power was stacked against them, and it still is ...

Many of the workers who were involved in those earlier strikes are pretty old now; we should get their stories. All of them contributed to what is happening to us. Those are our saints, yet we don't even know who many of them are. I see their stories as crucially important to give us a sense of perspective, of history. There's a lot that is hidden, that is just in the heads and hearts of people. But many are already dead ...

It's from the strikes of others that I've learned some very simple but meaningful things, very basic things, that have to be taken care of if you're going to exist. I learned that all strikes are decided in the first few weeks. In nearly all cases, the strike was broken in the first eight to thirteen days. A good strike can last about ten days with the emotion and the outrage, but from there on, it's just hard to pull. It becomes a lot of hard work.

Some organizers felt, too, that they couldn't organize unless they struck at the same time. That was a big mistake. The first decision we made was that there would be no strikes until we'd organized first. The concept of organizing a union without getting a contract didn't occur to earlier organizers.

Of course, they didn't have much of a chance anyhow, the power was so stacked against them. Besides terror and violence, the power of agribusiness is clear in the history of labor law in our country [that has excluded farm workers from laws beneficial to organized labor] . . .

SELECTION 4:
FLEXIBILITY AND ORGANIZING

It's very difficult I guess to capture the feeling of organizing in a book. I haven't seen a book yet that accurately describes the inside of a guy, how he feels about the conditions, what it's like to be an organizer. I guess it's because there are about a thousand things happening at the same time, so many that you couldn't possibly cover everything and make it readable.

It's not at all dramatic. It's long and drawn out. Most of it is anticipation. The victories come much later.

When we came to Delano, we said, "We're going to organize farm workers. We don't know how, but we have some ideas. We don't have anything planned because even life itself can't be planned, and we're dealing with a lot of lives, we're dealing with human beings."

In organizing, you don't have a detailed plan, like a Farm Worker Organizing Master Plan. It doesn't work that way. You can't say that if you take steps one, two, and three, then everything follows. That would be predicting human nature. No one can do that.

There are guidelines and there are certain inescapables that you must meet, and then you build around that. But you don't know, for instance, that tomorrow you can have three hundred people at a certain meeting. You just don't know.

And you can't organize by fluttering all over the place or being flighty. That's the worst thing you can do. You must stay with one thing and just hammer away, hammer away, and it will happen . . .

SELECTION 5:
NON-VIOLENCE AS A PRACTICAL TOOL FOR STRATEGY AND ORGANIZING

To us the boycott of grapes was the most near-perfect of non-violent struggles, because non-violence also requires mass involvement. The boycott demonstrated to the whole country, the whole world, what people can do by non-violent action.

Non-violence in the abstract is a very difficult thing to comprehend or explain. I'd read a lot, but all of it was in the abstract. It's difficult to carry the message to people who aren't involved. Non-violence must be explained in context.

People equate non-violence with inaction—with not doing anything—and it's not that at all. It's exactly the opposite.

In his autobiography, Malcolm X said, "I believe it's a crime for anyone who is being brutalized to continue to accept that brutality without doing something to defend himself. If that's how Christian philosophy is interpreted, if that's what Gandhian philosophy teaches, well then I will call them criminal philosophies."

But Gandhi never said not to do anything. He said exactly the opposite. He said, "Do something! Offer your life!" He said, "If you really want to do something, be willing to die for it." That's asking for the maximum contribution.

Often only talk results when a person with social concern wants to do something for the underdog non-violently. But just talking about change is not going to bring it about. Talk just gives people an out. Generally what happens is that people will study non-violently, read books, go to seminars where they discuss non-violence, and attend endless meetings. In most cases, they find some satisfaction in this and think they somehow are accomplishing something. But all the while, and right across town, the pot is brewing.

Non-violence is action. Like anything else, though, it's got to be organized. There must be rules. There must be people following.

The whole essence of non-violent action is getting a lot of people involved, vast numbers doing little things. It's difficult to get people involved in a picket line, because it takes their time. But a person can be persuaded not to eat a grape–and we persuaded millions not to eat grapes—that's involvement, that's the most direct action, and it's set up in such a way that everybody can participate.

Non-violence also has one big demand—the need to be creative, to develop strategy. Gandhi described it as a moral jujitsu. Always hit the opposition off balance, but keep your principles . . .

By and large, people oppose violence. So when government or growers use violence against us, we strategize around it. We can respond non-violently, because that swings people to our side, and that gives us strength.

First, of course, the workers have to understand non-violence. Gandhi once said he'd rather have a man be violent than be a coward. I agree. If he's a coward, then what good is he for anyone? But it is our job to see he's not a coward. That's really the beginning point of our training.

And while the philosophy of non-violence covers physical, verbal, and moral behavior, we haven't achieved that goal. If we can achieve it, we're saints—which we're not. We're still working on eliminating physical violence, though that isn't all, by any stretch of the imagination. After workers begin to understand physical non-violence among people, then we also apply it to property and go on from there.

SELECTION 6:
KEEPING THE UNION ALIVE AND VITAL

We're confident—not overconfident. It's just a matter of doing what we've always done since we started the Movement, working very hard and not giving up and doing the work that must be done to win.

But if we're not careful, we can begin to misunderstand and mismanage the whole idea of the trust that the workers have given us to lead and direct and administer and wrestle with the problems that we've had.

I've learned two very big things that I knew and had forgotten. The same methods that we used to build a Union, very effective in the beginning, still apply today and much more so. We thought because we had contracts that there were other things we could do. But I'm convinced we can't. We've got to do exactly when we did back in 1962, 1963, 1964. We must go back to the origins of the Union and do service-center work. The contracts are no substitute for the basic help we provide workers in all aspects of their lives. In some cases we thought that this work didn't deal with what we consider to be trade union business. But they deal very directly with human problems.

The second thing I know from experience is that, whenever a critical situation hits us, the best source of power, the best source of hope, is straight from the people. It's happened to me so often.

There's a Mexican *dicho* that says there's always a good reason why bad news comes. And I think that in our case probably this will save the Union. I think that we were making a terrible mistake in the direction of the Union. We were isolating ourselves from the workers.

When I'm out with the workers, they teach me every single day. It's an amazing thing. Obviously I don't know everything, I just know a little bit. Perhaps because I've made more mistakes than anybody else, I've had a chance to learn more than anybody else. But still, the workers teach me every single day as I teach them.

What happens is that in most unions and most societies—be it the church, politics, or whatever—there is a tremendous pull away from people and into paper work and into direction at the top away from people.

The power came from the people, but no sooner is that power acquired than the man who got the power begins to isolate himself from people. There is so much competition for his time that the workers lose out, sometimes even with their consent.

And in our present struggle, we must organize not only among farm workers but also among consumers. So we are pulled by two constituencies, and we must remain in contact with both.

SELECTION 7:
LOOKING AHEAD

Once we have reached our goal and have farm workers protected by contracts, we must continue to keep our members involved. The only way is to continue struggling. It's just like plateaus. We get a Union, then we want to struggle for something else. The moment we sit down and rest on our laurels, we're in trouble.

Once we get contracts and good wages, we know the tendency will be for the majority to lose interest, unless the Union is threatened or a contract is being renegotiated. The tendency will be for just a few to remain active and involved, while everybody else just holds out until something very big happens. That's true of other unions that we've seen; that's true of other institutions; that's true of our country.

To avoid that, to keep people's attention and continuing interest, we've got to expand and get them involved in other things. The Union must touch them daily.

Our best education, the most lasting, has been out on the picket line. But when the initial membership gets old and dies off, the new people coming in won't have had the same experience of building a Union. So we must get them involved in other necessary struggles.

Poor people are going to be poor for a long time to come, even though we have contracts, and economic action is an exciting thing for them. If they see an alternative, they will follow it. And we've probably got now the best organization of any poor people in all the country. That's why we can go any place in California where there are farm workers and get a whole group of people together and in action. We are hitting at the real core problems.

After we've got the contracts, we have to build more clinics and co-ops, and we've got to resolve the whole question of mechanization. That can become a great issue, not fighting the machines, but working out a program ahead of time so the workers benefit.

Then there's the whole question of political action, so much political work to be done taking care of all the grievances that people have, such as the discrimination their kids face in school, and the whole problem of the police. I don't see why we can't exchange those cops who treat us the way they do for good, decent human beings like farm workers. Or why there couldn't be any farm worker judges.

We have to participate in the governing of towns and school boards. We have to make our influence felt everywhere and anywhere. It's a long struggle that we're just beginning, but it can be done because the people want it.

To get it done, there's a lot of construction work needed with our members. Many are not citizens, and others are not registered to vote. We must work toward the day when a majority of them are citizens with a vote.

But political power alone is not enough. Although I've been at it some twenty years, all the time and the money and effort haven't brought about any significant change whatsoever. Effective political power is never going to come, particularly to minority groups, unless they have economic power. And however poor they are, even the poor people can organize economic power.

Political power by itself, as we've tried to fathom it and to fashion it, is like having a car that doesn't have any motor in it. It's like striking a match that goes out. Economic power is like having a generator to keep that bulb burning all the time. So we have to develop economic power to assure a continuation of political power.

I'm not advocating black capitalism or brown capitalism. At the worst it gets a black to exploit other blacks, or a brown to exploit others. At the best, it only helps the lives of a few. What I'm suggesting is a cooperative movement . . .

As a continuation of our struggle, I think that we can develop economic power and put it into the hands of the people so they can have more control of their own lives, and then begin to change the system. We want radical change. Nothing short of radical change is going to have any impact on our lives or our problems. We want sufficient power to control our own destinies. This is our struggle. It's a lifetime job. The work for social change and against social injustice is never ended . . .

Once I was giving a talk in Monterey about the Christian doctrine. When I got through, one man came back and said, "It's very radical, very socialistic."

I didn't say anything but was convinced that it was very Christian. That's my interpretation. I didn't think it was so much political or economic.

Actually, I can't see where the poor have fared that well under any political or economic system. But I think some power has to come to them so they can manage their lives. I don't care what system it is, it's not going to work if they don't have the power.

That's why if we make democracy work, I'm convinced that's by far the best system. And it will work if people want it to. But to make it work for the poor, we have to work at it full time. And we have to be willing to just give up everything and risk it all . . .

Fighting for social justice, it seems to me, is one of the profoundest ways in which man can say yes to man's dignity, and that really means sacrifice. There is no way on this earth in which you can say yes to man's dignity and know that you're going to be spared some sacrifice.

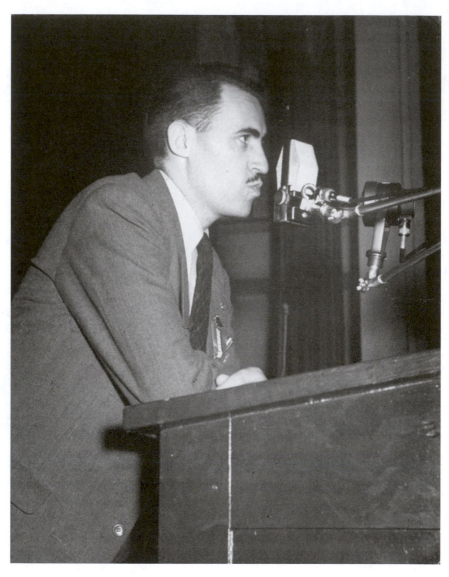

James Matles.

CHAPTER 16

JAMES MATLES

James Matles (1909–1975) was born Eichel Matlis Fridman in Rumania, of Jewish working-class parents, his name quickly becoming "Americanized" —as was the case with so many immigrants—upon his arrival in the United States in 1923. The young worker soon became involved in left-wing labor activity in the Metal Workers Industrial Union, affiliated with the Trade Union Unity League (TUUL). This had been organized to compete with the narrower and relatively ineffectual craft unions of the AFL.

Matles's energy and talents attracted the attention and mentorship of seasoned Communist labor organizer William Z. Foster, and he soon rose to key leadership positions in the TUUL. By 1934, however, Matles's union had evolved into a radical component of the International Association of Machinists inside the AFL—in the explosive year that saw general strikes of industrial workers in Minneapolis, Toledo, and San Francisco, bringing on the nationwide upsurge of industrial organizing.

Upon his death, *Time* magazine (unrelentingly anti-communist, pro-business newsweekly that it was) wrote a surprisingly positive obituary of James Matles, seeking to sum up how Matles's life story played out:

> When John L. Lewis set up the Congress of Industrial Organizations in 1935, Matles practically singlehanded converted his AFL-affiliated colleagues in the International Association of Machinists into a new union, which he called the United Electrical, Radio and Machine Workers of America. Under that umbrella name, it became one of the CIO's most influential arms. As director of organization for the U.E., Matles gained a reputation as a left-leaning leader as well as an articulate, precise negotiator. In 1949 the U.E. was ousted from the anti-Communist CIO, and Matles was briefly deprived of his U.S.

citizenship by a federal judge in 1957 on the ground that he had lied about his Communist ties when applying for naturalization more than 20 years earlier. The case went to the Supreme Court, where the decision was overturned. For three decades, Matles was a major force in shaping labor policy in the United States.

As was all too often the case with such newsweeklies, some of the facts were garbled. When the United Electrical workers (UE) was established in 1936, this was the work of Julius Emspak, James Carey, and others—Matles bringing his group of dissident machinists into the UE in 1937. In what he called "the dirty years" of the 1950s, Matles was never actually deprived of his citizenship. The effort to do this, in the intense period of Cold War anti-communism, was part of a government legal onslaught targeting the UE—and, like the other cases, it was simply dropped in the late 1950s, as Supreme Court decisions upheld civil liberties promised in the Bill of Rights.

Under the leadership of organizing director Matles, secretary-treasurer Emspak, and president Carey (replaced in 1940 by Albert Fitzgerald), UE membership rose from 33,000 in 1936 to more than 600,000 in 1947. It was one of the top three in the CIO. According to critical labor historian Robert Zieger, "the overall record of Communist-influenced unions with respect to collective bargaining, contract content and administration, internal democracy, and honest and effective governance was good." He cites UE in particular as "notable for fair and efficient administration, innovative cultural and educational programs, and positive responses to the distinctive problems of minority and female workers." One of the fiercest opponents of the UE's left-wing leadership in the 1940s, Monsignor Charles Owen Rice, later reflected that Matles and those around him were "good organizers technically and in terms of spirit, aggressiveness, and courage," and that "for the most part on the right side of battles legislative and social," they were also "good trade unionists . . . financially honest and dedicated."

With the hardening of the Cold-War confrontation between the United States and the USSR in the post-World War II years, and an accompanying tidal wave of anti-communism sweeping the U.S. political scene, the fortunes of UE and other left-wing unions in the CIO changed dramatically. By 1950, they had all been forced out of the CIO and were battered by intensified employer and government attacks. The UE was raided over and over again by a newly established anti-communist CIO affiliate, the International Union of Electrical workers (IUE), and other rival unions.

Unlike most of the other unions expelled by the CIO, however, the UE survived, with 150,000 members and a relatively high degree of morale. Ironically, while denounced as a "Communist union," the UE leadership indignantly rejected the Communist Party perspective, in the mid 1950s, that the UE should dissolve in order to allow its members to re-enter "labor's mainstream" in the unified AFL–CIO—an approach that resulted in membership losses. By the mid 1950s, UE membership stood at 75,000, but the increasingly dramatic decline of U.S. industry would further deplete its ranks to about 40,000 by the 1990s.

Director of organization for many years, Matles shifted to the position of secretary-treasurer upon the death of Julius Emspak in 1962. As the writings and speeches presented here indicate, he was tireless in his efforts to promote his vision of a radical "rank and file unionism" and an elemental class-consciousness. "A legendary workaholic who personified UE's principles of frugality and a spartan lifestyle," one union staffer recounted, "his plan after his formal retirement had been to continue working for the union, training staff and local officers, but without accepting any pay beyond his pension and Social Security." A few days after announcing his retirement and seeing his successor elected, he died of a massive heart attack.

The obvious desire of this lifelong labor radical to pass on insights from many years of struggle, with an explicit awareness of being part of a tradition going all the way back to the beginnings of U.S. working-class experience, makes it an appropriate conclusion for this volume.

Sources for Biographical Sketch

Ronald L. Filippelli and Mark D. McColloch, *Cold War in the Working Class: The Rise and Decline of the United Electrical Workers* (Albany, NY: State University of New York Press, 1995).

James J. Matles and James Higgins, *Them and Us: Struggles of a Rank-and-File Union* (Englewood Cliffs, NJ: Prentice Hall, 1974).

Notes to the author from Al Hart, editor of *UE News*.

Time magazine, September 29, 1975.

Robert H. Zieger, *The CIO, 1935–1955* (Chapel Hill, NC: University of North Carolina Press, 1995).

Sources for Selections

Section 1: James J. Matles and James Higgins, *Them and Us: Struggles of a Rank-and-File Union* (Englewood Cliffs, NJ: Prentice Hall, 1974), pp. 301–304.

Section 2: James J. Matles, *The Role of Labor Today: Reflections on the Past Throw Light on the Road Ahead* [speech from 1975], pamphlet (United Electrical, Radio and Machine Workers of America), pp. 5–6.

Section 3: Albert J. Fitzgerald and James J. Matles, *A Little Bit of UE History You Should Know*, pamphlet (New York: UE, 1968), pp. 14–19.

Section 4: James J. Matles, *Leadership Guide to UE Contract Negotiations*, pamphlet (New York: UE, approximately 1971), pp. 4–6, 9–10.

SELECTION 1:
LEARNING FROM THE RISE OF THE CIO (1974)

In the spring of 1972 old-timer Wobbly and UE Local 107 leader, John Schaefer, now retired after forty-two years on the job as a skilled pipefitter in the Westinghouse turbine works of South Philadelphia, sat with a few old UE friends in the living room of his home, where many a group had gathered for discussion over these years. The union friends were discussing the impact upon the labor movement of the changing composition of workers in the shops, among whom were many young workers of different backgrounds and temperaments.

In 1971 the members of traditionally militant UE Local 107 had concluded the third strike for a new contract in thirty-seven years of the local's existence. It lasted five and a half months, reminiscent of the historic 1955–56 ten-month struggle. "Johnny," one of the group observed, "the young fellows shaped up pretty good in the strike last year."

"Pretty good on the whole," said Schaefer. "Pretty solid." His wife, Maggie, thought that was an understatement. "Now Schaefer," she said, "they were as militant as the people in 1955. Not a single scab in five and a half months." Schaefer agreed that was true. "They've got militancy, the young fellows," he said. "No question about it. The militancy was there. But have they got the working class consciousness?" Schafer continued:

> Some teaching and learning has to be going on in working class prin-
> ciples, some study of past struggles. Reading about them, discussing
> them, picking up from there the principles for conducting recent
> struggles. And I'm not sure the rank-and-file, militant as it is, is
> getting that kind of education nowadays. I may be wrong. But from
> where I sit, I don't see much of it.

... The history of the labor movement shows that over and over again American workers have conducted struggles on the industrial front as fierce and determined as those in which workers anywhere on earth have engaged. Nevertheless ... class-consciousness has been slow in its growth. One measure of its low level could be found in the fact that even after one hundred years of working people's struggles in the United States, it remained the only industrialized country where no labor party had been organized. The most politically powerful and class-conscious corporate class in the world had managed to keep the working class tied to the long-established political system dominated by two major [pro-capitalist] parties.

Eugene V. Debs once observed:

> Ten thousand times has the labor movement stumbled and fallen
> and bruised itself and risen again; been seized by the throat and

choked into insensibility; enjoined by the courts, assaulted by thugs, charged by the militia, shot down by regulars, frowned upon by public opinion, deceived by politicians, threatened by priests, repudiated by renegades, preyed upon by grafters, infested by spies, deserted by cowards, betrayed by traitors, bled by leeches, and sold out by leaders. But notwithstanding all this, and all these, it is today the most vital and potential power this planet has ever known.

In the first half of the twentieth century more than thirty years of labor movement struggle took place, with advances and setbacks, before conditions prepared the ground for the rise of industrial unionism which Debs, among others, had foreseen as natural evolution. During those years a great world war, and all-out corporate assault on the American labor movement, and a vast economic depression in the United States—throwing millions out of work and shaking the corporate [capitalist] system to its depths—created conditions for a rebellion by working people. This rebellion assumed the form of a movement to organize the unorganized in mass production industry. CIO industrial unionism was born.

The leadership for such unionism emerged from the rank-and-file in the auto industry, steel, electric manufacturing, the machine industry, the rubber, glass, oil and chemical industries; from among the metal miners, longshoremen, the seamen, the transport workers, and from shops and plants all over the country. Most of them were young leaders. The movement had impact on the established leaders of the AFL. The old guard dug in to resist industrial unionism. Other AFL leaders, while not changing long-established policies and methods of running their own unions, recognized and accepted the challenge for the organization of the mass production industries.

They threw the energies, the resources, the manpower of their unions into the fight. They provided the indispensable element of their own experienced trade union leadership to the new movement, giving the young industrial union leaders not only guidance but full rein to get on with organizing the unorganized. Thus was the American labor movement realigned, strengthened and its membership increased by millions.

The CIO objective of the 1930s—to implant industrial unionism in the shops of mass production—had been achieved. But the drive toward long-range objectives—organizing the millions of workers still unorganized, developing a strong independent political movement, redistributing the national wealth and income—was derailed by the corporate anti-labor offensive conducted during a quarter-century of cold and hot war. In the seventies, then, these objectives still remain to be won.

The ground for historic changes in the American labor movement which make possible the realization of important objectives has always been prepared by the pressures which the corporate class exerts upon working people. This powerful class, striving relentlessly for increased productivity and higher profits, brings into being the objective conditions which produce change in the labor movement. Intolerable burdens are imposed upon workers in the shops. Severe economic strain is inflicted upon working-class families.

Labor leadership, new or established, does not create movements. It is the other way around. Seeds for change in the labor movement are sown among rank-and-file workers by conditions forced upon them. It is from this ground, from among these seeds, that new leadership springs to lead the struggle for change.

Selection 2:
A Class-Conscious Perspective on Roosevelt's
New Deal (1975)

When we look back to the Thirties we often think about Franklin D. Roosevelt. We think of FDR sometimes as the savior of our people, the great humanitarian. It is true, Roosevelt was not Tom Girdler of Republic Steel who had the strikers shot down in Chicago. No, FDR was not that kind of a man. He was what you would call a liberal man.

But Franklin D. Roosevelt did represent the corporate interests in America and he knew that the set-up was in trouble. He knew that the policies and actions of Herbert Hoover and Wall Street were running it into the ground. He knew and understood the trouble that was boiling in America and the rebellion that was arising in America and that you couldn't settle it with guns, as Hoover was doing—shooting down the veterans and the hunger marchers.

Roosevelt knew that this system had to make concessions in order to save itself, and he proceeded on a course to do just that, to save the corporate [capitalist] system in America. But most of the bosses were too dumb to realize what he was doing for them. They were too dumb to appreciate it.

But he saved the system. Yes, under the pressure of the millions, he gave ground. He put through some of the outstanding labor and social legislation of our time: the minimum wage and hour law, the Wagner Act, unemployment compensation, social security. Not since those early years of the New Deal have we seen a single gain of special importance to the working people and to the people of America. Not one significant piece of social legislation of the same magnitude.

When the system was saved, they clamped down again.

Yes, we have made progress, the working people have made progress in 40 years. They made progress but for every bit of progress they made they had to drag the system along, kicking and scratching and screaming all the time. Not a single concession was made willingly, no matter what the working people have done for the system, not a single concession.

SELECTION 3:
LEARNING FROM THE DECLINE OF THE CIO (1968)

At the time the CIO was organized in 1936, John L. Lewis was about ten years younger than Walter Reuther is today; Hillman was about twelve years younger than Fitzie is today. They were the old men of the CIO.* They were the ones who put their organizations, their funds and their manpower at the disposal of the unorganized workers in the steel, auto, textile and rubber industries.

Most of us in UE were in our twenties or early thirties. The electrical industry was the only mass production industry that was organized with our own sweat, our own manpower and our own money. What the CIO did for us Young Turks was to turn us loose and give us encouragement and moral backing.

Then we had four years of war, and during the war our unions continued to grow but, of course, we had to operate under different conditions. Our main objective then was to win the war and the CIO put its membership at the disposal of our country. Hundreds of thousands of us answered the President's greetings and the rest of our membership worked back at home to make victory possible.

CIO "Big Three" Strike in 1946

When we came out of that war we picked up where we left off and in January 1946 the labor movement witnessed the greatest demonstration of unity among working people. The Steel Workers, Automobile Workers and Electrical Workers shut down these three largest mass production industries to straighten out accounts with our bosses that we were not able to straighten out during the war.

While the corporations were engaged in war profiteering, we were working and sweating and bleeding. And when the war was over they wanted to just keep going on going the way they had, but we wanted to do something for our people and the greatest strike movement took place in America. The "Big Three" of the CIO got together on the initiative of this Union. Julius Emspak, who was then our Secretary-Treasurer, presented the proposal on behalf of this Union at a meeting of the CIO unions that we ought to go out for a $2.00 a day increase in pay. That was the demand agreed upon by the "Big Three."

---

* John L. Lewis, president of the UMW, was fifty-six years old, and Sidney Hillman, president of the Amalgamated Clothing Workers, was forty-nine years old in 1936, when both became central leaders of the Committee for Industrial Organization, later renamed the Congress of Industrial Organizations. In 1968, UAW President Walter Reuther and UE President Albert J. Fitzgerald were each sixty-one years old—in contrast to many older top labor leaders (such as AFL–CIO President George Meany, who was seventy-four).

The three industries said "No," and the plants and steel mills from California to New England went down. By the time the fight was over, we had scored one of the most impressive victories. We gained 18½ cents an hour and we went back victorious. The first post-war CIO convention took place in Atlantic City in October of 1946, several months after the great strikes.

CIO Leaders Become "Labor Statesmen"

We of UE checked into the convention hotel and, like we always did—I remember as though it were yesterday—Fitz [UE President Albert J. Fitzgerald], Jules [Emspak] and I took $3.50 rooms, and so did the rest of the UE delegation. At the end of the first day of the convention a caucus took place of the Young Turks, the militants in the CIO, from the Transport Workers, N.M.U. [National Maritime Union], Longshoremen, Auto Workers, Mine-Mill and Smelter Workers, and some of the others.

When Fitz, Jules and I went into that caucus we found ourselves in a big, fancy suite and, lo and behold, a bartender rolled in a bar with all the trimmings. I remember Fitz, Jules and I looking at each other in amazement. "Something has happened to us during the war years. Something has surely happened." After the meeting we said to each other that the CIO was losing its spark and losing its drive. We saw a change in our CIO associates. Instead of being organizers and picket line leaders, they talked and acted like "labor statesmen." They were more concerned with what the newspaper editors said about them than what their membership thought about them.

I recall we got up before that Convention and we said that too many CIO leaders were now sitting in swivel chairs, that we have to get out of those swivel chairs and get back to the factory gates or the CIO will go down the drain. We pleaded that we continue the drive to organize the millions of unorganized and to militantly fight for our membership, and the hell with what the newspapers say.

Some of you here will remember that one of our roughest fights during the big GE and Westinghouse strikes took place at the gates of the Philadelphia GE plant where our GE strikers, helped by our Westinghouse strikers from Lester, marched on the GE plant to put on a mass picket line in face of an injunction that forbade mass picketing.

Some of you remember the now nationally famous picture of mounted cops trampling our strikers. Well, a large number of these strikers were arrested and charged with inciting to riot. The trial of these strikers was coming up in Philadelphia while we were at the CIO Convention in Atlantic City.

I left the Convention to take a train to Philadelphia to be in court when the trial opened. I was standing in line at the Penn Railroad Station in Atlantic City to buy my ticket. There were two ticket windows—one for Coach and one for Pullman tickets. As I looked at the Pullman ticket line there was Chick Federoff, Regional Director of the Steelworkers. "Where are you going,

Chick?" I asked. "To Philadelphia," said Chick. "What the hell are you doing on the Pullman line?" Chick looked at me and all of a sudden yelled out, "I forgot, we must get off our swivel chairs and get down to the factory gates. Isn't that what you said yesterday, Jim?" With that he moved over to my line and bought a coach ticket to Philadelphia. The ride was only 1½ hours, but Chick complained all the way to Philadelphia. The seat was hard, the car was dirty and he didn't like it a damn bit. Chick Federoff was now a "labor statesman" and he loved it.

The Employers Drive for Taft–Hartley Law

The employers, when they analyzed what happened to them during the big 1946 strikes and how we came out of those strikes, raised the cry of "Labor Monopoly" and launched a most intensive red-baiting drive to destroy the CIO. The Steelworkers, the Auto Workers and the Electrical Workers, by combining their efforts and striking together for a $2.00 a day raise, were, according to the bosses, committing a crime. They introduced the Taft–Hartley bill in Congress so that never again would we be able to challenge their power.

When the Taft–Hartley bill was introduced, the UE got up before the Executive Board of the CIO and said, "We have to take that fight on right here and now before that bill becomes law." And we proposed the unthinkable. We proposed that the CIO call a general protest strike against that bill to stop its enactment. We couldn't get the support of the CIO; we couldn't get the CIO off its can to make the fight against the Taft–Hartley bill and it became law in June 1947.

Most CIO Unions Succumb to Taft–Hartley

Between June 1947, when Taft–Hartley was enacted, and November 1947, when the CIO Convention took place in Boston, the leaders of the Auto Workers, Textile Workers, and several other CIO unions had caved in and submitted to Taft–Hartley by signing the non-Communist affidavits.

The UE, the Steelworkers, the West Coast Longshoremen, and several smaller CIO unions still held out and abstained from signing the affidavits. In the AFL, most of its leaders willingly rushed to embrace the Taft–Hartley law, but the United Mine Workers, who were then in the AFL, and the Typographical Union of the AFL held out and refused to cave in to the Taft–Hartley Board.

John L. Lewis Raps AFL Leaders for Bowing to Taft–Hartley

While the 1947 CIO Convention was going on in Boston, the AFL Convention was going on in San Francisco at the same time. John L. Lewis stood up before that entire pack of gutless AFL leaders and just ripped the hell out of them for groveling before the Taft–Hartley Board. He said, "I don't think the Federation has a head. I think its neck has just grown up and haired over." Lewis walked out of that Convention and the Mine Workers pulled out of the AFL.

On the same day that Lewis castigated the AFL leadership at the San Francisco convention, we of UE fought to hold the line against Taft–Hartley at the CIO Convention. We warned those who had already caved in that Taft–Hartley is no chow line, and all that labor can get on that line is poison that will kill the CIO. It was the Taft–Hartley issue in 1947 that created the first serious split in the CIO.

UE Protests CIO Dictation of Political Policies

Then came 1948 with a Presidential election. The labor statesmen in the CIO issued an edict to the effect that any union that did not line up behind [Democratic President Harry] Truman was a traitor to the CIO. Fitzgerald and Emspak stood up at the CIO Executive Board meeting and said, "You are not going to dictate to this membership, and you can go to hell." They said that the CIO should not be the tail to any political party, that the CIO has to be an independent force that acts independently politically and doesn't tie itself to any politician or political party that can take the CIO for granted.

That was the second major fight that we had in the CIO.

Some think even up to the present day that our UE Convention endorsed [Progressive Party candidate] Henry Wallace for president. Our Convention did no such thing. There were some among us who individually supported Wallace, but our Convention took the same position in 1948 as we have taken here today on the Presidential election—precisely the same position. No endorsement of any Presidential candidate.

CIO Retaliates With Raid on UE

When the CIO leadership failed to get us to knuckle under, then the raiding started against UE. The Auto Workers and Steelworkers started a concentrated effort to raid UE shops and Locals.

The 1949 UE Convention warned that the CIO, having lost its early militancy, was becoming indistinguishable from the AFL and that there was no room for two AFLs in America—one being too many already. The UE warned that unless the CIO returned to its original militant rank and file policies it would be swallowed up by the AFL and go out of existence.

UE Withdraws From CIO

The UE 1949 Convention demanded an end to raiding and cannibalism in the CIO and, finally, the UE Convention issued an ultimatum to the CIO that unless raiding against the UE stopped forthwith, the UE would stop paying per capita [dues] to the CIO and withdraw.

Following the UE Convention and before the 1949 CIO Convention, the UE General Officers and Vice presidents met with Phil Murray and the CIO leaders and presented the UE Convention demands to them. Murray and the CIO leaders refused to meet the UE demands. The UE General Executive Board met and decided to put the UE Convention decision into effect. We stopped the payment of per capita to the CIO and pulled out. We never went near the CIO Convention. We just told them to go to hell.

AFL–CIO Merger

From 1949 until 1955 the CIO was going down, down, down, until finally no working man in America was able to tell it apart from the AFL, and in 1955, while we were walking the picket lines in Westinghouse during Christmas and New Year's, the AFL and CIO got together for what they called a merger. We said at the time that the merger did not represent any unity of the working people in order to fight for a better life. We said that it was a swallowing-up by the AFL of the CIO and that it was a sad and dark day for American labor.

Politicians, labor leaders, professors, intellectuals and liberals, all of them hailed the merger as a great achievement for labor. Everyone asked us: "Why don't you go in there? How about you? Why don't you get into the mainstream?" And we said, "That stream is polluted and we want no part of it."

I am reciting these historic facts for the many young people in our Union and for the older ones who have forgotten . . .

Selection 4:
Rank and File Unionism

It is our firm position that we would rather have a thousand contract settlements rejected by the rank and file than have a back door sweetheart agreement signed by any union officer without the approval of the rank and file . . . Here we have a rank and file union where never once were demands drawn up or strikes called or strikes called off, or contracts signed without the approval of the membership. Here we have a union with rank and file elected negotiating committees, where people from the shop, assisted by representatives from the International and District negotiate their own contracts. In spite of this we still have some contract settlements that are being rejected by the membership . . .

Trade Union Objectives

First, why do proposed contracts get rejected? In my judgment this is principally because the members are under tremendous economic pressures and, as a result, they fully expect that the union will extract a contract settlement that will meet all their basic needs. When the union negotiators fail to accomplish this they reject the settlement. This is the fundamental reason why settlements get rejected.

What workers do not understand, and what we ourselves have to understand, is that the American trade union movement, including unions like UE, are organizations with limited objectives.

The UE constitutional provision that sets out our principal objective states:

> We realize that the struggle to better our working and living conditions is in vain unless we are united to protect ourselves collectively against the organized forces of the employers.

That is as far as the UE Constitution goes. It accepts the fact that we will be struggling all our lives to protect and improve our standard of living under the corporate profit system. The very nature of the corporation requires it to constantly strive for a higher and higher profit. If a union is to secure a contract settlement that fully meets the needs of its members, the corporation would have to forgo all or most of its profits. Since the corporation is not a philanthropic institution the contract settlement will at best represent only what can be extracted from the corporation.

Origins of American Unions

When unions were first started in America, they were organized by European Socialist immigrants and by others with a radical ideology. When these leaders founded the American trade unions, they incorporated provisions in their constitutions which declared that the workers were entitled to the full fruits of their labor (which by the way was also Lincoln's philosophy).

It is a historical fact that the American trade union movement not only abandoned these principles but many of its leaders went further and proclaimed that in this county we have achieved a classless society and that the corporations and the workers belong to the same class.

The founding convention of our union in 1936 rejected this garbage about the classless society but at the same time we didn't include in our constitution the objective of securing for our members the full fruits of the labor. The subject was not even debated by the founders of UE. As I have already stated, we simply dedicated ourselves to a continuous struggle to extract from the corporations an ever higher price for our labor. The membership has to understand this.

But there are other reasons why contract settlements are rejected by the rank and file.

Drawing Up Union Demands

During my years in the labor movement, I have sat in at many membership meetings where contract demands were drawn up and I have watched this process. These union demands consist of three categories. In the first category are immediate economic and non-economic demands that must and can be realized in that round of negotiations. The second category includes pioneering objectives. Some of these you may or may not get in that round of negotiations, but it is extremely important that these basic pioneering demands be pressed. For example, the first time that we made the demand for paid holidays for production workers in GE and Westinghouse was in 1939. We made it every year but did not achieve a breakthrough until 1947 . . .

Ceiling-Walking Demands

So you have the immediate demands that must be realized right in that particular round and you have broader objectives that you may or may not get in that round but you have to press for in every way you can. Then you have what we call ceiling-walking demands.

There is no excuse at all for just anyone raising his hand at a membership meeting and saying "put it in, what can we lose?" By putting in a ceiling-walking demand you are undermining and discrediting the other sound demands. You are not helping yourself one iota. I will give you an example of such a demand: In one of our plants the shift tool operators and helpers in one department took turns for an hour or so to take a nap [a practice discovered and banned when a new management for the plant was installed] . . . When the contract came up for renewal, the department . . . wanted to write into the contract the right to catch their forty winks on the third shift . . .

For obvious reasons such demands are just plain ceiling walking. Therefore you fight it out at the membership meeting. You sift through the demands, argue it out and you don't create pie in the sky expectations that will act as booby traps at the ratification meeting.

At the same time, when drawing up the demands, remember that, as important as wages, cost of living protection, health insurance, pensions, vacations and paid holidays may be, there are other real issues of deep concern that do not fall into the economic category and frequently overshadow money issues. These so-called "little issues" may tip the scale in favor of ratification when you go before the membership with a settlement proposal. These demands involve working conditions, the dignity of the worker on the job, his treatment by supervision, health and safety conditions, protection against speedup, etc. These are demands that the rank and file must win in order to make their daily grind on the job more bearable. Remember, man does not live by bread alone.

Mobilizing Support

After you put in your demands, the next job is the mobilization of the membership in support of the demands they have adopted. Too often during negotiations the negotiating committee keeps parading in and out of the management office day after day, looking important with their impressive and bulging briefcases, while the membership sits on its hands waiting for the big day when the committee is going to call them together and deliver the goods. We seem to forget that no matter how smart we think we are at the bargaining table, we aren't worth much if the membership is not actively engaged in support of the negotiating committee while it is doing its work at the bargaining table.

Contact With Key Local Leaders

The most crucial single job that the negotiating committee must handle while the negotiations are going on, is to constantly keep in touch with the Local Executive Board members, shop stewards and with other key people who may not hold any elected position but who have influence in the shop. You know that these shop leaders can take you on at the ratification meeting and give you a rough time if they are kept in the dark during the entire course of the negotiations and are given no opportunity to play a part in the shaping of the settlement. In a rank and file union you have to keep your shop leadership posted on the problems that you face day by day at the bargaining table . . .

Level With the Membership

When you lead negotiations or when you lead a strike, forget about local elections. If you level with the membership, if you take them into your confidence, chances are good that come what may, they'll return you to office. But even if you should get dumped at the next election, don't forget that you were elected to lead. If you have a member on your committee who doesn't have the guts to stand up and be counted, make him resign and get someone who will remember that a leader is there to lead . . .

Meaning of Rank and File Unionism

. . . From time to time we hear some of our leaders complain that the trouble with UE is that we "suffer" from too much democracy. This is a fallacious idea. Even in a union like ours, we tend to practice democracy more like a ritual than as a vibrant living thing.

Rank and file unionism requires much more than the right to cast a ballot. It requires that each member have a full opportunity to get a piece of the action. Today, we must exert a special effort to actively engage the young, the black, the chicano, the Puerto Rican, and the woman member.

A law that would muzzle the rank and file would put the stamp of approval on the back door sweetheart contract and would give the greatest boost to corrupt business unionism from one end of the country to the other.

Any effort to enact such legislation must be fought with every ounce of energy and determination by every union man and woman in America.

NOTES

Chapter 1 Understanding Labor Radicalism

1   Loyd D. Easton and Kurt H. Guddat, eds., *Writings of the Young Marx on Philosophy and Society* (Garden City, NY: Anchor Books, 1967), pp. 257–258.

2   The chasm between Marx and tyrannies associated with his teachings (and the parallel with Jesus and those using his name in vain) is discussed in Paul Le Blanc, *Marx, Lenin, and the Revolutionary Experience: Studies of Communism and Radicalism in the Age of Globalization* (New York/London: Routledge, 2006); also see Geoff Eley, *Forging Democracy: The History of the Left in Europe, 1850–2000* (New York: Oxford University Press, 2002). Among the many valuable discussions of Marx as a theorist deeply committed to freedom and democracy are: Kevin M. Brien, *Marx, Reason, and the Art of Freedom*, Second Edition (Amherst, NY: Humanity Books, 2006); Richard N. Hunt, *The Political Ideas of Marx and Engels*, 2 vols. (Pittsburgh, PA: University of Pittsburgh Press, 1974, 1984); and of course the works of Hal Draper; for example, his collected essays in *Socialism From Below*, ed. by E. Haberkern (Atlantic Highlands, NJ: Humanities Press, 1992). Michael Löwy's fine study situating Marx in the workers' movement and examining essentials of his thought can be found in *The Theory of Revolution in the Young Marx* (Chicago, IL: Haymarket Books, 2005).

3   A useful historical survey can be found in Chris Harman, *A People's History of the World* (London: Verso, 2008). For a summary of humanity's early economic development, see Ernest Mandel, *Marxist Economic Theory*, vol. 1 (New York: Monthly Review Press, 1968), pp. 23–131, 174–177.

4   On this "dual revolution" see E. J. Hobsbawm, *The Age of Revolution, 1789–1848* (New York: New American Library, 1962).

5   See Paul M. Sweezy, *The Present as History* (New York: Monthly Review, 1962), p. 205; Paul M. Sweezy, *The Theory of Capitalist Development* (New York: Monthly Review Press, 1968), pp. 57–59, 79–83; Ben Fine and Alfredo Saad-Filho, *Marx's Capital* (London: Pluto Press, 2004), 21.

6   Overviews of the Internationals are provided in a number of works, including: Wolfgang Abrendroth, *A Short History of the European Working Class* (New York: Monthly Review Press, 1972); Julius Braunthal, *History of the International,*

1864–1943, 2 vols. (New York: Frederick A. Praeger, 1966); Duncan Hallas, *The Comintern* (New York: Haymarket Books, 2008). Useful works focusing on Marxism's connection with the Internationals include: August H. Nimtz, Jr., *Marx and Engels: Their Contribution to the Democratic Breakthrough* (Albany, NY: State University of New York Press, 2000); Ernest Mandel, *The Place of Marxism in History* (Atlantic Highlands, NJ: Humanities Press, 1994), and Paul Le Blanc, *From Marx to Gramsci* (Amherst, NY: Humanity Books, 1996).

7   V. I. Lenin, "Draft and Explanation for the Social Democratic Party" (1895), cited in Paul Le Blanc, *Lenin and the Revolutionary Party* (Amherst, NY: Humanity Books, 1993), p. 26.

8   Raymond Williams, *Keywords: A Vocabulary of Culture and Society* (New York: Oxford University Press, 1983), pp. 87–93; Raymond Williams, *Culture and Society, 1780–1950* (New York: Harper and Row, 1966), p. xvi; A. L. Kroeber and Clyde Kluckohn, *Culture: A Critical Review of Concepts and Definitions* (New York: Vintage Books, no date [first published 1953]), pp. 82, 112, 141, 83, 84 (in order of use).

9   Eleanor Leacock, "Marxism and Anthropology," in Bertell Ollman and Edward Vernoff, eds., *The Left Academy: Marxist Scholarship on American Campuses* (New York: McGraw-Hill, 1992), 267–268.

10 V. I. Lenin, "Critical Remarks on the National Question," *Collected Works*, vol. 20 (Moscow: Progress Publishers, 1972), pp. 23–24. In a somewhat similar vein, Raymond Williams comments that "there is clearly that we can call alternative to the effective dominant culture, and there is something else that we can call oppositional, in a true sense," in Raymond Williams, *Problems in Materialism and Culture* (London: Verso, 1980), p. 40.

11 Leon Trotsky, *Problems of Everyday Life, and Other Writings on Culture and Science* (New York: Monad/Pathfinder Press, 1973), p. 19; Phil Gasper, ed., *The Communist Manifesto: A Roadmap to History's Most Important Political Document* (Chicago, IL: Haymarket Books, 2005), pp. 58–59.

12 Karl Marx, *The Eighteenth Brumaire of Louis Bonaparte*, in Karl Marx and Frederick Engels, *Selected Works*, vol. 1 (Moscow: Progress Publishers, 1973), p. 398.

13 E. P. Thompson, *Customs in Common: Studies in Traditional Popular Culture* (New York: The New Press, 1993), pp. 16, 13, 12 (in order of use); E. P. Thompson, *The Making of the English Working Class* (New York: Vintage Books, 1966), pp. 9–10, 11.

14 Herbert Gutman, *Work, Culture and Society in Industrializing America* (New York: Vintage Books, 1977), pp. 18, 15 (in order of use); Herbert Gutman, *Power and Culture: Essays on the American Working Class*, ed. by Ira Berlin (New York: Pantheon Books, 1987), p. 381.

15 Eleanor Marx and Edward Aveling, *The Working-Class Movement in America*, ed. by Paul Le Blanc (Amherst, NY: Humanity Books, 2000), pp. 70–72, 76, 77, 78, 79, 143, 146, 151.

16 There are ample materials demonstrating the historical phenomenon of this labor–radical sub-culture in the United States; for example: Philip S. Foner, *History of the Labor Movement in the United States*, 10 vols. (New York: International Publishers, 1947–1994); Mari Jo Buhle, Paul Buhle, and Dan Georgakis, eds., *Encyclopedia of the American Left*, Second Edition (New York: Oxford University Press, 1998); Nicholas Coles and Janet Zandy, eds., *American Working-Class Literature: An Anthology* (New York: Oxford University Press, 2006); Laura Hapke, *Labor's Text: The Worker in American Fiction* (New

Brunswick, NJ: Rutgers University Press, 2001); Edith Fowke and Joe Glazer, eds., *Songs of Work and Freedom* (New York: Dover, 1973); David Montgomery, *Beyond Equality: Labor and the Radical Republicans* (New York: Alfred A. Knopf, 1967); Franklin Rosemont and David Roediger, eds., *The Haymarket Scrapbook* (Chicago, IL: Charles H. Kerr, 1986); Joyce Kornbluh, ed., *Rebel Voices, An IWW Anthology*, Revised Edition (Chicago, IL: Charles H. Kerr, 1988); John Graham, ed., *Yours for the Revolution: The Appeal to Reason, 1895–1922* (Lincoln, NE: University of Nebraska Press, 1990); Oscar Ameringer, *If You Don't Weaken* (New York: Henry Holt, 1940); James Weinstein, *The Decline of Socialism in America, 1912–1925* (New York: Vintage Books, 1969); Bryan Palmer, *James P. Cannon and the Origins of the American Revolutionary Left, 1890–1928* (Urbana and Chicago, IL: University of Illinois Press, 2007); Michael Denning, *The Cultural Front* (London: Verso, 1998).

17 Key aspects of the 1930s power shift are discussed in Art Preis, *Labor's Giant Step: Twenty Years of the CIO* (New York: Pathfinder Press, 1972), pp. 3–81; Robert H. Zieger, *The CIO, 1935–1955* (Chapel Hill, NC: University of North Carolina Press, 1995), pp. 6–190; David Brody, *Workers in Industrial America: Essays on the 20th Century Struggle* (New York: Oxford University Press, 1981), pp. 82–119; and Nelson Lichtenstein, *State of the Union: A Century of American Labor* (Princeton, NJ: Princeton University Press, 2002), pp. 20–53. The interplay of left-wing organizations and militants with the larger struggles comes through in such works as Charles Rumford Walker, *American City: A Rank and File History of Minneapolis* (Minneapolis, MN: University of Minneapolis Press, 2005); Farrell Dobbs, *Teamster Rebellion* (New York: Monad/Pathfinder Press, 1972); Sol Dollinger and Genora Johnson Dollinger, *Not Automatic: Women and the Left in the Forging of the Auto Workers' Union* (New York: Monthly Review Press, 2000); and—in a somewhat different vein—in Steve Rosswurm, ed., *The CIO's Left-Led Unions* (New Brunswick, NJ: Rutgers University Press, 1992), and Judith Stepan and Norris Maurice Zeitlin, *Left Out: Reds and America's Industrial Unions* (New York: Cambridge University Press, 2003).

18 On the labor–radical sub-culture of the German working class, see Evelyn Anderson, *Hammer or Anvil: The Story of the German Working-Class Movement* (Almeda, CA: Center for Socialist History, 2007); Vernon L. Lidtke, *The Alternative Culture: Socialist Labor in Imperial Germany* (New York: Oxford University Press, 1985); Mary Nolan, *Social Democracy and Society: Working Class Radicalism in Dusseldorf, 1890–1920* (New York: Cambridge University Press, 2002); Eric D. Weitz, *Creating German Communism, 1890–1990* (Princeton, NJ: Princeton University Press, 1997). Also see Pierre Broué, *The German Revolution, 1917–1923* (Leiden, The Netherlands/Boston, MA: Brill, 2005), pp. 14–16, 627–646. A related study can be found in Helmut Gruber, *Red Vienna: Experiment in Working-Class Culture, 1919–1934* (New York: Oxford University Press, 1991).

19 Antonio Gramsci, *Selections from the Prison Notebooks*, ed. by Quinton Hoare and Geoffrey Nowell-Smith (New York: International Publishers, 1973), pp. 16, 199, 204–205, 232–233, 340.

20 Leon Trotsky, "The United Front for Defense" (February 23, 1933), in Leon Trotsky, *The Struggle Against Fascism in Germany*, ed. by George Breitman and Merry Maisel (New York: Pathfinder Press, 1971), p. 367.

21 Antonio Gramsci, "On Fascism 1921" and "Democracy and Fascism," in David Beetham, ed., *Marxists in the Face of Fascism* (Manchester, UK: Manchester University Press, 1983), pp. 83, 84, 85, 121.

22 Frank Lovell, "The Socialist Purpose: To Educate the Working Class," in Paul Le Blanc and Thomas Barrett, eds., *Revolutionary Labor Socialist: The Life, Ideas, and Comrades of Frank Lovell* (Union City, NJ: Smyrna Press, 2000), p. 133; Ernest Mandel, *The Meaning of the Second World War* (London: Verso, 1986), pp. 169, 45, 159–168.

23 Frank Lovell, "The Cataclysm: World War II and the History of American Trotskyism," in Le Blanc and Barrett, p. 135; Michael D. Yates, *In and Out of the Working Class* (Winnipeg, Canada: Arbeiter Ring Publishing, 2009), p. 45.

24 Steve Nelson, with James R. Barrett and Robert Ruck, *Steve Nelson, American Radical* (Pittsburgh, PA: University of Pittsburgh Press, 1981), pp. 284–285.

25 Among other sources, see: Harry Braverman, *Labor and Monopoly Capital: The Degradation of Work in the Twentieth Century* (New York: Monthly Review Press, 2003); Lizabeth Cohen, *A Consumer's Republic: The Politics of Mass Consumption in Post-War America* (New York: Vintage, 2003); Mike Davis, *Prisoners of the American Dream: Politics and Economy in the History of the U.S. Working Class*, Second Edition (New York: W. W. Norton, 2000); David M. Gordon, Richard Edwards, and Michael Reich, *Segmented Work, Divided Workers: The Historical Transformation of Labor in the United States* (Cambridge: Cambridge University Press, 1882); George Lipsitz, *Rainbow at Midnight: Labor and Culture in the 1940s* (Urbana, IL: University of Illinois Press, 1994); Kim Moody, *An Injury to All: The Decline of American Unionism* (London: Verso, 1988).

26 James P. Cannon, "Trade Unionists and Revolutionists," *Speeches to the Party* (New York: Pathfinder Press, 1973), pp. 57, 58.

27 John C. Leggett, *Race, Class and Political Consciousness: Working-Class Consciousness in Detroit* (New York: Oxford University Press, 1968), pp. 52, 53.

28 Stanley Aronowitz, *False Promises: The Shaping of American Working-Class Consciousness*, Revised Edition (Durham: Duke University Press, 1992), p. 95; James Boggs, *American Revolution: Pages From a Negro Worker's Notebook* (New York: Monthly Review Press, 1963), pp. 15, 16.

29 Sol Chick Chaikin, *A Labor Viewpoint: Another Opinion* (Monroe, NY: Library Research Associates, 1980), p. 220; Archie Robinson, *George Meany and His Times, A Biography* (New York: Simon & Schuster, 1981), p. 294. Also see Paul Buhle, *Taking Care of Business: Samuel Gompers, George Meany, Lane Kirkland and the Tragedy of American Labor* (New York: Monthly Review Press, 1999).

30 Arch Puddington, *Lane Kirkland, Champion of American Labor* (Hoboken, NJ: John Wiley & Sons, 2005), pp. 6–7, 115.

31 Michael Yates, *Why Unions Matter*, Second Edition (New York: Monthly Review Press, 2009), p. 189; Les Leopold, *The Man Who Hated Work and Loved Labor: The Life and Times of Tony Mazzocchi* (White River Junction, VT: Chelsea Green Publishing Co., 2007), pp. 410, 437–438, 440.

Chapter 2 Revolutionary Currents in the U.S. Labor Movement

1 Some of these points can be found in the classic collection, J. B. S. Hardman, ed., *American Labor Dynamics* (New York: Harcourt, 1928). Also see Simeon Larson and Bruce Nissen, eds., *Theories of the Labor Movement* (Detroit: Wayne State University Press, 1987).

2 Surveys providing ample demonstration of these points include: Samuel Yellen, *American Labor Struggles 1877–1934* (New York: Pathfinder Press, 1974); Sidney Lens, *Labor Wars: From the Molly Maguires to the Sit-Downs* (Chicago, IL:

Haymarket Books, 2009); Jeremy Brecher, *Strike!*, Revised and Updated Edition (Boston, MA: South End Press, 1997); Sharon Smith, *Subterranean Fire: A History of Working-Class Radicalism in the United States* (Chicago, IL: Haymarket Books, 2006). Also see Paul Le Blanc, *A Short History of the U.S. Working Class* (Amherst, NY: Humanity Books, 1999).

3   It is helpful to be able to place the history of U.S. labor in a broader historical context. One popular radical synthesis is provided by Howard Zinn's *A People's History of the United States* (New York: HarperCollins, 2005), although Eric Foner's *Give Me Liberty!: An American History*, Second Edition (New York: W. W. Norton, 2008), provides an outstanding overview with some differences in interpretation. Ronald J. Takaki's *A Different Mirror: A History of Multicultural America*, Second Edition (New York: Little, Brown and Co., 2008) offers an eloquent survey. Louis M. Hacker's classic *The Triumph of American Capitalism* (New York: Simon & Schuster, 1940) remains, in some ways, unsurpassed. Also see the rich syntheses of Sean Wilentz, *The Rise of American Democracy: Jefferson to Lincoln* (New York: W. W. Norton, 2006), and Alan Dawley, *Struggles for Justice: Social Responsibility and the Liberal State* (Cambridge, MA: Harvard University Press, 1993).

4   See especially Pauline Meier, *American Scripture: The Making of the Declaration of Independence* (New York: Vintage, 1998). A useful synthesis is provided by Edward Countryman, *The American Revolution* (New York: Hill and Wang, 1986). Two worthwhile, if somewhat divergent, interpretations are offered in Gordon S. Wood, *The Radicalism of the American Revolution* (New York: Vintage, 1993), and Gary B. Nash, *The Unknown American Revolution: The Unruly Birth of Democracy and the Struggle to Create America* (New York: Penguin, 2006).

5   Thomas Paine, "Agrarian Justice," in Philip S. Foner, *The Complete Writings of Thomas Paine*, 2 vols. (New York: Citadel Press, 1969), vol. 1, p. 617. Also see Eric Foner, *Tom Paine and Revolutionary America* (New York: Oxford University Press, 1976).

6   Philip S. Foner, *The History of the Labor Movement in the United States*, vol. 1 (New York: International Publishers, 1962), pp. 106–107, 110. Also see Sean Wilentz, *Chants Democratic: New York City and the Rise of the American Working Class, 1788–1850* (New York: Oxford University Press, 1984).

7   Foner, *The History of the Labor Movement in the United States*, vol. 1, p. 107.

8   Frederick Douglass, *My Bondage and My Freedom* (New York: Dover, 1969), pp. 160–162 Also see Bruce Levine's fine study, *Half Slave, Half Free: The Roots of the Civil War*, Revised Edition (New York: 2005)

9   Foner, *The History of the Labor Movement in the United States*, vol. 1, p. 275.

10 See Eric Foner, *Free Soil, Free Labor, Free Men: The Ideology of the Republican Party Before the Civil War* (New York: Oxford University Press, 1995), and Mark A. Lause, *Young America: Land, Labor, and the Republican Community* (Urbana, IL: University of Illinois Press, 2005).

11 Foner, *The History of the Labor Movement in the United States*, vol. 1, p. 292.

12 Foner, *The History of the Labor Movement in the United States*, vol. 1, p. 132; Frances Wright, "Statement on Nashoba," in Albert Fried, ed., *Socialism in America, From the Shakers to the Third International, A Documentary History* (Garden City, NY: Anchor Books, 1970), p. 116. Also see Celia Morris, *Fanny Wright, Rebel in America* (Urbana, IL: University of Illinois Press, 1992).

13 See Peter N. Stearns and John Hinshaw, *The ABC–CLIO World History Companion to the Industrial Revolution* (Santa Barbara, CA: ABC–CLIO, 1996).

14 Foner, *The History of the Labor Movement in the United States*, vol. 1, pp. 230–234, 279–282.

15 Paul Le Blanc, "The Absence of Socialism in the United States: Contextualizing Kautsky's 'The American Worker,'" *Historical Materialism*, vol. 11, no. 4 (2003), pp. 135–141; Eric Foner, *Free Soil, Free Labor, Free Men: The Ideology of the Republican Party Before the Civil War* (New York: Oxford University Press, 1995); Karl Obermann, *Joseph, Weydemeyer* (New York: International Publishers, 1946); Bruce Levine, *The Spirit of 1848: German Immigrants, Labor Conflict, and the Coming of the Civil War* (Urbana, IL: University of Illinois Press, 1992); Mark A. Lause, *Young America: Land, Labor, and the Republican Community* (Urbana, IL: University of Chicago Press, 2005).

16 Jonathan P. Grossman, *William Sylvis, Pioneer of American Labor* (New York: Columbia University Press, 1945), pp. 229–237; Foner, *History of the Labor Movement*, vol. 1, p. 311.

17 Charlotte Todes, *William Sylvis and the National Labor Union* (New York: International Publishers, 1942), pp. 91–92.

18 David Montgomery, *Beyond Equality: Labor and the Radical Republicans, 1862–1872* (New York: Alfred A. Knopf, 1967), pp. 249–260; Foner, *History of the Labor Movement*, vol. 1, pp. 364–369; Friedrich A. Sorge, *Labor Movement in the United States: A History of the American Working Class to 1890* (Westport, CT: Greenwood Press, 1977), pp. 100–102, 134–137.

19 See Philip S. Foner's useful study, *The Workingmen's Party of the United States: A History of the First Marxist Party in the Americas* (Minneapolis, MN: MEP Publications, 1984).

20 *Labor Standard*, July 28, 1877. Also see Philip S. Foner, *The Great Labor Uprising of 1877* (New York: Monad Press/Pathfinder Press, 1977), and Robert V. Bruce, *1877: Year of Violence* (Indianapolis, IN: Bobbs-Merrill, 1959).

21 Aspects of this analysis were developed in an unpublished Masters research paper in the History Department of the University of Pittsburgh—Paul Le Blanc, "Pioneers of American Socialism: The Workingmen's Party of the United States" (1978), some of which found its way (with partial acknowledgment and a different interpretive twist) into Philip S. Foner's, *The Workingmen's Party of the United States*. Foner follows Selig Perlman (in John R. Commons and Associates, *History of Labor in the United States*, vol. 2. (New York: Macmillan Co., 1918)) in projecting a sharply defined "Marxist vs. Lassallean" factional dispute onto the WPUS split—but there is no clear evidence that this is how the protagonists identified themselves or each other. On Daniel De Leon and related matters, see David Herreshoff, *Origins of American Marxism* (New York: Monad Press/ Pathfinder Press, 1973).

22 An exploration of the remarkable Chicago movement can be found in an unpublished Masters research paper in the History Department of the University of Pittsburgh—Paul Le Blanc, "Revolutionary Socialism in America, 1878–1887" (1979). The outstanding published works are: Henry David, *The History of the Haymarket Affair* (New York: Collier Books, 1963, originally published 1936); Paul Avrich, *The Haymarket Tragedy* (Princeton, NJ: Princeton University Press, 1984); Bruce Nelson, *Beyond the Martyrs: A Social History of Chicago's Anarchists, 1870–1900* (New Brunswick, NJ: Rutgers University Press, 1988); David Roediger and Franklin Rosemont, eds., *Haymarket Scrapbook* (Chicago, IL: Charles H.

Kerr Co., 1986); and James Green, *Death in the Haymarket: A Story of Chicago, the First Labor Movement, and the Bombing That Divided Gilded Age America* (New York: Anchor Books, 2007).

23   "The AFL, 1886 Preamble," in Albert Fried, ed., *Except to Walk Free: Documents and Notes in the History of American Labor* (Garden City, NY: Anchor Books, 1974), p. 153.

24   Samuel Gompers, *Seventy Years of Life and Labor, An Autobiography*, vol. II (New York: E. P. Dutton & Co., 1925), pp. 222–223.

25   Foner, *History of the Labor Movement*, vol. 1, p. 520.

26   Foner, *History of the Labor Movement*, vol. 2 (New York: International Publishers, 1955), pp. 56–92.

27   James Maurer, *It Can Be Done* (New York: Rand School Press, 1938), quoted in Le Blanc, *A Short History of the U.S. Working Class*, p. 50.

28   See Stuart B. Kaufman, *Samuel Gompers and the Origins of the American Federation of Labor, 1848–1896* (Westport, CT: Greenwood Press,1973), and Bernard Mandel, *Samuel Gompers, A Biography* (Yellow Springs, OH: Antioch Press, 1963).

29   Sorge, pp. 211–212; Carolyn Ashbaugh, *Lucy Parsons, American Revolutionary* (Chicago, IL: Charles H. Kerr Co., 1976), p. 58.

30   Philip S. Foner, ed., *The Autobiographies of the Haymarket Martyrs* (New York: Monad Press/Pathfinder Press, 1977), p. 43.

31   Sorge, p. 210.

32   Foner, *The History of the Labor Movement in the United States*, vol. 3, (New York: International Publishers, 1964), p. 386. Among the important studies of the Socialist Party of America, led by Eugene V. Debs, in the first two decades of the twentieth century are Ira Kipnis, *The American Socialist Movement, 1897–1912* (Chicago, IL: Haymarket Books, 2004); James Weinstein, *The Decline of Socialism in America 1912–1925* (New York: Vintage Books, 1967); Ray Ginger, *The Bending Cross: A Biography of Eugene Victor Debs* (Chicago, IL: Haymarket Books, 2007); and Nick Salvatore, *Eugene V. Debs: Citizen and Socialist*, Second Edition (Urbana, IL: University of Illinois Press, 2007). Also worth considering is the essay by James P. Cannon, "Eugene V. Debs and the Socialist Movement of His Time," in James P. Cannon, *The First Ten Years of American Communism, Report of a Participant* (New York: Lyle Stuart, 1962), pp. 245–276.

33   Henry M. Tichenor, ed., *Labor and Freedom, The Voice and Pen of Eugene V. Debs* (St. Louis, MO: Phil Wagner, 1916), p. 120.

34   Ibid., pp. 125, 172–173.

35   Joyce Kornbluh, ed., *Rebel Voices: An IWW Anthology*, New Expanded Edition (Chicago, IL: Charles H. Kerr Co., 1988), p. 138.

36   Ibid., p. 196.

37   Elizabeth Gurley Flynn, "The Truth About the Paterson Strike," in Kornbluh, p. 215.

38   Ibid., p. 209.

39   Peter Cole, *Ben Fletcher, The Life and Times of a Black Wobbly* (Chicago, IL: Charles H. Kerr Co., 2007), pp. 104–105.

40   Kornbluh, pp. 26–27. In addition to Kornbluh, works on the IWW worth consulting include: Philip S. Foner, *The History of the Labor Movement in the United States, Vol. 4: The Industrial Workers of the World, 1905–1917* (New York: International Publishers, 1965); Melvyn Dubofsky, *We Shall Be All: A History of the IWW* (New York: Quadrangle, 1974); Fred Thompson, *The IWW:*

Its First Seventy Years (Chicago, IL: Charles H. Kerr Co., 1976); Stewart Bird, Deborah Schaffer, and Dan Georgakas, eds., *Solidarity Forever: An Oral History of the Industrial Workers of the World* (Chicago, IL: Lake View Press, 1985); Franklin Rosemont, *Joe Hill: The IWW and the Making of a Revolutionary Workingclass Counterculture* (Chicago, IL: Charles H. Kerr Co., 2002).

41 This interpretation draws from James P. Cannon, "The I.W.W.—The Great Anticipation," in Cannon, *The First Ten Years of American Communism*, pp. 277–310.

42 William Z. Foster, *From Bryan to Stalin* (New York: International Publishers, 1937), pp. 74, 76; William Z. Foster, *American Trade Unionism: Principles and Organization, Strategy and Tactics, Selected Writings* (New York: International Publishers, 1947), p. 66.

43 See David Brody, *Labor in Crisis: The Steel Strike of 1919* (Philadelphia, PA: J.P. Lippincott Co., 1965).

44 On the first ten years of U.S. Communism (including the TUEL and its transformation into the TUUL), see Theodore Draper, *The Roots of American Communism* (New York: Viking, 1957) and *American Communism and Soviet Russia* (New York: Viking, 1960), as well as Bryan Palmer, *James P. Cannon and the Origins of the American Revolutionary Left, 1890–1928* (Urbana, IL: University of Illinois Press, 2007). Also see Philip S. Foner, *History of the Labor Movement in the United States, Vol. 9: The TUEL to the End of the Gompers Era* (New York: International Publishers, 1991) and *History of the Labor Movement in the United States, Vol. 10: The TUEL, 1925–1929* (New York: International Publishers, 1994).

45 Paul Le Blanc, "Brookwood Labor College," *Encyclopedia of American Social Movements*, vol. 2, ed. by Immanuel Ness (Armonk, NY: M. E. Sharpe, 2004), pp. 596–603; A. J. Muste, "My Experience in Labor and Radical Struggles," in Rita James Simon, ed., *As We Saw the Thirties: Essays on Social and Political Movements of a Decade* (Urbana, IL: University of Illinois Press, 1967), pp. 125–150.

46 See, for example, Irving Bernstein, *The Turbulent Years: A History of the American Worker, 1933–1941* (Boston: Houghton Miflin Co., 1971), pp. 217–317.

47 Le Blanc, *A Short History of the U.S. Working Class*, p. 85; A. J. Muste, "Trade Unions and the Revolution" (1935), in Nat Hentoff, ed., *The Essays of A. J. Muste* (New York: Simon & Schuster, 1970), p. 194.

48 The outstanding biographies are Saul Alinsky, *John L. Lewis, An Unauthorized Biography* (New York: Vintage Books, 1970), and Melvyn Dubofsky and Warren Van Tine, *John L. Lewis, A Biography* (New York: Quadrangle Books, 1977). Dubofsky and Van Tine challenge aspects of Alinsky's classic (originally published in 1949)—unfortunately, five years after his death. However, Sanford D. Horwitt provides a capable defense in *Let Them Call Me Rebel: Saul Alinsky, His Life and Legacy* (New York: Vintage Books, 1992), pp. 91, 94, 216–221.

49 A range of perspectives, and much information, on this matter can be found in: Robert H. Zieger, *The CIO, 1935–1955* (Chapel Hill, NC: University of North Carolina Press, 1995); Art Preis, *Labor's Giant Step: Twenty Years of the CIO*. New York: Pathfinder Press, 1972); Bert Cochran, *Labor and Communism, The Conflict that Shaped American Unions* (Princeton, NJ: Princeton University Press, 1977); Mary Heaton Vorse, *Labor's New Millions* (New York: Modern Age Books, 1938); Ben Stolberg, *The Story of the CIO* (New York: Viking Press, 1938); Len DeCaux, *Labor Radical, From the Wobblies to CIO: A Personal History* (Boston, MA: Beacon Press, 1970). Also see Paul Le Blanc, "Revolutionary Vanguards in

the United States During the 1930s," in John Hinshaw and Paul Le Blanc, eds., *U.S. Labor in the Twentieth Century: Studies in Working-Class Struggles and Insurgency* (Amherst, NY: Humanity Books, 2000).

50 Lewis, quoted in Vorse, pp. 294–295.
51 DeCaux, pp. 242–243.
52 James Matles, "The Role of Labor Today," in Hinshaw and Le Blanc, *U.S. Labor in the Twentieth Century*, pp. 360–361; similar points can be found in David Milton, *The Politics of U.S. Labor: From the Great Depression to the New Deal* (New York: Monthly Review Press, 1982), and David Brody, *In Labor's Cause*, pp. 175–220.
53 See Bert Cochran's study, *Labor and Communism*, cited in note 49, and Preis, *Labor's Giant Step*, pp. 323–416. Among the most informative recent studies are: Judith Stepan-Norris and Maurice Zeitlin, *Left Out: Reds and America's Industrial Unions* (New York: Cambridge University Press, 2003); Steve Rosswurm, ed., *The CIO's Left-Led Unions* (New Brunswick, NJ: Rutgers University Press, 1992); Robert W. Cherny, William Issel, and Kiernan Taylor, eds., *American Labor and the Cold War: Grassroots Politics and Postwar Political Culture* (New Brunswick, NJ: Rutgers University Press, 2004), and Shelton Stromquist, ed., *Labor's Cold War: Local Politics in a Global Context* (Urbana, IL: University of Illinois Press, 2008). Two book-length case studies worth consulting are John Hoerr, *Harry, Tom, and Father Rice: Accusation and Betrayal in America's Cold War* (Pittsburgh: University of Pittsburgh Press, 2005), and Rosemary Feurer, *Radical Unionism in the Midwest, 1900–1950* (Urbana, IL: University of Illinois Press, 2006).
54 Michael Harrington, *Socialism* (New York: Bantam Books, 1973), pp. 305–329.
55 Jervis Anderson, *A. Philip Randolph, A Biological Portrait* (Berkeley, CA: University of California Press, 1986), pp. 323–332; I. F. Stone, "The March on Washington" (1963), in *In a Time of Torment* (New York: Vintage Books, 1968), pp. 122–124.
56 A. Philip Randolph, "Introduction," in *A "Freedom Budget" For All Americans* (New York: A. Philip Randolph Institute, 1966), pp. iii–v.
57 Anderson, pp. 344–345; Martin Luther King, Jr., "Where Do We Go From Here?" (1967), in James M. Washington, ed., *A Testament of Hope: The Essential Writings and Speeches of Martin Luther King, Jr.* (San Francisco, CA: HarperCollins, 1986), p. 602.
58 See Leon Fink and Brian Greenberg, *Upheaval in the Quiet Zone: 1199/SEIU and the Politics of Healthcare Unionism*, Second Edition (Urbana, IL: University of Illinois Press, 2009).
59 For different aspects of the story of the United Farm Workers, see: Randy Shaw, *Beyond the Fields: Cesar Chavez, the UFW, and the Struggle for Justice in the 21st Century* (Berkeley, CA: University of California Press, 2008); Miriam Pawel, *The Union of Their Dreams: Power, Hope, and Struggle in Cesar Chavez's Farm Worker Movement* (New York: Bloomsbury Press, 2009); Marshall Ganz, *Why David Sometimes Wins: Leadership, Organization, and Strategy in the California Farm Worker Movement* (New York: Oxford University Press, 2009). For another key figure in the farm workers' struggle, see Craig Scharlin and Lilia V. Villanueva, *Philip Vera Cruz: A History of Filipino Immigrants and the Farmworkers Movement*, Third Edition (Seattle, WA: University of Washington Press, 2000).
60 Valuable works on this period include: Maurice Isserman, *If I Had a Hammer . . . : The Death of the Old Left and the Birth of the New* (New York: Basic Books, 1987); Van Goss, *Rethinking the New Left: An Interpretive History* (New York:

Palgrave Macmillan, 2005); Clayborne Carson, *In Struggle: SNCC and the Black Awakening of the 1960s* (Cambridge, MA: Harvard University Press, 1995); Kirkpatrick Sale, *SDS* (New York: Vintage Books, 1974); Max Elbaum, *Revolution in the Air: Sixties Radicals Turn to Lenin, Mao and Che* (London: Verso, 2006); Barry Sheppard, *The Party: The Socialist Workers Party, 1960–1988, Volume 1: The Sixties* (Chippendale, Australia: Resistance Books, 2008).

61 Harvey Swados, "The Myth of the Happy Worker" (1957), in *A Radical's America* (Boston, MA: Little, Brown and Co., 1962); C. L. R. James, *American Civilization* (Oxford, UK: Blackwell, 1993); Harry Braverman, "The New America," *American Socialist*, July 1957, and also *Labor and Monopoly Capital, The Degradation of Work in the Twentieth Century* (New York: Monthly Review Press, 1974).

62 See Raymond Williams, *Keywords: A Vocabulary of Culture and Society*, Revised Edition (New York: Oxford University Press, 1983), pp. 61–67, and Paul Le Blanc, *From Marx to Gramsci* (Amherst, NY: Humanity Books, 1996), p. 126.

63 George Breitman, quoted in Paul Le Blanc, "Writer, Organizer, Revolutionary: The Life and Legacy of George Breitman," in Anthony Marcus, ed., *Malcolm X and the Third American Revolution: The Writings of George Breitman* (Amherst, NY: Humanity Books, 2005), pp. 381–382.

64 Quoted in Les Leopold, *The Man Who Hated Work and Loved Labor: The Life and Times of Tony Mazzocchi* (White River Junction, VT: Chelsea Green Publishing Co., 2007), pp. 277–278.

65 Dan Georgakas and Marvin Surkin, *Detroit: I Do Mind Dying, A Study in Urban Revolution* (New York: St. Martin's Press, 1975); Paul F. Clark, *The Miners' Fight for Democracy: Arnold Miller and the Reform of the United Mine Workers* (Ithaca, NY: ILR Press/Cornell University Press, 1981); Dan La Botz, *Rank-And-File Rebellion: Teamsters for a Democratic Union* (London: Verso, 1990).

66 Judith Coburn, "Ed Sadlowski Strides Toward Bethlehem," *Village Voice*, February 7, 1977, p. 15; *Time*, February 21, 1975 (available online at: www.time.com/time/magazine/article/0,9171,913481,00.html, accessed October 6, 2010).

67 See Richard Rashke, *The Killing of Karen Silkwood: The Story Behind the Kerr-McGee Plutonium Case*, Second Edition (Ithaca, NY: Cornell University Press, 2000).

68 Quoted in Les Leopold, *The Man Who Hated Work and Loved Labor: The Life and Times of Tony Mazzocchi* (White River Junction, VT: Chelsea Green Publishing Co., 2007), pp. 394–395.

69 Arch Puddington, *Lane Kirkland: Champion of American Labor* (Hoboken, NJ: John Wiley & Sons, 2005), p. 129.

70 A good case study of the Hormel strike is offered in Peter J. Rachleff, *Hard-Pressed in the Heartland: The Hormel Strike and the Future of the Labor Movement* (Boston, MA: South End Press, 1999).

71 Richard A. Brisbin Jr., *A Strike Like No Other Strike: Law and Resistance during the Pittston Coal Strike of 1989–1990* (Baltimore, MD: Johns Hopkins University Press, 2002); Tom Juravich and and Kate Bronfenbrenner, *Ravenswood: The Steelworkers' Victory and the Revival of American Labor* (Ithaca, NY: ILR Press/Cornell University Press, 2000).

72 Warren R. Van Tine, *The Making of the Labor Bureaucrat: Union Leadership in the United States, 1870–1920* (Amherst, MA: University of Massachusetts Press, 1973), pp. 33, 56.

73 The triumphant several-decades-long campaign is beautifully described and documented in Kim Phillips-Fein, *Invisible Hands: The Making of the*

Conservative Movement From the New Deal to Reagan (New York: W. W. Norton, 2009). Its impact is capably analyzed in Patricia Cayo Sexton, *The War on Labor and the Left: Understanding America's Unique Conservatism* (Boulder, CO: Westview Press, 1991).

74   Kim Moody, *U.S. Labor in Trouble and Transition: The Failure of Reform From Above, The Promise of Revival From Below* (London: Verso, 2007), p. 11.

75   Relevant works include: Trevor Blackwell and Jeremy Seabrook, *A World Still to Win: The Reconstruction of the Post-War Working Class* (London: Faber and Faber, 1986); Kim Moody, *Workers in a Lean World: Unions in the International Economy* (London: Verso, 1997); Ronaldo Munck, *Globalisation and Labour: "The Great Transformation"* (London: Zed Press, 2002); Paul Mason, *Live Working or Die Fighting* (London: Vintage Books, 2008).

76   Michael D. Yates, *Why Unions Matter*, Second Edition (New York: Monthly Review Press, 2009), p. 205.

77   Mike Parker and Martha Gruelle, *Democracy is Power: Rebuilding Unions from the Bottom Up* (Detroit, MI: Labor Notes, 1999), p. 64; Sheila Cohen, *Ramparts of Resistance: Why Workers Lost Their Power and How to Get It Back* (London: Pluto Press, 2006), pp. 2, 3.

78   Dan Clawson, *The Next Upsurge: Labor and the New Social Movements* (Ithaca, NY: ILR Press/Cornell University Press, 2003), pp. 13–14, 20.

79   Frank Lovell, "Toward an Understanding of Working-Class Radicalization," in Paul Le Blanc and Thomas Barrett, eds., *Revolutionary Labor Socialist: The Life, Ideas, and Comrades of Frank Lovell* (Union City, NJ: Smyrna Press, 2000), pp. 179, 181; Bill Fletcher, Jr. and Fernando Gapasin, *Solidarity Divided: The Crisis in Organized Labor and a New Path Toward Social Justice* (Berkeley, CA: University of California Press, 2008), p. 24.

80   Carl Sandburg, *The People, Yes* (New York: Harcourt, Brace and Co., 1936), p. 286.

BIBLIOGRAPHY

This bibliography seeks neither to reproduce all sources that can be found in the reference notes on previous pages nor to provide an exhaustive compendium of relevant literature. It offers a number of introductory works on U.S. labor and labor radicalism that help provide an overview for the material presented here, plus some of the more useful substantial works helping to contextualize and elaborate on the issues dealt with in this volume.

Adamic, Louis. *Dynamite: The Story of Class Violence in America*. New York: Viking Press, 1931.

Brecher, Jeremy. *Strike!* Revised and Updated Edition. Boston, MA: South End Press, 1997.

Brenner, Aaron, Benjamin Day, and Immanuel Ness, eds. *The Encyclopedia of Strikes in American History*. Armonk, NY: M. E. Sharpe, 2009.

Brody, David. *In Labor's Cause: Main Themes on the History of the American Worker*. New York: Oxford University Press, 1993.

Buhle, Mari Jo, Paul Buhle, and Dan Georgakas, eds. *Encyclopedia of the American Left*, Second Edition. New York: Oxford University Press, 1998.

Buhle, Paul. *Taking Care of Business: Samuel Gompers, George Meany, Lane Kirkland and the Tragedy of American Labor*. New York: Monthly Review Press, 1999.

Coles, Nicholas and Janet Zandy, eds. *American Working-Class Literature, An Anthology*. New York: Oxford University Press, 2007.

Commons, John R. and Associates. *History of Labor in the United States*, 4 vols. New York: Macmillan Co., 1918–1935.

Countryman, Edward. *The American Revolution*. New York: Hill and Wang, 1985.

Dawley, Alan. *Struggles for Justice: Social Responsibility and the Liberal State*. Cambridge, MA: Harvard University Press, 1993.

Dubofsky, Melvyn. *Industrialism and the American Worker, 1865–1920*. Arlington Heights, IL: AHM Publishing Corp., 1975.

Dubofsky, Melvyn and Warren Van Tine, eds. *Labor Leaders in America*. Urbana, IL: University of Illinois Press, 1987.

Fletcher, Bill, Jr. and Fernando Gapasin. *Solidarity Divided: The Crisis in Organized Labor and a New Path toward Social Justice*. Berkeley, CA: University of California Press, 2009.

Foner, Eric. *Give Me Liberty!: An American History*, One-Volume Edition. New York: W. W. Norton, 2004.

Foner, Philip S. *History of the Labor Movement in the United States*, 10 vols. New York: International Publishers, 1947–1994.

—— *Organized Labor and the Black Worker, 1619–1981*, Second Edition. New York: International Publishers, 1982.

—— *Women and the American Labor Movement*, 2 vols. New York: Free Press, 1979, 1980.

Foner, Philip S. and Ronald L. Lewis, eds. *Black Workers: A Documentary History from Colonial Times to the Present*. Philadelphia, PA: Temple University Press, 1989.

Fried, Albert, ed. *Communism in America: A History in Documents*. New York: Columbia University Press, 1997.

—— ed. *Socialism in America, From the Shakers to the Third International: A Documentary History*. Garden City, NY: Anchor Books, 1970.

Gutman, Herbert. *Power and Culture: Essays on the American Working Class*, ed. by Ira Berlin. New York: Pantheon Books, 1987.

—— *Work, Culture, and Society in Industrializing America*. New York: Adolph A. Knopf, 1976.

Hacker, Louis M. *The Triumph of American Capitalism*. New York: Columbia University Press, 1947.

Hinshaw, John and Paul Le Blanc, eds. *U.S. Labor in the 20th Century: Studies in Working-Class Struggles and Insurgency*. Amherst, NY: Humanity Books, 2000.

Kessler-Harris, Alice. *Out to Work: A History of Wage-Earning Women in the United States*. New York: Oxford University Press, 2003.

Le Blanc, Paul. *A Short History of the U.S. Working Class: From Colonial Times to the Twenty-First Century*. Amherst, NY: Humanity Books, 1999.

Lens, Sidney. *Labor Wars: From the Molly Maguires to the Sit-Downs*. Chicago, IL: Haymarket Books, 2009.

—— *Radicalism in America*. New York: Thomas Y. Crowell Co., 1969.

Levine, Bruce C. *Half Slave and Half Free: The Roots of Civil War*, Revised Edition. New York: Hill and Wang, 2005.

Lichtenstein, Nelson. *State of the Union: A Century of American Labor*. Princeton, NJ: Princeton University Press, 2003.

Lynd, Alice and Staughton Lynd, eds. *Rank and File: Personal Histories by Working-Class Organizers*. New York: Monthly Review Press, 1988.

McPherson, James M. *Abraham Lincoln and the Second American Revolution*. New York: Oxford University Press, 1992.

Montgomery, David. *Beyond Equality: Labor and the Radical Republicans, 1862–1872*. New York: Alfred A. Knopf, 1967.

Moody, Kim. *An Injury to All: The Decline of American Unionism*. London: Verso, 1988.

—— *U.S. Labor in Trouble and Transition: The Failure of Reform From Above, the Promise of Revival From Below*. London: Verso, 2007.

Morris, Richard B., ed. *The U.S. Department of Labor Bicentenniel History of the American Worker*. Washington, DC: U.S. Government Printing Office, 1976.

Ness, Immanuel, Dario Azzellini, Marcelline Block, Jesse Cohn, Clifford D. Conner, Rowena Griem, Paul Le Blanc, Amy Linch, Soma Marik, and Ayokunle O. Omobowale, eds. *International Encyclopedia of Revolution and Protest, 1500 to the Present*, 8 vols. Malden, MA/Oxford, UK: Wiley-Blackwell, 2009.

Preis, Art. *Labor's Giant Step: Twenty Years of the CIO*. New York: Pathfinder Press, 1972.

Schlager, Neil, ed. *St. James Encyclopedia of Labor History Worldwide*, 2 vols. Farmington Mills, MI: St. James Press, Thomson/Gale, 2004.

Smith, Sharon. *Subterranean Fire: A History of Working-Class Radicalism in the United States*. Chicago, IL: Haymarket Books, 2006.

Stearns, Peter N. and John H. Hinshaw. *The ABC–CLIO Companion to the Industrial Revolution*. Santa Barbara, CA: ABC–CLIO, 1996.

Takaki, Ronald. *A Different Mirror: A History of Multicultural America*, Revised Edition. New York: Back Bay Books, 2008.

Weir, Robert E. and James P. Hanlan, eds. *Historical Encyclopedia of American Labor*, 2 vols. Westport, CT: Greenwood Press, 2004.

Wilentz, Sean. *Chants Democratic: New York City and the Rise of the American Working Class, 1788–1850*. New York: Oxford University Press, 1984.

Yates, Michael. *Why Unions Matter*, Revised Edition. New York: Monthly Review Press, 2009.

Zieger, Robert H. *The CIO, 1935–1955*. Chapel Hill, NC: University of North Carolina Press, 1995.

Zinn, Howard. *A People's History of the United States*. New York: Harper Perennial Classics, 2005.

INDEX